The Railway Workers
1840 – 1970

by the same author

A GLOSSARY OF RAILWAYMEN'S TALK
Ruskin History Workshop
Pamphlet No. 1 1970
VICTORIAN RAILWAYMEN
History Workshop
Volume 1 1976

The Railway Workers
1840–1970

FRANK McKENNA

FABER AND FABER
London · Boston

First published in 1980
by Faber and Faber Limited
3 Queen Square London WC1N 3AU
Printed in Great Britain by
The Bowering Press Ltd
Plymouth and London
All rights reserved

British Library Cataloguing in Publication Data

McKenna, Frank
The railway workers, 1840–1970.
1. Railroads—Great Britain—Employees—History
I. Title
301.44′44   HD8039.R12G8

ISBN 0–571–11563–2

For my wife, Sylvia

There is a King, and a ruthless King,
Not a King of the poet's dream;
But a tyrant fell, white slaves know well
And that ruthless King is Steam.

E. P. Mead, *An Anthology
of Chartist Literature*

Contents

	List of Illustrations	*page*	13
	Foreword		15
	Preface		17
	Acknowledgements		19
1.	The Railway Company: A Victorian Leviathan		21
2.	The Rise and Fall of Company Loyalty		40
3.	Signalmen and Guards		65
4.	Ashpits and Offices: The Engine Shed		88
5.	Engine Cleaners and Firemen		109
6.	Engine-Drivers		151
7.	The Double Homers		190
8.	Language on the Railway		230
9.	The Tyranny of the Clock		242
	Appendix to Chapter 5		255
	Appendix to Chapter 9		256
	Notes		261
	Index		271

Illustrations

Between pages 28 and 29

1. Matthew Kirtley and Midland Railway staff, locomotive department, Derby, *c.* 1860 (Photo: A. B. Longbottom)

2. Bagster's clock (1837); now in the office of Sir Peter Parker, British Rail Headquarters (Photo: British Rail)

3. Dial of the Bagster Clock (Photo: British Rail)

4. Massed ranks: staff and officers at Strood, Kent, 1924 (Photo: Ron Bennet)

5. State, Church and Army: a nameplate ceremony for a diesel locomotive, 1960s (Photo: British Rail, London Midland Region)

6. Army officer and trade union official: Colonel Sir Ian Walker-Okeover and Mr John Ratcliffe, Secretary, ASLEF Branch, Cambridge Street (Photo: British Rail, London Midland Region)

7. Regimentals: a Great Central guard, 1907 (Radio Times Hulton Picture Library)

8. The aristocrats of the line—an exception: Great Central engine-driver, 1907 (Radio Times Hulton Picture Library)

9. Polish and shine on the Great Central Railway. A Marylebone porter, 1907 (Radio Times Hulton Picture Library)

10. Great Central Railway carter, 1908 (Radio Times Hulton Picture Library)

11. Low Fell signal box, 1914 (Photo: Mrs Greenwell)

12. Pride in uniform: Walter Stephens, a passenger guard at Paddington, *c.* 1904

13. Carriage-cleaning staff at Bournemouth West, *c.* 1925

Between pages 92 and 93

14. The Vigilants (Photo: R. Lunniss)

15. New faces at King's Cross, 1965: Bob Lunniss and a new recruit (Photo: John Bull)

16. Jim Swain with two other engine cleaners, King's Cross, 1933 (Photo: J. Swain)

17. Women engine cleaners, 1941 (Photo: Ron Payne)

18. Mrs Pat Forward working as a tube cleaner at Kentish Town engine sheds, 1942 (Photo: *Picture Post*)

19. 'The Binch', Polmadie, Glasgow, 1947 (Photo: British Rail)

20. Locomotive for lodging: LNER express locomotive type A.4., fitted with corridor tender (Photo: P. Townend)

21. Banbury Lodge, Great Western Railway (Photo: British Rail)

22. Facing the future: part of the Old Oak Common Hostel, London, 1949 (Photo: British Rail)

23. North Road Lodge, Plymouth, Great Western Railway (Photo: John Parsons)

24. Crewe Lodge, Mill Street, 1845 (Photo: Mr W. Davis)

25. Rugby Lodge (Photo: Mr V. Wolfe)

26. Immingham Lodge (Photo: Mr R. Dane)

27. Mallaig Lodge

28. A lodging basket (Photo: Driver Bert Hooker)

29. Mrs E. Maillard at the keyboard of 'The Nunnery', Sheffield (Photo: E. Maillard)

30. The Midland Pullman (Photo: British Rail, London Midland Region)

31. A Kentish Town driver and second man ready to take out the Midland Pullman in the mid-1960s (Photo: British Rail, London Midland Region)

Foreword

The history of British railways has usually been written from one of two points of view: as a history of companies or as a history of machines, of engineering. There are good reasons why that should have been so. The most readily available evidence arises from the companies themselves: the hundreds of them in the Victorian age, the four big ones of 1923–47, the state organization that has taken over from them since 1948. The impulse to write the history of railways, to turn to the subject at all, has arisen most commonly from an interest in some aspect of their engineering, a romantic feeling for the steam locomotive (and why not?—it was one of man's great creations), a curiosity about devices, such as signals or turntables.

All this literature is now very extensive. And yet it remains patchy and incomplete. If we leave engineering aside, its strength has lain in the treatment it has accorded to the companies; but they have been seen almost wholly from one point of view, as entities in themselves, projectors and developers of railway systems, in exciting rivalry with one another—a rivalry that has sometimes extended to an absurd partisanship in the authors of the books that recount it. That is history written from the board-room, the offices of the managers and chief engineers alone.

But there is more to the history of these companies than this, and much more to the history of railways. Though railways were mechanical contrivances, their machinery was in the hands of men, and the men themselves have received strangely little attention compared with that which has been lavished on the machines. That is true right through the industry. We have no good biography of any railway chairman save George Hudson, none of Glyn or Gooch or Watkin. If, among managers, we now have studies of Huish and Herbert Walker, they stand alone: we have none yet of Allport or Birt or Gibb. As for the rest of the companies' servants—and at one time there were more than half a million of them—they remain almost entirely anonymous. One of them emerges here or there as the centre of a tragedy or the butt of a comic anecdote. Where are the others, in their hundreds of thousands?

They make some appearance in the histories of trade unions, and P. W. Kingsford did something to reveal them to us in his *Victorian*

Railwaymen ten years ago. In this book Frank McKenna has gone
further than anyone before him towards showing us what railwaymen
have been like, the sort of lives they led and the work they performed,
from the 1840s down to our own time.

That nobody should have tried to do this before is not to be attributed solely to blindness or indifference. Real difficulties lie in the way of
anyone who attempts the task. Very few ordinary railwaymen have
ever been articulate, able to record their experience and to pass any
useful judgement upon it. The great majority of them have lived and
died unknown, and it is no easy matter to recover their histories, as
individuals, now.

It may not be easy, but here, in generous measure, it has been done.
There are sources for the kinds of information we need, which have
been inadequately worked in the past: the most notable of them being
the long series of reports on accidents, sometimes full-scale inquiries,
of the Inspecting Officers of the Board of Trade. There are the railway
newspapers, and the voluminous evidence given by railwaymen, and
on their behalf, at public investigations. But Frank McKenna has been
able to cast his net much more widely. He has read voraciously and
corresponded with many people who have told him just what he, and
we, wish to know. He has been a railwayman himself, which at once
gives him the advantage (denied to nearly all railway historians) of
writing of what he knows about, and feels for, from the inside. This
has given him a point of view—here and there, as he indicates very
fairly himself, a *parti pris*, perhaps even a prejudice. He sees the railway service without illusions. Those who think of it romantically will
do well to reflect on some of the more unpleasant realities he forces
us to face.

Yet this is not a work of denigration, or complaint. It shows a larger
mind than that, a desire above all to do justice. Through his previous
experience, his accumulated observation and reflection, McKenna is
better able than any previous writer to tell us how railwaymen worked.
He gives us here a book about a way of life, of substantial importance
in British society for the past hundred years and more. It is recalled
and recorded, sometimes with indignation and compassion, to make an
original book, affording a valuable contribution to our knowledge and
understanding of railways.

JACK SIMMONS
Emeritus Professor of History
University of Leicester

Preface

There is a vast and informative body of literature dealing with British railways, but twenty years as engine cleaner, fireman, main-line driver, trade-union representative and compulsive scribbler convinced me that social historians needed a book which described the work, workplaces and tools of railway workers in action. I make no claim to being a railway historian, the subject is too vast and varied for anything except a fragmented view. The work is necessarily subjective, although I hope not vindictive in any way.

This book is not about entrepreneurs, directors, architects and engineers. They appear, but it is with the effects of their policies on the lower participants that we are concerned. In the days when steam was king the railways of Britain were maintained by an army of 600,000 industrial workers, who were divided into a complicated structure of grades which bred division and insularity—a special railway 'separatedness'. This industry opened up every continent to industrial and commercial development and added many new dimensions to life in the nineteenth and twentieth centuries. The tradition of the railway from the earliest time was that 'the train must go through'; 'stopping the job', 'working to rule', 'putting on the big hammer', even 'going slow' were activities inimical to railway workers. This book looks at our railway system from a different angle—that of the people who could put their divisions to one side and, by united activity, put the actions of governments to naught.

London 1980   FRANK McKENNA

Acknowledgements

This book is a combination of many skills and much dedication. Its themes and structure were formulated and consolidated in Oxford in the early 1970s when Raf Samuel and David Selbourne, tutors at Ruskin College, opened my awareness to the possibility of such a volume. Jim Fyrth of the University of London was always available with sound advice and Professor Jack Simmons of Leicester University made invaluable suggestions on tightening the text. Professor D. S. Landes of Harvard University alerted me to the importance of railway time and the history of clocks and watches. Norman Whitney, Kathy Wallace and John Landen of Ealing College of Higher Education helped sharpen my sense of the significance of language in industrial contexts, and Sylvia Mann cross-checked my references with great expertise. Joni Clark deserves credit for her initial typing without which we would not have got started. To Timothy O'Grady I owe a special debt for his meticulous copy editing and helpful suggestions. Frank Pike of Faber and Faber really got the project under way and I am especially grateful to Nicole Foster of the same firm for guiding the material to its conclusion.

The Associated Society of Locomotive Engineers and Firemen, the National Union of Railwaymen, British Rail Public Relations Officers and J. Edgington of the Railway Museum, York, met my requests with great courtesy. Harry Evans of Gwent let me view a Great Western Railway watch and Vernon Brown of London sent me photographs of the famous Roscopf railway watch. David Trimbell of Gloucester furnished interesting material on 'Railway Time' and K. Phillips of Peterborough provided an interesting discussion on time and railway mileage. J. Good of the Horological Department at the British Library was extremely helpful in my search for information on specialized time-keeping devices such as the Swindon Works Time Clock of 1839. Derek Howse of the National Maritime Museum allowed me to view the manuscript of his book *Greenwich Time and the Discovery of the Longitude*.

Martin Hicks of the Doncaster branch of ASLEF kindly loaned me his huge file of newspaper cuttings on the 1949 unofficial stoppages against an extension of lodging turns by enginemen, and Eddie Coules, ASLEF organizer, loaned me his files on the same issue when it erupted in 1952. Without letters and views of rank and file members of the ASLEF and the NUR this previously unrecorded chapter of railway history could not have been written. To all those who gave of their memories our thanks are due.

To my own family a special thank you. They have lived with this book for a decade.

1

The Railway Company:
A Victorian Leviathan

Against the unlimited resources of the secured monopoly of
custom, and the absolute unity of will enjoyed by these modern
Leviathans . . . the quarter of a million pounds of the strongest
union and the clamour of one or two thousand obstinate and
embittered workmen are as arrows against ironclads.
                                   —SIDNEY AND BEATRICE WEBB,
                                        Industrial Democracy, 1897

In the fifteen years which separated the battlefield of Waterloo from
the opening of the Liverpool and Manchester Railway, the power of steam
revolutionized economic, political and social relationships within the
British Isles. Only one year after Wellington's victory and three short
years after Christopher Blackett and William Hedley successfully railed
Puffing Billy on the Wylam Colliery Railway, the old society began to
splinter under the pressures of the new propellant. The double prong
of steam power and its running mate, the demand for Parliamentary
reform, so rocked established economic and political power that habeas
corpus, the legal basis of British freedom, was suspended by a government which genuinely feared a popular uprising.

On 23 May 1822 the first rails of the Stockton and Darlington Railway were positioned at St John's Wells near Stockton, and in 1824, on
the eve of the repeal of the Combination Acts, the company was
authorized to carry passengers in trains hauled by steam locomotives.
The Steam Engine-Makers' Society was founded in 1824 and one year
later the Stockton and Darlington was in business. The age of railway
steam did not begin, however, until George Stephenson, that practical
Tynesider, left the Stockton and Darlington Railway to become engineer
on the first truly passenger railway in the world—the Liverpool and
Manchester Railway.

George Stephenson made the Liverpool and Manchester Railway the
great experimental railway of the world, an undertaking which connected with sinews of iron the industries of the north-east and the commercial power of Liverpool and Manchester. As early as 1828, the
double-chimneyed locomotives, the *Lancashire Witch* and *Twin Sisters*,

were hauling spoil to Liverpool and Manchester railway embankments, a proceeding of some embarrassment to the Stockton and Darlington, which at that time was using horses as well as locomotives to haul its trains. The conquest of the 'quaking bog' at Chat Moss and the carving of this line through the Lancashire brownstone are great monuments to Stephenson and the men who built it. The line itself was highly speculative, for until 1837 the formation of joint stock companies was dependent upon private Acts of Parliament. Companies could be formed, but not of limited liability. Railways were largely financed by risk money, but the railway moneys of the 1840s created a vast industry which at its zenith employed 600,000 workers in Britain and opened up five continents.

In 1830, the directors of the Liverpool and Manchester discussed the problem of to whom should fall the honour of opening the first truly steam-hauled railway. In the view of the directors one man was superbly equipped to perform this ceremony: the Prime Minister of Great Britain —the Duke of Wellington.

In 1830, the Duke of Wellington occupied a lone pinnacle based upon many years of unbroken military and civil success. He was known, however, to be hostile to the new form of transport. He was confident that trains would never supersede the new macadamized roads, at that time enjoying huge acclaim, nor would they ever run at more than twenty miles per hour. He was unabashed in saying that popularization of railway travel might encourage the working classes to aspire to things beyond their true position in life. The Iron Duke, whose tatterdemalion forces had consigned La Grande Armée to the dusty and echoing sidings of history, disliked any challenge to authority and cheerfully admitted his opposition to any reform of Parliament, an institution famous in 1830 for rotten boroughs and the purchasing of votes. To the delight of the directors of the L. and M., Wellington agreed to perform the opening ceremony. This was a significant change of attitude by the Prime Minister and placed a seal of approval on the ambitions of the railway company. Once again the Duke of Wellington, the 'silver penny' of his social group, had turned the tide of history.

At 9.30 a.m. on 15 September 1830, the Duke of Wellington entered the Crown Street premises of the Liverpool and Manchester Railway and occupied the sumptuous coach prepared for him by the company. As the notes of 'See, the Conquering Hero Comes' died in the trumpets of the triumphal band, a small gun fired the signal to start the procession. Unfortunately, the wadding from the round removed the eye of a labourer who was standing nearby. It was the start of an eventful day for the Duke. On the journey to Manchester one of the train engines threw a wheel and during its repair a following engine rammed the rear of this train. Mr William Huskisson descended from the first train and was killed, thereby becoming the first passenger to die in a railway accident.

At about 5.45 in the evening, after a journey described by the Duke as 'stupendous' and 'magnificent', the train was met outside Manchester, not only by the Fifty-Ninth Regiment, but also by a huge crowd of demonstrators who displayed their hostility to the Duke by hooting, cat-calling and shouting, or by standing in silence as the Duke's carriage passed.

The city of Manchester in 1830 was already a 'cottonopolis'. Soon to become a terminus of the world's first passenger railway, the city was a place where great wealth and terrible poverty squatted uneasily together, united by the power of steam but divided by the inequality of its rewards. On two previous occasions, the impact of steam technology and the demand for Parliamentary control of unbridled economic development had seen blood flow on the streets of the city.[1] To many radicals, the Iron Duke represented this repression, and they were determined to demonstrate their hostility to the great defender of the hated system. The mood of the city was very ugly and a confrontation with the Duke's entourage was avoided only by the withdrawal of his train back along the railway. The opening of the railway recalled the distant trumpets of vanquished Bonapartism, the brutal treatment of the Blanketeers and the breeze-borne slogans of demonstrators savaged in the Peterloo outrage of 1819.[2] Britain's bristle-hard commander tasted defeat at Manchester in 1830 but his life and character draw together for us the disparate strands of railway development, radical politics and Parliamentary reform.

In 1830, Britain possessed less than 100 miles of fully operative railway, yet by 1850 mail- and stage-coach had finally surrendered to the deep impatient cough of the steam locomotive. By 1875, Britain had 6,000 miles of track in operation, most of it double, and the satisfying smack of engine buffer on wagon headstock was as familiar in Melton Mowbray as it was in Manchester.[3] Staff and investment grew accordingly. Between 1830 and 1847, the first year for which reliable figures are available gives the permanent staff of the companies as 47,000. By 1860, the total had risen to 112,000. Despite these large numbers, the industry rapidly became capital intensive; by the 1860s it was of the order of £3,000–4,000 for every man employed.

The railways altered the appearance of Britain as marshes were drained, valleys bridged, rivers crossed and mountains tunnelled, in a bewildering variety of styles and materials. In urban areas the railway companies provided a new street architecture of offices and warehouses, mainly in brick. On town and city fringes appeared new engine sheds and miles of windy, desolate sidings, creating and sustaining within the environment a new generation of shapes, shadows and sounds.

The railways of east London, in creating new vistas, were often responsible for the destruction of much that was old and bad; in the main the effect was beneficial, with the construction of new buildings and the paving and lighting of streets. This was, of course, the result of necessity rather than altruism, and the clearing and building was accompanied by severe overcrowding. This was certainly true of the arrival of the Eastern Counties Railway in Bethnal Green in the 1840s. This railway had a profound effect on the area, in particular the disclosing and cleaning of putrefaction during the building of the line. The railway cleared a swath through this foul and putrid area and the dispossessed tenants were crowded into the remaining houses. One historian has recorded: 'All the space enclosed between a hoarding on either side of the Eastern Counties Railway, a distance of about forty to sixty feet, was one enormous ditch of thickly putrefying matter . . . a row of twenty-two houses of two flats with cesspools in front are being built parallel to and within ten feet of this disgusting scene. A ditch has been dug on either side of the railway to prevent the arches of the railway being damaged.'[4]

Such sights are reminiscent of Bermondsey, where a magnificent viaduct constructed by the London and Greenwich Railway was responsible for clearing one of the most unhealthy areas along the Thames. Bermondsey had once been a spa noted for its lively social life, but had degenerated to the extent that, previous to the coming of the railway, it was dubbed 'the Venice of drains'. Mr. R. H. G. Thomas has recorded that:

[The railway] was to run for nearly a mile through a densely built-up area near London Bridge, crossing more than a dozen streets between there and Spa Road, Bermondsey, and for this reason . . . a viaduct [was planned] to carry the railway twenty-two feet above the ground; an additional reason for the elevated railway was that the land lay below the Thames high-water mark, and was naturally marshy. . . . For a distance of about three-quarters of a mile from London Bridge a large population lived in the utmost squalor, crowded together in a district which contained an incredible number of tiny courts, alleys and yards . . . frequent outbreaks of cholera there had led doctors and others to suggest schemes of slum clearance.[5]

The building of the railway, carried on 870 brick arches from London Bridge to the Greenwich terminus, was a triumph of organization carried out with military precision, and many disease-ridden hovels which passed for homes were cleared away. The viaduct ranks as one of the greatest brick structures of all time.

The success of the new industry fulfilled the prophecy of George Stephenson—that railways would change the world. The coming of the railway brought about a scientific and metallurgical revolution, a renaissance created by the impact of smooth wheels on smooth rails. Information was exchanged at far greater speed, and medical men, publishers and politicians were able to obtain details of the newest ideas and methods arising in other countries.

Who were the workers behind this enormous, spreading industry? Where did they come from and under what conditions did they live and work in the years when private ownership ruled unchecked? According to the railway historian Michael Robbins, the coal-pits and engine houses of the Durham and Northumberland coal-fields were drawn upon heavily for engine-men and mechanics. Lancashire was another fruitful source.[6] Vast numbers came straight from the farm. In 1850, the farm labourer was earning around 10s. per week; on the railway he could almost double that—a good enough reason to swap his hoe for a head-lamp. Itinerant independent harvesters, haymakers and thatchers provided another significant area of recruitment for the industry; according to David Morgan:

> Jack Lenten, a Warwickshire thatcher, the cleverest labourer in the village, went off to Lunnon when the haymaking came on. When he returned the farmers told him he might go in the winter where he had been in the summer. He had to get another place, but they would never again let Jack gain a settlement. Jack was sent to his own parish to find that his cottage was pulled down. When the railways came Jack got a job as a ganger.[7]

The Enclosure Acts and the Poor Law of 1834 played an important part in providing the companies with the labour needed. In Wiltshire, between 1760 and 1820, enclosures covered more than a quarter of the county. A general concentration of land holdings, of which enclosures were just a part, caused mass unemployment in the area until 1840, when the Great Western Railway decided to build a railway works, engine shed and artisans' houses in the area. As a result of this decision, Swindon, a small town which did not enforce the Acts of Settlement, grew from 2,495 souls in 1841 to a town of 45,000 in 1901.[8]

In the early days, the companies had the pick of the labour market not committed to apprenticeships. How sought-after a railway job was can be seen from the following, a testimonial from a group of people recommending a man for employment on the Great Western Railway:

> The humble petition of William Bullock, a resident inhabitant of the Parish of Steventon in the County of Berks., respectfully shewed that your petitioner is anxious to obtain employment as a Porter on your

line of Railway. We the undersigned inhabitants of the said Parish recommend him as being a sober, honest, industrious person as a candidate for that office; he therefore solicits the kind approval of your honourable company hoping they will be pleased to grant him an early appointment and should he be the object of your choice will no doubt to the utmost of his abilities merit your confidence and approbation in discharging the duties committed to his care.[9]

From the earliest days, and long before the economy drifted into the depression of the 1860s, potential railway workers needed to provide references from a variety of sources before they could hope for consideration, let alone appointment—doctors, teachers, and clergymen being especially valued as proposers. Men aspiring to managerial positions on the Great Western Railway needed impeccable sponsors, and H. A. Simmons, who wrote under the pseudonym Ernest Struggles, commented that, 'You may have to run down to get a testimonial from the parson of the village where you lived, and a line from the farmer with whom you lived as bailiff; but, perhaps, the house agent's reference will do instead.'[10] To be fair, railways did not confine the need for impeccable references to those desiring lower- or middle-ranking posts.

At the beginning of the railway age the countrymen of England worked within squirearchies which had altered little since feudal times. Squirearchical power demanded obedience and quiescence; in return, the estate worker achieved a poorly paid, but often secure position. In the villages and small towns of the old society there was little opportunity for class organizations to develop. Trade unions and working-class political agitation groups had little chance of success against the entrenched power of the landed gentry, often backed by the Church and the town merchants. Rank, degree and authority were reflected in the pattern of seating in the churches, where front pews were reserved for the squire and his family, the middle rows for the estate managers and bailiffs, and the rear seating for the labourers and their families. H. A. Simmons has written:

The people at the village of Hinehoe were most exemplary. It was one of those parishes where the squire ruled the parson, and the parson ruled the people. Any man who did not touch his hat to the parson and attend church was an outlaw, unworthy of soup tickets and parish relief, and if he fell ill he might get better as he could; but if, on the other hand, he was respectful in his conduct, and if his wife picked up news or gossip for the curate as to what his neighbours and their wives and families did—then he was a worthy man, and could afford to lose one day a week and spend it at a public house, while his wife went for food and scraps to the mansion.[11]

Here the gossip of the village was transferred by regulatory whisper into the ear of the parson. Many country parsons fell in behind the new authority created by the railway companies, as unpaid service for the lord of the manor was transmuted into paid service in the industrial enterprise. One such notable was Dr Elliot, Bishop of Gloucester, who urged that agitators be thrown into the village horsepond.[12] The stringency of church views was soon backed by a legal sanction. One example was that any person found guilty of throwing wood or stone upon the railway was liable to penal servitude for life.

Arriving fresh from such a rigidly authoritarian background, the docile countryman made an ideal employee. The London and South-Western Railway was very keen on recruiting countrymen; after three decades of steam a staff magazine writer could comment:

> . . . looking at the general intelligence and powers of organization of the higher grades of our uniformed staff, we need not inquire further of what that raw material is capable . . . coming from the country they have as a rule a deal of shrewdness and a certain amount of hard-headedness against which the blandishments of agitators have hitherto been levelled in vain. . . . If they do their duty faithfully towards the Company, their advancement is sure.[13]

Slipping from one type of feudal power to another caused little difficulty for the countryman, particularly as his wages on the railway were so much better. Bonuses, too, were possible. On the London and Greenwich Railway the company paid a monthly bonus to engine crews who could reduce the amount of coke burned in fireboxes. By reducing consumption to sixteen pounds per mile, the driver could earn 5s. and his stoker 2s. 5d. For a reduction to fifteen pounds per mile the rates were 12s. and 6s. respectively—big rewards in the 1830s. And while in the countryside stratification was rigid, on the railway there was an opportunity to move up the ladder of promotion. A porter could aspire to station-master, an engine cleaner to express-train driver, an apprentice to works manager. The railway offered prospects—a career open to talents. Old concepts of obligation, although replaced by new concepts of service, were open to challenge, and this, to a countryman with some acumen and years of service, provided access to a new world. This situation appertained in railway workshops, and one writer discovered:

> I find the works at Bow have been in operation about twelve years, and cover about five acres, employing about 750 hands in their present juvenile condition.
> The labour is chiefly skilled, and even when it is not it is well remunerated and never too hard . . . it is most likely to be in the

future as it was in the past, that the greatest men of coming generations will be recruited not from the ranks of the apprentices, who are
most natty in dress and the greatest dandies, but those who are
least afraid to touch iron, hot or cold, or do such work rough or
smooth which comes their way.[14]

The same was true three-quarters of a century later. On leaving
school, Ritson Graham of Carlisle went to work on a farm, normal employment for young men in his area. But service in the First World War
unsettled him and he now needed a job with money and status. Before
he could join the Midland Railway sheds at Durran Hill, Carlisle, his
local vicar had to stand as guarantor. Ritson Graham went on to become
a trade unionist, a writer and broadcaster on the flora and fauna of
Cumberland, mayor and, eventually, freeman of the city of Carlisle.[15]

Jim Swain was born in Kingsbury, Middlesex, then completely rural.
In 1914, his father was working as a farm labourer, sixty-two hours a
week for a wage of 22s. Swain was the eldest of six children and the
income he received for the two jobs he did—4s. a week delivering gro-
ceries, and 5s. per week on a paper round—bridged the gulf between survival and disaster for the family. After many casual jobs Jim Swain
became an engine cleaner on the Great Northern Railway and carved
out for himself a notable career as a trade unionist, trainmen's inspector, and social activist.[16]

With such inducements, the smocked, unshaven villager was lured
over the dyke and introduced into a world where night and day had
little significance. Decked in uniform, buttoned and badged, he slotted
effortlessly into the hierarchy of railway grades. There was no room
here for the 'idiocy of the countryside'. Many of the men took to the
system like cream to coffee; from barn and byre, field and fold they were
recruited, and within a decade they were working in and around the
new industrial architecture, as over bridges of trestled wood and viaducts of stone and brick the trains of Britain went about their business. Michael Reynolds wrote lyrically, 'From tending nibbling sheep
and reposing on a bed of heather, he obtained a berth in a running
shed.'

But while the company looked favourably on him for his industrious-
ness, the countryman did occasionally feel the rancour of his colleagues
from the town. At the turn of the century the country versus town argument was raging in the Swindon works of the Great Western Railway,
and one writer commented:

> The workmen who come from the village are usually better natured
> than those who are strictly of the town. On the whole, though, they
> make the most congenial of mates, they work much harder and are

1. Matthew Kirtley and Midland Railway staff, locomotive department, Derby, c. 1860. Matthew Kirtley (the central figure in the front row, in light suit and hat) was MR locomotive superintendent from 1844 to 1873.

2. Bagster's clock (1837); now in the office of Sir Peter Parker, British Rail Headquarters. Notice the letter from C. A. Bagster to Richard Creed displayed at the back of the case.

3. Dial of the Bagster Clock.

4. Massed ranks: staff and officers at Strood, Kent, 1924.

5. State, Church and Army: a nameplate ceremony for a diesel locomotive, 1960s.

6. Army officer and trade union official: Colonel Sir Ian Walker-Okeover and Mr. John Ratcliffe, Secretary, ASLEF Branch, Cambridge Street.

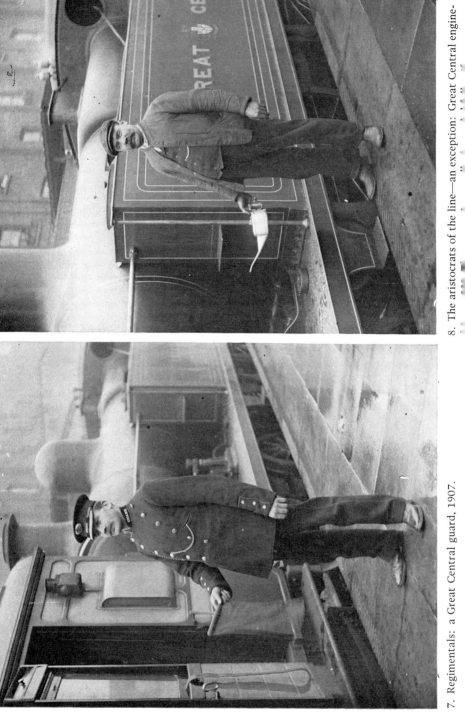

7. Regimentals: a Great Central guard, 1907.

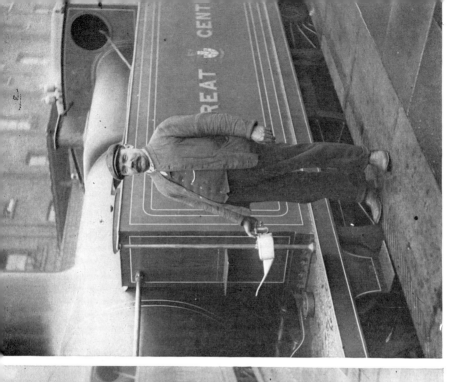

8. The aristocrats of the line—an exception: Great Central engine-

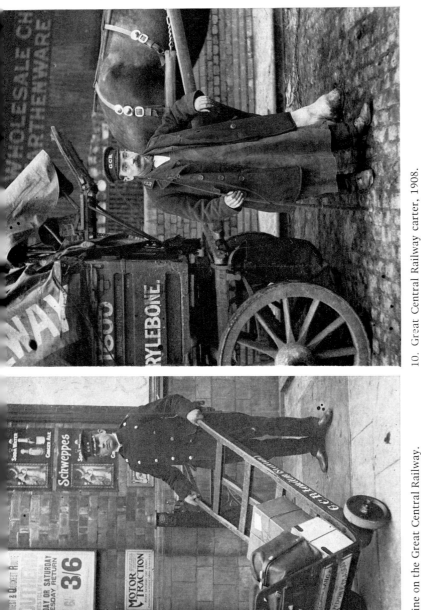

9. Polish and shine on the Great Central Railway.
A Marylebone porter, 1907.

10. Great Central Railway carter, 1908.

11. Low Fell signal box, 1914.
J. Dent, W. Fleming,
G. Thomson and H. Greenwell.

12. Pride in uniform:
Walter Stephens,
a passenger guard at
Paddington, *c*. 1904.

13. Carriage-cleaning staff at Bournemouth West, *c*. 1925. 'Although not provided
with uniform [only caps] we managed to maintain a matter [*sic*] of
self-respect, especially during the visit of H.R.H. the Prince of Wales'

more conscientious. They dress more roughly than their confreres of
the town; the last named would not dream of wearing corduroys in
the works. The countryman is fresh and tractable, open to receive
ideas and impressions of things. He brings what is practically a virgin
mind to the work; he is struck with the entire newness of it all, and
enters heart and soul into the business.

He is usually more active and vigorous, both in brain and body,
than is the other, and even when he falls short in actual intelligence
and knowledge of things, he more than makes up for it with pains-
taking effort; he is very proud of his situation.

Many of the town workmen, especially the more highly skilled
classes and journeymen, though village-born themselves show considerable hostility for the country hand newly arrived in the shed,
even after he has worked there many years and proved himself of
exceptional ability. They consider him at all times an interloper and
a waster, and make no secret of their dislike and antipathy to him.
They often curse him to his face and tell him that 'if it was not for
the likes of him we would have gotten higher wages. All you blokes
is fit for is cow banging and cleaning out the muck yard; you ought to
be made to come here and work for 10s. a week,' they say. All this
has little effect on the countryman and he seldom deigns to reply to
it.[17]

As late as 1919, Mr Harry Core was told that the locomotive superintendent for the Great Western Railway at Worcester, when congratu-
lating prospective drivers, advised them to 'keep good control of the
firemen, because the majority of locomotive-men were recruited from
the land and were of low mentality and little education'.[18]

One of the major sources of this enmity was the countryman's docility,
the very quality which made him attractive to his employer. In the
early days agitation was a rarity among railway workers, and Bristol men
were warned that there were plenty of agricultural labourers earning
9s. per week who were ready to replace militant railway workers. Roland
Kenney, a capstanman from Oldham, observed: 'It is the excessive
supply of labour coming from the agricultural districts which enables
the companies to readily replace servants agitating for wage increases.'[19] Kenney continued:

I have worked with some of these agricultural labourers—these plough
boys, to whom the wages of goods porter or carman mean prosperity.
The lightness of the work and the certainty of promotion . . . were
the baits which lured them from the countryside. I worked at a
goods yard where these countrymen were employed, and they were
certainly responsible for the low rate of wages, 16s. 10d. for a seventy-

hour week; they were the victims of specious promises and official hypocrisy.

The founding of the railway companies created a completely new problem in the recruitment, training and control of large bodies of workers across a wide range of skills. The most pressing problem was the establishment of undisputed authority, upon which a timetabled service was dependent. As with almost any large group, things occasionally got out of hand. When the Eastern Counties Railway arrived at Romford in Essex in 1839, the local men taken on by the company turned out to be rather wild fellows. From the newly built engine shed the men had the habit of frequenting a beershop near the works, and after such visits the men confused visitors by altering round the road signs. According to local documents, 'the calm of Romford was restored only when the Eastern Counties moved their twenty engines to Stratford, east London.'[20] Discipline was maintained with a singular harshness. Backing up the regime was a system of by-laws and Parliamentary Acts,[21] as quoted by the Great Western *Rule Book* of 1863: 'It shall be lawful for any officer or agent of the Company to seize or detain any engine-driver, porter, etc., who shall be found drunk, and convey such person before a Justice of the Peace, and such person may be committed for a period not exceeding six months.'

Apart from discipline, there were entirely new and special problems of costing and administration which had to be solved. Capital, technology and labour rapidly created difficulties quite new in industrial relations. An important confrontation arose over the new machinery and the physical labour required to service it. The technology which created the *Royal Scot*, the *Cornish Riviera* and the *Golden Arrow* was mocked by the widespread practices of men working in dusty, dark and draughty engine sheds, gas-lit signal boxes and in the hell-holes of the ashpits. The reward of investment was highlighted by the smallness of the wages paid. The aristocracy of the engine-drivers contrasted with the humbler echelons such as porters. Central policies contrasted with local methods. The *Rules and Regulations*, if carried out, simply meant the work would stumble into stoppage. Loyalty to the needs of the company was challenged by loyalty to family, grade, union and eventually to social class.

The only precedent for large-scale organization was the armed services and it was to these that the companies turned for their model. From the 1830s to the present, railway labour-control techniques and terminology have reflected many aspects of military life. The essential difference between railway work and the armed forces appeared when the railway workers realized that by carrying out their orders to the letter they would reduce the train services to a shambles. This 'working to rule' turns the concept of obligation upside-down.

The companies quickly constructed a hierarchy of grades which were based on the manifold tasks involved in the preparation and dispatch of trains. At first, little training was given and staff turnover could be high without serious inconvenience to the service. However, the companies quickly saw the need for literate as well as obedient staff. A large company needed a strong ethic, and this could be seen in the demands of the Great Western Railway. In 1837, those seeking employment in the company were asked to write these words: 'Zealously try to excel. Industry is commendable. Perseverance deserves success. Quietude of mind is a treasure.' In 1837, many people in Britain would have been hard put to copy that, let alone take it down as dictation. The railwaymen were from the beginning ruled by instructions as detailed as those of the Koran. They were the first 'organization men', stitched firmly into the fabric of their company, noted for punctuality, cleanliness and the smart execution of orders. A railway worker was 'in the service'. He reported for duty, and left it only after being relieved. Failure to report for duty meant he was absent without leave. He took unpaid leave only after written permission had been granted; unauthorized leave could lead to suspension, fines, dismissal and even prosecution. The military terminology was evident as early as 1830, when on the opening of the Liverpool and Manchester Railway 'orders of the day' were issued to the participants.

A number of military men appeared as railway officers: Captains Laws and Binstead on the Lancashire and Yorkshire, Coddington on the Caledonian, Eborall on the North-Western, and O'Brien on the North-Eastern. London's first railway, the London and Greenwich, was masterminded by a Woolwich-born army officer, Lieutenant-Colonel George Thomas Landman, who had built brick forts for the British Army in America during the tussles of 1812. Landman was assisted by Lieutenant George Walter, late of the Royal Marines. These commanding officers saw their task as fending off invasion of the territories they had been chosen to defend. In 1850, Captain William O'Brien became General Manager of the North-Eastern Railway and during his tenure his company fought off a series of attempted incursions. One writer has commented: 'It was with no ordinary satisfaction that Captain O'Brien, and those with him, had organized the defence of the North-Eastern during the most perilous part of its existence. . . . Not a position of importance had been surrendered, not an inch of territory lost.'[22]

Pay differentials on the railway reflected military hierarchies. In May 1847 the head of the Topographical Department of the Board of Trade was Captain Harness, and he enjoyed a salary of £600 per year. His assistant, Lieutenant Galton, earned £250 per year. On the Railway Commission, Major Brandreth received the handsome salary of £1,500 per year. At this time many railway workers were in receipt of less than £50 per year; few of them aspired to £100 per year.

Of the military men who chose railways as their second career, the most important was probably Mark Huish.[23] Nottingham-born of Dissenting parents, Mark Huish was at twenty-three a cadet in the army of the East India Company; by 1824 he was registered as an ensign with the Sixty-Seventh Regiment, Bengal Native Infantry. As a lieutenant he was, by 1826, personal escort to Lord Amherst in the newly raised Sixth Extra Regiment. As quartermaster and interpreter to this regiment, Huish mastered administrative techniques which he later placed at the disposal of his employers.

Mark Huish began his railway career on 3 November 1837 as Secretary to the Glasgow, Paisley and Greenock Railway. His salary was £200 annually and he was required to find sureties of £1,000. In 1841, Huish was appointed Secretary and General Manager of the Grand Junction Railway; four years later his salary was £1,250 annually, proof of his ability and status. Huish, despite his mistakes, was a new type of manager. On the Grand Junction Railway he advised the directors on general policy, represented them at select committees investigating the railway industry, and dealt with labour problems. Not only responsible for the general direction of policy, he was also the public face of the company. His experience was an important influence in the amalgamation which formed the London and North-Western Railway Company in 1846, of which he became the General Manager at a salary of £2,000 per year. His attitude to the company was one of zealous regard for all aspects of its policy. From 1846 to 1858 he was one of the foremost managers of the Victorian age. According to Professor T. R. Gourvish:

> His activities were similar to those expected of today's top managers in large-scale companies . . . he comes close to George Steiner's ideal, the charismatic leader of men . . . a business statesman in dealing with government and community leaders . . . a vigilant seeker of opportunities who is willing to come to grips with and solve problems.

Huish's reports were testimony to his ability not only as a practical railway officer, but also as a contributor to improvements in the techniques of management. His policy was simply the pursuit of victory for the organization he managed. His accomplishments read like a string of martial campaigns—the Octuple, the Six Towns Agreement, and the Secret Treaty, which he negotiated with the Midland Railway, are examples of his militaristic stewardship.

In the first week of Huish's reign at Euston, Queen Victoria was riding

North-Western metals between Euston and Crewe; at one point the train was running on a quarter of a mile of rail raised one foot above the soft clay preparatory to repacking. Responding to this near-disaster Huish embarked on a 'heavy metal policy'—anything which attempted to delay him should be taken over or shouldered aside.

Huish's great achievement was the Euston Confederacy, an alliance of companies incuding the Midland, the Lancashire and Yorkshire and the Eastern Counties. The aim of this alliance was to isolate Edmund Denison's Great Northern Railway. The Confederacy prevented Great Northern engines taking water at Retford, and Denison's trains were held up so that the Humber Ferry was missed. The track to Grimsby was obstructed by placing blocks on the line. In 1852, when the Great Northern attempted to encroach upon Midland territory, the first of its engines was denied access and driven into a shed where, after the tracks behind it were drawn, it miseried for seven months. Such activities were bound to create enmity and as the Confederacy began to crumble, Huish was the obvious scapegoat. His resignation in 1858 was the end of an age.

As Manager of the London and North-Western, Huish laid the foundations for one of the most advanced industrial structures in the world. In the 1850s, rising costs, fierce competition and government intervention made Huish's task difficult, but he nevertheless devised methods of accounting and control necessary to the conduct of his employer's business. The pricing and pooling system of his Confederacy was a massive contribution to railway working.

Under Huish, many haphazard previous practices were replaced by a sharper understanding of the role and status of an executive officer. Huish became and remained a railway manager, never achieving the status of a director of the company he served so well. Perhaps he was too aristocratic, too egocentric for his colleagues, for by 1858 he was undone. In his twelve years of office the ex-Bengal Lancer had seen the company's revenue increase by 50 per cent. According to Gourvish, 'Huish also professed a concern for the conditions in which railway men worked. His sympathy for the cause of a half-day holiday was publicized in 1856, when it was revealed that he had closed certain London and North-Western offices in Manchester, Liverpool and London on Saturday afternoons. . . .' Huish was described as 'a gentleman whose character stands high for Christian principles'.

In the years 1846–58, Mark Huish was raised to an exalted position. His new style of management and command of so many levers of power was certain to create jealousy and hostility. On his resignation, the company awarded their charismatic captain a free pass for life, but decided against a pension. In retirement he became a director of the

Isle of Wight Railway—the position denied him on the London and North-Western. Huish gave evidence to the 1867 Royal Commission on Railways, was active in the problems of Irish railways and arbitrated in a number of inter-company disputes. In retirement he was able to indulge in his Nonconformist ideals. He favoured religious instruction for the labouring classes and in 1863 obtained the appointment of a scripture reader for men constructing the Isle of Wight Railway. The doyen of the railway captains died, aged fifty-eight, in 1867, and is buried at St Boniface's Graveyard, Combe Wood, Isle of Wight. From the concept of service in feudal England and the uncompromising style of Mark Huish and other military men on their industrial manors, we can trace many contemporary theories of management.

The industry had a loyal police system designed to support such authoritarian rule. From the earliest days the companies wanted smart willing men to act as police and also give a good impression. The police, along with the rest of the industrial army, were easily recognizable by uniform, badges and buttons. The staff took pride in wearing the livery and insignia of the company they served, the company coat-of-arms being the supreme heraldic device. Uniformed staff and an effective system of policing gave an aura of discipline and pride in the task.

The London and North-Western's 1847 *Rule Book* insisted that 'every person receiving a uniform must appear on duty clean and neat.' The station-masters in this company made a daily inspection of the staff, ensuring that the railway servants on duty were clean in person and clothes, shaven, and with shoes brushed.

On the Eastern Counties Railway the staff of 1845 were controlled by railway police assisted by a manager and a number of inspectors; uniforms included top hats, tail coats and brass buttons. Many stations had sergeants of police assisted by a station clerk who issued tickets.

On the London and South-Western, the grade of policeman outnumbered all others. They were dressed in swallow-tailed, chocolate-coloured coats, dark trousers and tall, leather-crowned hats. Their duties were to preserve order in all the stations and on the line of railway, give and receive signals, assist in cases of accident, caution strangers of danger and remove intruders of all descriptions. They were also to guard the company's premises and to convey the earliest information on every subject to their appointed station and superior officers.

Discipline was maintained on every level. On 3 December 1847, a transfer clerk on the London and South-Western was dismissed for exercising with gun and dog on Battersea Fields. He was on sick leave at the time. An employee who left the same company without proper notice was prosecuted and sentenced to three weeks' hard labour, a

warning being issued to the staff. In 1848, the Great Western dismissed
a clerk at Abingdon for betting on a horse race, and dismissed a porter
who issued a writ against the company for fining him 1s. for a misdemeanour. The Great Western also threatened a guard with dismissal
unless he kept up his membership of the provident society operating
within the company. On the North-Eastern Railway, the driver of any
train was obliged to open any gates which were closed to his path;
failure to comply meant a fine of £2, more than two weeks' wages.

In a period when the Great Northern would suspend for the most
trivial offences, and the North-Western discharged a ganger for leaving
his post to obtain a cup of tea, at least one railway worker believed that
the companies had in their employ officials 'whose sole duty it was to
harass men by giving them arbitrary orders, by spying on them and by
generally acting the part that became known by its French term, "agent
provocateur". It was this bullying and arbitrary treatment management
were anxious to preserve.'[24]

This sort of treatment was to span many years. In 1935, Mr Walter
Stephens, a machine operator on the Great Western, spoke up on behalf
of a non-unionized group of railway workers. As a consequence of this
action the famous paternalism of the Great Western turned sour, and
Mr Stephens was transferred, without appeal, to a 'punishment' job.
This was a tour of duty starting at 1.45 p.m. and ending at 1.30 a.m.
Mr Stephens was employed for seventy-two hours per week on a guil-
lotine—a paper-cutter—for the princely sum of £1.[25] From such evidence
we can deduce that the companies, diverse in origin as they were, still
managed a common policy of labour control.

Such labour control, with its constituent elements of low pay and
long hours, was particularly evident in plate-laying, a labour-intensive
task which was by no means a 'punishment' job. Mr Will Thorne worked
on a plate-laying gang six days of twelve-hour shifts for the sum of 21s.
per week. The working day was 6.00 a.m. until 6.00 p.m., and the track
had to be made good before the men could leave the site. Sunday duty
was compulsory. If, through illness, a man failed to report for duty on
Sunday, his wages for the following Monday were forfeited. The plate-
laying ganger had power of wage determination and was very harsh
on men known to be members of the Amalgamated Society of Railway
Servants. There were no 'glassbacks' on the Tondu gang. It did not take
young Thorne long to understand what was meant by the railway
worker who 'penned' on behalf of the plate-layer.

He is the most neglected man in the service. The company decorate
him not with buttons, nor care for him in sickness, nor treat him as
traffic men are treated. He is the outcast of the railway system,

drudging on in his dangerous work, exposed to all weathers, receiving in return the scantest pay, and with little prospect of any promotion to a higher and more remunerative grade . . . hard work, danger and exposure are encountered and borne by him, that he and his family might bite an honest crust out of a pittance ranging from 17–20s. per week.[26]

These plate-layers were expected to act as retrievers of any items of equipment which might be lost from moving vehicles; all such items had to be returned to the stores with a letter showing where the equipment had been found. They were also forbidden to burn unsightly line-side grass on embankments over which sporting rights had been rented by the company. A Great Western Railway memorandum of 1 August 1905 drew attention to the fact that partridge nests had been destroyed at Carmarthen and that 'in future nests should not be unnecessarily destroyed.'[27]

The main-line railways were not alone in their cavalier treatment of plate-layers. On the Lynton and Barnstaple Light Railway—born 1898, interred 1935—the management were so keen on preserving a glossy image that plate-layers, just prior to the First World War, were not allowed on the station platform at Lynton, but had to 'slink by on the track'.[28]

It is not surprising in such circumstances that the desire to avoid punishment, suspension or fines was occasionally tempered with an urge to defy these sanctions under the very noses of authority. Within his own area even a booking clerk would sometimes display the bulldog spirit. H. A. Simmons has left us a fascinating picture of a daring young man employed on the Great Western Railway in the 1860s:

'Now, Mr British public,' said Joe, rubbing his hands, 'it wants just seven minutes to the time of train starting, I'll give you gruel!' And so saying he opened the slide for tickets. At least four hands were thrust into the office through the aperture, and twenty voices were heard asking for tickets to different places. Joe decided on one place first, and calling out that all those who wanted tickets for that place would be served first, Joe proceeded to issue the tickets.

The fare was 7s. 11d. Joe handed the ticket, and receiving in most cases half a sovereign, he promptly put down one penny, called out '9s.', and then adding 1s. change, said 'ten', handing out another and another with a sleight of hand that was marvellous.

He had not calculated it right, as 7s. 11d., 1d. and 1s. only made 9s., and each passenger was thus defrauded of 1s. So I told him of the mistake. . . .

'Ernest, my boy,' said he, 'that's bunce.'

'Bunce,' said I. 'What's that?'

'You are green,' said Joe. 'Why bunce is makings . . . if you think you're going to be on a railway and go straight, I tell you once for all, you will find your mistake out. Why, there is old Peltum, the superintendent, and that Calcraft, the auditor, if they are to catch you £1 short in your cash, they would have you up before the board the very next Wednesday, and "sack" is the name for it, straight off. Besides, if a fellow doesn't dress well and keep himself respectable, Peltum would shift him to the goods, and there you can't make a stiver, and you must go in rags for the rest of your life. Do you think the directors imagine for one moment that 22s. 6d. per week keeps me? Not they. They know all about it; and when they appoint booking clerks, they ought to say, "There's a place for you; we know you can't live on what we pay you, but go in and do the best you can for yourself; but, by George, don't let us catch you." '[29]

Normally, however, honesty was a fetish on the railways. From the earliest days the companies instilled in their staffs the tenets of the sanctity of private property lost or found on railway premises. Although engine-drivers engaged in 'ratting'—the stealing of corks and oil trimmings from one another's engines—the respect for private property was a potent concept among railway workers.[30] Even today, railway workers are very concerned with preserving this image of uniform honesty, even to the point where they will not report the misdeeds of others for fear of shattering it. F. S. Williams discovered this on the Midland many years ago, and wrote:

> Perhaps the chief difficulty in the prevention of offences of this kind among railway servants arises from the false code of honour which exists among the men themselves—a code, unhappily, found also elsewhere—which hinders them from actively repressing crimes which they would not themselves commit, or even perhaps countenance, but which they will not expose.[31]

The instrument at the heart of the entire disciplinary structure was the almighty *Rule Book*. Its role can be divided into three phases throughout railway history. The first of these was one in which the *Rule Book* was simply the company edict; no appeal against its strictures was possible. The second phase opened with the Railway Disciplinary Procedure of 1912. Here the stringency of the *Rule Book* was relaxed; men accused of misdemeanours were issued with charge sheets and could ask for formal hearings at which they could bring witnesses for their defence. The book remained tightly structured, however, and in the 1930s the men learned to turn this to their advantage as a bargaining weapon. The Vigilance Movement showed them that 'working to rule' made them virtual masters of the stations and depots; it allowed them to express their grievances without resorting to the dreaded step of 'stopping the job'. The third phase in the saga of the *Rule Book* is its popularization. Although engine-men, guards and signalmen will often insist on 'having it by the book', there is now a widespread acceptance of the need to interpret it in a more moderate way on both sides.

The dangerous nature of railway work meant that rules and regulations as stringent as those of the armed services were needed. It was important for railway workers to appreciate that their own safety, as well as that of the passengers, depended upon correct application of the rules. The printed commands, backed by suspension and dismissal, represented an attempt not only to keep the men in their places but also to control behaviour in any foreseeable circumstance. When the unforeseeable occurred, men whose normal role it was to observe a rule to the letter became innovators, responding to emergencies in ways which restored equilibrium to the system.

The need to observe the rules was demonstrated on various occasions. On 10 May 1848 the noon express from Exeter ran at full speed into a horse box and van which, contrary to rule, had been pushed foul of the main line, despite the fact that signals were clear for the express. Six passengers were killed and thirteen injured, a heavy price for an illegal shunting movement. On 10 October 1874, a failure in communication between an inspector and a telegraph clerk led to rule breaking and a collision near Norwich on the Great Eastern which cost the lives of twenty-one people, including five railway workers. In 1875 thirteen passengers were killed and seventy-three injured in a crash at Abbots Ripton on the Great Northern Railway. Item six of the findings of the inquiry placed a large responsibility on the signalman for neglecting to carry out the rules regarding the placing of detonators and the provision of proper handlamp signals.

A considerable amount of the responsibility for such accidents as these, however, must be placed on the companies' policy of overworking underpaid men, and the reason why accidents were not ten times the level they were was due to the praiseworthy loyalty of these exhausted souls to the task at hand. In any case it was mostly the men themselves who suffered from such accidents. Railway work was as dangerous as it was arduous, and the slaughter went on until the last quarter of the nineteenth century. Between 1874 and 1876, 2,249 railway workers were killed and 10,305 injured. According to a survey conducted in 1865, the risk of accidents was fifty times greater among railway servants than railway travellers. Accidents to railway workers were categorized as acts of God and the companies were long reluctant to accept responsibility for accidents and sickness among the staff. This reluctance also extended to some of their passengers. In 1867 the South-Eastern Railway was trying to obtain a limit of £100 in compensation paid to victims of railway accidents. 'We have', it was declared, 'to pay large sums of money to people of a low class of life, and there is a desire on the part of solicitors and others to connive at attempts to extort large sums of money from the railways.' There is no doubt where the loyalties of the South-Eastern lay.

Given such attitudes it is not surprising that in the early days the men occasionally resented the *Rule Book* and all it implied. A version of the railway commandments which appeared in the *Railway Service Gazette* on 5 April 1873 ably demonstrates what it must have been like to work for those leviathans.

The Railwaymen's Ten Commandments

1. Thou shalt have no occupation but this.
2. Thou shalt not seek the benefits of a trade union.
3. Thou shalt make all thy application in vain.
4. Remember the Sabbath day—work for nothing.
5. Honour thy official and carry tales.
6. Thou shalt use all thy skill.
7. Thou shalt commit 300 rules to memory.
8. Thou shalt not have any time for meals.
9. Thou shalt not make any complaint, except for the waste-paper basket.
10. Thou shalt not covet any superior position—thou shalt obey thine official, be his manservant, his gardener, his ass, or anything short of being his neighbour.

2

The Rise and Fall of Company Loyalty

Once a railwayman, always a railwayman.
—SIR JOHN ELLIOT

What is man made for except to reform what man has made?
—RALPH WALDO EMERSON

In the early 1970s the director of the New York Centre for Residential Security Design, Mr Oscar Newman, aroused great interest with his theory of defensible space. Mr Newman's hypothesis was that the behaviour of social groups was determined by their ability to mark off for themselves a clearly defined area in which the writ of the group would run. Without such territorial rights, Newman argued, a group would suffer from environmental alienation, and the frustration of these groups would manifest itself in unsocial behaviour and the eventual destruction of the area and its artefacts.[1]

The railway companies of the 1840s employed neither anthropologists nor sociologists, but they were not unaware of the desire of individuals and groups to establish a little elbow room. When a company employed a man, it expected him to stay at his post, and he was fined if found in places where he had no business. Within his limited territory, however, a man could often create his own administrative system. The companies sensed that well-defined boundaries made for clearly established relationships and that the long hours and harsh discipline could be compensated for by the ability of the railway worker to stamp his individuality over a certain area or stretch of ground.

The result was the railway 'bailiwick'. Trapped in space and time, railway workers learned how to defend their space. However humble his status, control of his own thinking and of the technology he operated was always in the grasp of the railway worker. Very quickly the engineman was referring to 'my engine', the signalman to 'my box' and the shunter to 'my yard'. The engines, wagons and staff of other companies were quickly dubbed 'foreigners', even though the premises of rival companies were often only a few hundred yards apart. All grievances and union matters were discussed and initiated on the bailiwicks, and national agreements came to reflect the needs and customs of this sovereign territory. Thus was created a new form of industrial anthropology, a tribalistic grouping of men based on an elaborate division of labour, a hierarchy of groups and a ritualistic adherence to territory, myth, symbolism and insignia unknown outside the specified boundaries.

From the earliest days, the railway companies sought a new type of loyalist, nothing less than a prototype, an 'organization man'. They achieved an outstanding success, and for more than a century the workers demonstrated a loyalty to newly founded traditions and working methods unique in British industrial history. In the railway industry, the Protestant ethic, militarism and nineteenth-century paternalism met and were cemented into specific loyalties which retained their potency long after the amalgamation of disparate companies in 1923, or the advent of public ownership in 1948. How did such loyalties originate, and why is it that no other industrial or commercial undertaking has ever been able to initiate and maintain the corporate image engineered by the railway companies?

The fundamental gregariousness of man, the need for acceptance and the desire to belong and to be seen to belong to a differential group were the basics for the companies' success; second was the unprecedented way in which the owners handed over the tools of production to the workers, thus establishing a proprietary interest in the care and maintenance of the equipment. The slogan 'the train must go through' was never a platitude to railway workers, but a daily, indeed lifelong challenge to their loyalty and ingenuity. An additional element of this new style of labour control was the encouragement of a whole range of company-encouraged social activities, ranging from Fur and Feather Societies to Rifle Volunteer Units, which tied men to a corporate identity even in their leisure hours.

Working for a railway company involved a man in a mass of contradictory thoughts. A natural desire for freedom clashed daily with the need to swallow his pride and curb his tongue when injustice was observed. There was a fear of freedom too, for freedom meant the glutted labour market, the freedom to starve.

Despite the fines and the suspensions and the fear of freedom, a specific loyalty was born, flourished and was difficult to eradicate. The men of the Highland Railway typified this attitude:

In a word, the HR man looked upon himself as part and parcel of the system. He would proudly resent the idea of being looked upon as a serf, a slave, a menial or a bottom dog. Not in his wildest dreams did it ever occur to him to strike . . . for improved conditions of living. He succeeded in 'making ends meet' . . . for he knew contentment, and contentment is a jewel not to be found in the possession of many who have accumulated much of the world's filthy lucre.[2]

Loyalty can go no further than the case of the Inverness ticket-collector; O. S. Nock describes his activities: '. . . between trains, and quite voluntarily, [he] spent the time sweeping the square, and making the place look smart and tidy. This was a self-appointed task, and quite unrewarded financially; but it was typical of the Highland Railway employees' sense of pride in the company.'[3]

More than half a century later Alan Butler met a similar approach by porters on the Western Region of British Railways, and he has written:

My workmates, nearly all older men, had known nothing else but railway work. Despite the poor pay, they believed in the service they were giving. Most of them had waited fifteen years for promotion, and this slow progress had given them a strong sense of the brotherhood of railwaymen.

While working at Clifton Down as a porter my attention was drawn to the case of a porter who was about to retire after fifty-five years' service on a pension of 1s. per week. For many years he had paid into an old railway pension fund, but through inadequate support by the men concerned, the original promise of 5s. per week did not materialize and the surviving members of the fund had to take what remained from a rapidly diminishing fund. Yet even nationalization of the industry and the prospects of better pensions had not killed off their pride in the Great Western Railway.[4]

The numerous accidents to railway servants which meant loss of work also meant loss of earnings, the man's suffering becoming almost immediately aggravated by poverty. A railway worker, when incapacitated, could appeal to his employer; in the case of rejection he could appeal to his comrades and, as a last resort, to the public. If accident or illness was prolonged and the sources of assistance atrophied, the workhouse was the final humiliation. For the company, the most usual way to discharge its debt to a permanently disabled man was the provision of a small lump sum, financed mainly by fines for disciplinary offences; if a man was injured, but not wholly disabled, he could be kept on in the company in a lower post and at a smaller wage. In the days when men faced injury in a hundred ways, this concession by the employer promoted a specific loyalty, as one observer found when he visited one of the new railway towns:

. . . at Wolverton are to be observed an extraordinary number of young couples, young children, young widows, also a considerable number of men who have lost a finger, hand, arm, or leg. All, however, whether whole or mutilated, look for support to 'the Company', and not only their services and their thoughts, but their parts of speech are more or less devoted to it: for instance, the pronoun 'she' almost invariably alludes to some locomotive engine; 'he' to 'the chairman', 'it' to the London Board.[5]

Because of this terror of accidents and sickness, railway workers in the 1840s and 1850s went 'fund mad'. On the London and South-Western Railway at this time staff welfare was catered for by the company's Friendly Society.[6] The company's annual contribution to this fund was augmented by the proceeds from lost property sales and staff fines. The directors reported that most of the men had joined a casualty fund paying 1d. per week, which the company matched. Superannuation for clerks was begun and for the needy retired the distastefully named Decayed South-Western Clerks Fund was established. By 1881 the South-Western could offer its staff the following societies: Medical Fund, Provident Fund, Widows and Orphans, Friendly Society, Staff Guarantee Club, and Institute Club, plus others.[7]

Two influences were at work here: first, the lack of national legislation on injuries and sickness; and second, the deep desire of the staff to pay for and control their own independence and security. The few coppers entering the coffers of many slate clubs could make only a small dent in the relief required by widows, orphans and injured men, but the cheerfulness with which the money was collected and dispensed by volunteers is evidence of the power of self-help theories promoted in England by men such as Samuel Smiles. Workmen's Compensation, National Insurance and the attempt to provide a comprehensive health service in Britain all have their origins in the desire of people in dangerous trades to protect themselves against economic blizzards which blew when injury or sickness struck down the breadwinner. The myriad railway friendly and benefit societies pointed unmistakably in one direction—security for all. By contrast, although 'no work, no pay' was the rule for railway servants, skilled officers of the companies who were temporarily immobilized did not forfeit salary. Provision against ordinary sickness was therefore not regarded as a common need by railway officers, who were not usually members of local provident clubs.

An interesting provident society was the Railway Benevolent Institution, an organization founded in May 1858 by railway officers from various companies. Its purpose was to give help to those members and their families who were deprived of adequate means of support. This institution marked itself off from its contemporaries by undertaking the maintenance, clothing and education of certain children who were impoverished. Until schools were established, the children were placed in private places selected by friends and approved by the board of the institution. Expenses for education, clothing and maintenance were met by the board out of disposable funds.

The treatment of children thus cared for contrasted oddly with the provisions made for the children of railway servants who were catered for at the Euston Day School in Seymour Street. At this establishment, built in 1853, charges were made for instruction according to the amount of wages received by the father. In 1867 the charges at the school were as follows:

For children of persons receiving	Each child per week
Less than 20s. per week	2d.
Above 20s., not exceeding 25s.	3d.
Above 25s., not exceeding 30s.	4d.
Above 30s., not exceeding 35s.	5d.
Above 35s.	6d.

The doyen of the railway provident societies was probably the Great Western Railway Engine-men and Firemen's Mutual Assistance Fund. Under this compulsory society, GWR engine-men could retire at sixty years of age with a lump sum of £100 and a weekly pension of 12s. 6d. The lump sum was equal to a year's earnings for a driver, and the weekly pension was equal to a third of his retirement wage.

Henry Kirtley, an engine-driver from Cheltenham, became Secretary of this fund, the MAS, in 1865 and was for many years its driving force. Kirtley actually became Locomotive Superintendent at Paddington, a remarkable achievement for a railway worker, and from this position he enrolled Great Western locomotive superintendents into the fund. An obelisk to his memory stands in Kensal Green Cemetery in London. In 1950, foot-plate staff at Newton Abbot and Banbury stopped work in defence of compulsory membership of the fund, a principle queried by the Railway Executive, at that time struggling with new proposals for railway pensions. The GWR men won their battle. The fund's report for 1965 indicated surplus funds of £1 million.[8] When the fund winds up in the year 2004 it will have given a century and a half of voluntary service to the engine-men of the Western Region.

Self-help, self-sacrifice and a sense of morality were important elements in the preservation of railway loyalty. Another example of morality was the attitude of railway managements and staffs in their approach to alcoholism and the temperance movement in Victorian England.

Weekends in Victorian cities were often enlivened by the sight of drunkards being forcibly ejected from licensed premises and later by weeping women searching for their besotted menfolk. Although the long and degrading hours of factory labour could be eased by drink-sodden oblivion, the railway companies would accept neither time-weathered customs of drink on the job nor legislative provisions of the Beer Shops Act, 1830, which allowed any householder to brew drink in his home. From their experiences with the railway navvies, who had roistered the industry into being, the companies had learned that alcohol and trains do not mix well. Drinking on duty was to have no place in the industry, and as early as 1840 railway workers discovered the worse for drink could be sent to the treadmill.

In London, the Railway Temperance Movement tackled the problem of the 'accursed trade', which in 1890 was worth £100 million annually.[9] The campaign against drink brought forth zealots of great resource and daring, including engine crews who carried out leaflet raids from moving engines. Humble and titled representatives of the Railway Temperance Movement campaigned against the 'Big D' alliance of Drink, Devil and Disease. In the search for converts and witnesses many fine tracts were written. Some grades had pamphlets specially written for them. *On the Line* was directed at the engine-men, *The Coupling Iron* went to shunters and *The Breakdown Gang* was offered to those who rerailed engines and wagons. *Are You Loaded?* pointed its message to the railway carter.

Speaking at Euston on 7 February 1908, the Venerable Archdeacon of London remarked that Britain was 'spending £142 million annually on intoxicating drinks, and that premature death through unsober habits claimed 120,000 victims annually'. In that year there were reputed to be 600,000 habitual drunkards in Britain; more than 300,000 charges of drunkenness were brought before the magistrates in 1907. According to the Archdeacon, the country had more than 160,000 public houses, and a total of 103,000 lunatics owed their incarceration to 'mazing their minds with alcoholic drinks.'

At the same meeting at Euston, Lord Stalbridge, Chairman of the London and North-Western Railway, argued that 'no railwayman has got any business whatsoever to lose the slightest particle of the power of the will, or the brain power which God has given him, by muddling it in any way by drink, making him incapacitated for duty either in the day or night.' The good Lord Stalbridge urged further: 'that of all people in the world, railwaymen ought to, and I assert they do, set an example of sobriety and good fellowship'. At this hugely successful meeting a new phrase was coined—'as sober as a railwayman'.

Another supporter of temperance connected the subject with Christianity. Lady Hope, whose ardour for temperance could not disguise her recognition of social class, remarked: 'They all took an interest in their servants. Why not in the railwaymen, who were equally their servants?'[10] She went on to congratulate the workers who were always at their posts doing their duty, and she referred to the guard who had told her that 'on one journey he had been offered strong drink on no less than seventeen occasions'. When he refused all blandishments he was accused of 'thinking himself better than they'. According to Lady Hope, railwaymen were 'a noble race of men but they were also poor sinners who needed salvation from the power of guilt and sin'; she made no reference to the policies of the companies in wages and hours.

The leading Parliamentary teetotaller was Mr Wilfred Lawson, who sat for the railway centre of Carlisle.[11] Known to his opponents as the 'Apostle of Slops', he described the right to brew beer as a 'licence to do harm'. The Railway Temperance Movement, born out of a distaste for drunkenness, compassion for its casualties, and a sense of responsibility for traveller and company, faced a united front of brewers, publicans and consumers. Although in 1872 Thomas Brassey, son of the railway builder, had agreed that trade societies had strenuously exerted their influence to suppress the vice of drunkenness,[12] the fact remained that in 1908 75 per cent of the 10,000 trade-union branches then existing met in public houses and a large part of the ritual was centred on 'drink stewards'. The association of trade unions with public houses is old in Britain's history. Nevertheless, although boxes existed in which committee members were allowed to dip for liquid expenses, many union branches fined members who brought liquor to the meetings. And while the temperance movement, despite its mighty efforts of public meetings and warning pamphlets, never prised away union meetings from licensed premises, the fact remains that for the present-day railway worker, the sanctions against drunkenness are identical to those of the 1840s —dismissal and the consequent loss of character.

In the promotion of loyalty the companies could not afford to ignore the social cement of church attendance and religious instruction, though no united policy was attempted. For many years Sunday duties on the railway were unpaid labour and despite the need to encourage the good behaviour which would stem from regular church-going, some companies were not unaware of the cash value lost if railway workers spent a large part of Sunday in company pews rather than on company duties. But on the London and Greenwich Railway there was no ambivalence. It was stated that:

. . . the directors intend on all occasions to prevent their men being employed during Divine Service on Sundays, as they have engaged two pews at St James's Church, Bermondsey, expressly for their accommodation, and have intimated their wishes that those who are in their employ should be constant in their attendance at Church.[13]

Great Western Railway Temperance Union.

President: CHAS. MORTIMER, Esq., J.P.

I shall be glad to have my name enrolled as a Member of the GREAT WESTERN RAILWAY TEMPERANCE UNION, and agree to the Declaration to which I have subscribed my name.

DECLARATION A.

I RECOGNISE my duty to exert myself for the suppression of Intemperance, and having become a Member of this Union, will endeavour, both by example and effort, to promote its objects.

Name ....

Address ....

Occupation ....

Dept. or Office ....

Date ....

DECLARATION B.

I RECOGNISE my duty to exert myself for the suppression of Intemperance, and having become a Member of this Union, will endeavour, both by example and effort to promote its objects, and in furtherance of this Declaration, I promise, with the help of God, to abstain from all Intoxicating Drinks as Beverages.

Name ....

Address ....

Occupation ....

Dept. or Office ....

Date ....

Recommended by ....

This form should be filled up and handed to the Branch Secretary or a member of the Branch Committee, or forwarded to the General Secretary, 14, Eastbourne Terrace, Paddington.

Fig. 1 Temperance Declaration Form (Reproduced by courtesy of Leonard Lean)

The North London Railway was tougher; it suspended train services during the time the directors were at church. The Taff Vale Railway, with a more oblique approach, used knowledge of church attendance as a means of granting promotion. It was on the London and North-Western, however, that the real alliance of mechanical and religious power was cemented. As one commentator on that industrial giant observed:

> Francis Webb . . . as head of the works . . . was an absolute autocrat, not only inside it, but out. He coerced politically those under his command, he coerced them religiously. His foremen were unexceptionally Conservatives, and intimidation of the rank and file through these was reduced to a system. That rank and file was predominantly Liberal and Nonconformist. For example, the living of St Paul's, Crewe, was in the gift of the railway, and to it, Webb appointed his brother (afterwards Canon A. H. Webb) in 1879. The church had been poorly supported. It was now filled on Sundays. The foremen, formed into a committee in the following year, saw to that on behalf of the brothers Webb. Dismissals were certainly not unaffected by the political convictions of those dismissed; nor were promotions.[14]

The London and North-Western Railway for many years took pride in advising its staff that arrangements existed for every man in the company to attend a service at least once on a Sunday. From Monday to Saturday workers on the LNWR laboured in the vineyard of the Webbs, but even on Sunday authority demanded the presence in church of those not manning railway yards and offices.

W. J. Gordon records:

> . . . as far back as 1857 Derby seems to have been the first centre, and the Midland the first railway where a distinct religious work was founded among the men employed . . . the directors of the company built a commodious hall in 1877. A little before this the men had begun to ask various ministers of the town to come and speak to them . . . Dr Tait, Bishop of London . . . Bishop Lonsdale . . . John Ashworth of Rochdale. . . . Breakfast and address would go on at the same time, and then when plates and cups [were] empty, the eager assembly join[ed] heartily in a song of praise at the close of the 'breakfast talk'.[15]

But this activity paled before what was occurring 120 miles away outside the Gothic fastness of the London terminus of the Midland, St Pancras Station. The station is named after a Christian boy martyred by the Roman Emperor Diocletian. By 1874, the platforms of the station were roofing a huge vault devoted to the storage of Burton ales. Within a few yards of this beer cathedral, representatives of the Total Abstinence

Movement took their stand in the railway arches and fulminated against the demon drink. Miller's *St Pancras—Past and Present*[16] discusses the testimony of Rev W. Ewart of Zion Presbyterian Church, Goldington Crescent: 'He has been undaunted by difficulties and opposition. . . . He has seen . . . the absolute necessity of promoting the Total Abstinence Movement as the only successful method for the prevention and cure of intemperance.'

Rev Ewart was part of a movement which eventually created the Railway Mission, an organization devoted to the promotion of Christian values among railway workers. By 1898, the mission had twenty-three full-time evangelists and missionaries, whose work was supported by voluntary contributions from rank and file railway workers. Its work continued through the 1970s but the affection felt by railway workers for the missionary does not extend to his talks and texts. The railway missionary has a capacity to glide into the company of railwaymen, but once he has gone the stilted conversation becomes relaxed and the taboo subjects are reinstated. The free tracts will gather dust on messroom shelves, until cleared by the watchful steward.

Staff on the West Highland Railway were fierce defenders of their own religious needs and obligations. When this company penetrated the West Highlands, it entered territory where religion had altered little since the Reformation. Churches were cobbled together from platform station rooms, the signalman often taking the role of beadle. Ministers who travelled long distances to service the flock appeared only at monthly intervals. Religion was a serious matter for the first Protestants who came north to man the line, as well as to the locally recruited labour. For them the Lord's Day meant exactly what the Ten Commandments said—rest. Sunday working on the railway was anathema to Highlanders, civil population and railway workers alike, and for this principle they were prepared to fight. In the summer of 1882, the West Highland Railway felt the full force of deeply held religious views. In May of that year the railway foolishly attempted to load and despatch a fish train from Strome Ferry. John Thomas has recorded the result:

On the last Sunday in May 1881 a fish train was loaded up at Strome Ferry on the Dingwall and Skye line and despatched to London. When the fact became known there was rage and consternation in the area. . . . What happened next was described in the following day's *Glasgow Herald*: 'At that moment a body of about fifty natives with clubs and bludgeons presented themselves on the quay and stated they would not allow the unloading of the vessels to go on. It was the Lord's Day and they would not permit such a desecration of the Sabbath for fear of a judgment from heaven. The crowd forcibly ejected a man in charge of the steamers and, on the crews of the steamers and the railway officials persisting in unloading the fish, threatened them with personal violence. A fight ensued and those belonging to the steamers and the railway company were completely overpowered and compelled to give up hope of unloading the vessels.

'Later that morning, when Highland Railway headquarters in Inverness were informed by telegraph of the situation at Strome Ferry, a special train was sent out, stopping at Dingwall on the way to pick up six policemen. They found Strome station and pier invested by some 150 angry and determined men. The police charged the crowd six times and were beaten back to stand cowed and impotent outside the station door. The Highland Railway then requested the military authorities for "a detachment of bayonets" but the request was refused. Strome stayed in rebel hands until someone shouted "Twelve o'clock", whereupon the demonstrators disappeared into the darkness. The fish, no longer fresh, left for London.'[17]

Railway work was often 'kept in the family'; sons followed their fathers into the industry and railway families often intermarried. Fathers and uncles already in the service would ask at shed, station or yard on behalf of younger members of the family seeking work. This was of great assistance to the companies in fostering loyalty as family honour became identified with the undisturbed progress of the companies. Sometimes the relationship was horizontal, when many members of the same family took up railway work, while at other times it was vertical —generation to generation. The Cornish family of Exeter is an example of vertical association, five sons becoming workers on the Great Western, as is the Lean family of Hanwell, London, whose association with the GWR can be traced to the apprenticeship of a Lean to none other than Richard Trevithick. John Lean, who was active in the 1850s, reported direct to Brunel on the construction of the line between Starcross and Teignmouth. Charles Lean worked on the Kilsby Tunnel, near Rugby, and the skills he learned in controlling water seepage in the Cornish mines would be crucial in saving the tunnel from abandonment. Charles Lean gave forty-nine years of service to the Great Western Railway, and the tradition of Western Leans is carried on today by Mr Leonard Lean, who works in the Paddington offices of British Rail, a living link with the first railwaymen of Britain.

From the earliest days the companies used housing policy as a means of staff control and for the preservation of company loyalty. A company cottage with attached garden provided an inducement for many prospective railway workers and was also a useful barrier to militancy. Railway housing began as a hotchpotch, when to meet early needs railway arches were filled up as habitations; later, old houses, stations, and even stables were renovated to house the staff. By the late 1840s, however, the attitude to staff housing was changing. In 1848, for example, when the Eastern Counties Railway moved its engine works from Romford, Essex, to Stratford in east London, 300 houses were built by the company for its workers.[18] By 1851, the Great Western had built a good deal of new Swindon. The housebuilder Rigby erected 300 cottages on land provided by the company. The blocks of houses were arranged in groups of three, each group having the blocks abreast of each other and running parallel with the railway. By 1897 the Midland Railway possessed 2,199 workers' cottages.[19] When the Manchester, Sheffield and Lincolnshire Railway entered Manchester, of the twenty acres purchased, eleven were set aside for staff housing.[20]

At Peterborough, the Great Northern Railway built an estate which became known as 'The Barracks', due to its military-style layout. There were 226 brick and slate houses, plumbed and flushed. The end houses in each terrace were larger than their neighbours, the original tenants being foremen.

A watershed in the provision of railway housing was described by Sir F. Head in 1855:

> ... Wolverton ... is a little red-brick town composed of 242 little red-brick houses—all running either this way or that way at right angles—three or four tall red-brick engine-chimneys, a number of very large red-brick workshops, six red houses for officers—one red beer-shop, two red public houses, and, we are glad to add, a substantial red schoolroom and a neat stone church, the whole lately built by order of a railway board, at a railway station, by a railway contractor, for railwaymen, railway women, and railway children; in short, the round cast-iron plate over the door of every house, bearing the letters LNWR, is the generic symbol of the town.[21]

In the same period, Head found on the windy Cheshire plain a village growing into the archetypal Victorian company town:

> The town of Crewe contains 514 houses, one church, three schools, and one town hall ... the new houses at Crewe were originally built solely for railway servants, yet it was soon found necessary to construct a considerable number for the many shopkeepers and others who were desirous to join the new settlement, and accordingly, of the present population of 8,000, about one half are strangers.[22]

At Horwich, on the Lancashire and Yorkshire Railway, staff education was provided for by a mechanics institute and a technical school, which were opened in 1888. In 1893 a public hall with seating for 900 was added. Later, the board placed eleven acres of land at the disposal of the institute committee, and this was laid out with bowling green, tennis courts and a cricket pitch. Of the 5,000 men and boys employed at Horwich in the 1890s, well over 2,000 of them were regularly associated with the facilities of the institute.

Railways in Scotland had, as may be expected, their own way of doing things. When the North British Railway developed the hillside town of Riccarton, it built cottages and provided gas capable of supplying 300 lights. A schoolhouse was built for the Riccarton children, and when they left school to learn a trade, they were given a season ticket worth £1 per year. A company recreation hall housed a library, concert hall and a variety of competitive games.[23] The Riccarton pioneers worshipped at first in the engine shed, then moved to the station waiting-room. Later the railway workers founded a local co-operative store, with a shop on the station platform. The books of the society were submitted periodically for the scrutiny of the company's directors.

In Glasgow, a railway job had status, and housing conditions for railway workers were commensurate with responsibility. Men stepped up in housing as they stepped up in grade. William McLagan has written:

> There were many railway properties adjoining the railway lines and these could be put into two categories: (1), small one room and kitchen and single apartment houses in tenement properties, particularly in Gorbals and Bridgeton; (2), two- and three-room flats with bathrooms near suburban stations such as Queen's Park and Mount Florida. The former were demolished, declared sub-standard by today's needs. In their day they were small, about eight foot by twelve foot, dingy, without inside bathroom or toilets. Rent and rates were very low compared with private houses in the same districts. The tenants would change with the times. First it would be drivers, then firemen, guards, then shunters or signalmen and then porters.[24]

In 1863, the Edinburgh and Glasgow Railway built houses for their workers in the Springburn district of Glasgow. The site they chose was Springburn Hill, which was surrounded by engine sheds, yards, and locomotive builders' works. On the steep slopes of the hill they built a series of spectacular terraces in the Scottish baronial style with elegant turret staircases and crow-stepped gables, examples of which can still be seen in certain parts of Edinburgh. They were built of fine grey sandstone and were known locally as 'The Blocks'. In their day they were 'workers' dwellings that had no equal', according to press statements of the time. Although this may have been true they still did not have bathrooms; toilets were shared between two families. The communal washhouse was used to wash clothes; bodies were catered for at the nearby

Springburn Public Baths. Working on engines was a very dirty job, but railwaymen were always noted for their cleanliness; both the kitchen sink for the body and the wash-house for the clothes were often in use. The houses at the top of the hill were of a better standard and were for the top drivers, engineers and supervisors, while the lower blocks were for other drivers and lower grades. One entered through a warren of passageways, each giving access to what is known in Glasgow as a 'single end', or one-roomed flat. They measured 12 ft by 8 ft and housed complete families. The only source of daylight was a small window about 3 ft above street level. Lighting was by gas.

A century after their construction these blocks could be seen by passengers coming into Glasgow from Edinburgh or the Western Isles. In the 1950s, although designated sub-standard by the local authority, they possessed an air of elegance few other blocks could boast. The rents of these houses before 1939 ranged from 7–10s. weekly, rates inclusive. The private building sector could not at this time offer anything comparable to railway accommodation. For the period, in both style and rents, the railway blocks were most desirable residences for workers.

Following the tenement tradition, the Caledonian Railway built a block of flats in Carlisle known as 'Caley Buildings', which incorporated the 'bed-in-the-wall'—the single end. There was, however, another side to this company's housing policies. In 1890, strikers at Motherwell were evicted with great violence from their rented cottages. Police and army were called in to carry out the eviction, and by way of retaliation the strikers did great damage to the glass roof of Motherwell Station. A medallion, inscribed 'Remember Motherwell 1890', was later struck to mark the occasion when company loyalty in Scotland was set at nought by the Caledonian Railway.

Far away to the south, the Great Western Railway, a pioneer in staff housing since Brunel made Swindon the powerhouse of the London–Bristol services, produced a fine example of railway housing when it helped to create Hayes Garden Village, Middlesex.[25] In the 1920s a plan to provide comfortable houses for Great Western employees was mooted. A company was formed which had the GWR as main guarantor. Only railway workers were to be considered as tenants. Land was acquired at Acton and Hayes, the only stipulation being that tenancy in Acton was restricted to engine-men, while other grades could apply for a Hayes tenancy. The company took no risks with engine-men; they had to live near the running sheds at Old Oak Common.

Each prospective tenant was asked to invest in the Great Western Housing Association (London) and a deposit was required as a sign of goodwill. Hayes Garden Village stands on what was originally the Lady Minet Estate. The houses were well built, with gardens front and back, the entire area planted out with trees shrubs and flowers. A long waiting-list developed, and the early tenants soon formed an association to improve the area further. Insurance schemes, which the railway industry repeatedly used to foster company loyalty, covered the tenants for a wide range of liabilities—the 'sick', 'thrift' and 'Christmas' sections being very popular.

One man fortunate enough to find a house on the Hayes estate was Mr Bill Parker, who has written:

> Should you be fortunate enough to get a house before you had accumulated £25 you could pay 2s. 6d. each week on top of your rent, which at that time was 10s. and 3s. 9d. for rates, making 13s. 9d. per week for a house with three bedrooms, living-room, kitchen, bathroom and a fair-sized garden, which was wonderful value. The usual waiting period was three years but it was well worth the wait. Trains left Paddington about one each hour all through the night and also left Hayes at various intervals so whatever turn of duty a man had to work he could always catch a train from Hayes or Acton, and as there were 580 houses on the Hayes Estate and 500 at Acton the night trains were always in use.[26]

Between 1939 and 1945 the sports field and flower plantations were developed as allotments, but after the war the ground was reclaimed, ploughed and re-seeded, the pitches again being much in demand. In 1971 I interviewed many Hayes tenants and I heard nothing but praise for the Great Western Railway, its traditions and its treatment of its workers.

In contrast to the scalloped greenery and tree-trimmed streets of the Hayes estate was the brick tenement in St Pancras known as Polygon Buildings, which for over nine decades housed workers of the London and North-Western Railway and its successors. It was a brick block-house, standing well back from the street and marked off by an iron railing. For almost a century it acted as both connecting link and dividing line between the termini of Euston and St Pancras. This area was the railway hinterland, its western side dominated by the Greek portico of Euston and its eastern extremity walled in by the Gothic station and utilitarian arches of St Pancras and Somers Town.

Polygon Buildings, erected by the London and North-Western Railway, in that period the richest limited company in Europe, represented failure and sadness, rather than the successful housing of the staff of a mighty corporation. The tenement was divided into flatlets, suitable for only the smallest families. There were no bathrooms; toilets and water taps were amenities to be shared. Yet low rents and good travelling facilities to depots and yards made Polygon Buildings an attractive proposition, especially for railway workers just making their way. In the 1950s rents for two-room flatlets were as low as 7s. per week. The properties were tied cottages, however. The company made this point quickly in 1871, when in nearby Camden Town it evicted from company cottages a number of engine-men who had embarked upon strike action.

The occupants of railway premises policed themselves. Bad behaviour was unacceptable in a living area where at any one time a third of the male population would be sleeping in daytime hours. Disorderly conduct produced its own social stigma. The children of railway workers were quickly taught good behaviour in the home, for good behaviour was an implicit part of the tenancy. A railway home was usually a quiet home, the door-knocker often screwed or muffled against unthinking callers. On railway estates such as the one at Carlisle, errand boys soon learned the art of a silent approach and tradesmen calling at the homes of shift workers developed a sense of occasion based on the sleeping habits of their customers which amounted almost to a social science.

The worst railway housing properties were as bad as anything in the field of Victorian dwellings. Yet in comparison with the offerings of the private builder, the barrack type of railway housing was often both advanced in concept and cheap to rent. The best efforts, such as the Great Western settlement at Swindon, were in line with the workers' homes produced by Robert Owen at New Lanark. The Hayes Garden Village is probably unique in British industrial history, providing we do not compare it with such places as Welwyn Garden City or Letchworth, which are really exercises in urban planning rather than industrial estates.

The aura of paternalism generated by the companies' housing policy was bolstered by concessionary travel rates. The privilege ticket and the free pass, especially when these were extended to cover the London Transport Authority and foreign countries, were great boons to railway families. There were always restrictions on free passes, especially in the high holiday period, but if the railway family were prepared to holiday late or early there was a world open to them which, until the advent of mass motoring and package holidays, was simply unavailable to millions. In my time on the railway, management had an ambivalent attitude towards concessionary travel. I doubt if even today the railways have decided whether such travel is part of the conditions of service of railway workers, or a concession by management. Such factors as I have outlined sufficed, in the days of high unemployment, to give railway workers a special status and aura in the community. In my view, the evidence shows that the companies obtained a high return in loyalty from their human investments.

By 1880, the demand for unswerving and uncomplaining loyalty to the company was being challenged on many sides, and not least in the columns of the all-grade union newspaper. One eloquent representative reproached his fellow men in the following terms:

> An unmanly spirit appears to possess the minds of the bulk of the London and North-Western staff. . . . Self-respect, a sense of independence, the dignity of labour, are, alas, all banished from the breasts of great numbers of the men. Like serfs . . . they toil and drudge on day by day, fearing the power that is over them, and startled by even a thought of offending it. . . . Under the dominion of social tyrants, who deny them the freedom of the country, they are submissive and subservient. . . . No king or emperor could reign over a people more surely than the chief of this line reigns over his subject servants.[27]

These are strong words, the phrases of a well-read, thinking man, attacking the fiefdom at Crewe but also castigating fellow railway workers for their lack of spirit.

But management at Crewe was more than paternalistic—it could also show the cloven hoof. At a meeting of the Amalgamated Society of Railway Servants at Crewe in 1880, it was recorded, 'Only last Sunday, at a specially convened meeting of the branch, not one London and North-Western locomotive man dared to attend. Outside the door of the meeting-house a son of their foreman had planted himself, and if any came as far they feared to enter, and turned their faces in another direction.'[28] Such activity contrasted wildly with the Christian ethic encouraged in the town, and it was finally counter-productive. Railway workers were coming to realize that service did not coincide with slavish acceptance of the companies' whims and that loyalty could be subdivided, even contradictory and painful.

What kind of loyalty could be expected of a man like John Jones of Oswestry, who worked for the Great Western Railway and told the Parliamentary Select Committee on Railway Hours in 1891: 'I have been shunting at Oswestry for five years. Throughout the period I have alternated between weeks of eighty hours and seventy-two hours, a fortnight of 152 hours ducking between vehicles, lifting and screwing up the engine and coach couplings.' The week began for Jones at 2.00 a.m. Monday, this turn ending at 6.00 p.m. Monday evening. In his time at Oswestry Jones regularly worked turns of thirty-six hours consecutively. He told the committee that he got so exhausted during those long stretches that 'it was impossible to attend to duty with safety to public or person'. Despite such overwork, the safety record of the Great Western

Railway was a regular feature in railway annals; the overburdened worker had a high loyalty—a loyalty to the job itself. No matter how irksome or onerous the task, it was tackled and completed.

The original demand by the company was for total loyalty from the staff. Before the days of railway trade unionism, appeals to the company were by memorial and petition. In 1871, the Amalgamated Society of Railway Servants promoted two new concepts: loyalty to grade and union. Later the railway workers, realizing their real ranking in society, burst their bonds in the great strike of 1911.

The old concept of loyalty, however, was still held by the representatives of the companies. Giving evidence to a Parliamentary commission one of them insisted, 'What I have found as regards the railway service has been that there is a devotion and a loyalty to the service, and especially to the company, which includes every branch of the service from the simple porter to the inspector and superintendent, who have perfect faith in each other.'[29]

What was the import of such a statement? Did it portray the viewpoint of a man who believed that the prevailing order of social ranking was justified and immutable, with the company as provider, protector and guide to the staff? Or was it just whistling in the dark? A refusal to recognize the coming upheaval in the industry? Were the companies really unconscious of the injustices perpetrated daily in their names, or was the obedience demanded by the companies a deliberately constructed shield to protect them from the wrath of men commanded with such inflexibility? Part of the answer to these imponderables came in 1911, a year noted for the publication of some of the highest ever railway receipts and the year of 'the great labour unrest'. A better definition would be 'the revolt of the railway slaves'.

A Blue Book (Cd. 6796, 1911) reported with due decorum that gross traffic receipts had achieved record proportions.

Passenger traffic receipts

1909	£51,205,000
1910	£52,758,000

Freight traffic receipts

1909	£59,447,000
1910	£61,419,000

In the first half of 1911 the LNWR paid 6 per cent and put away £100,000 to reserve, besides carrying forward a balance of £141,000. The Great Western paid 4½ per cent, and carried forward £120,426. . . . The Midland made a net increase of £181,000, and placed £30,000 to reserve.[30]

In comparison, the wages of almost half a million railway workers were hovering around 25s. per week. However, in order to understand the swift rush of events in 1911, it is necessary to examine the conditions and frustrations which were smouldering beneath the surface in the four years previous to the events of August of that year.

In 1907, the railway companies established a system of Conciliation Boards, talking shops which never got to grips with the grievances agitating the railway workers. Although practically nothing was conceded by the companies in the era 1901–7, the owners had in the same period managed to increase profits and also to reduce staff overall by 1,000 men. Not for nothing were the boards dubbed 'Confiscation Boards' by the railway workers, many of whom despaired of achieving justice by peaceful means. By 1911, it was obvious to many railway workers that the boards were nothing more than another means of oppression, and in August of that year, when Mr J. H. Thomas of the ASRS and Mr J. Bromley of ASLEF were in Liverpool investigating the effects of the dock strike, the leaders were made aware of the animosity that the railway rank and filers held for the Conciliation Boards. Conscious or not of a great turning point in railway history, the unions requested of the Government that unions and management should discuss the failures of the Conciliation Boards. The Liberal Government, however, was unprepared to take this step.

In reply, the unions sent an ultimatum to the companies, stating that 'within twenty-four hours all labour will be withdrawn from the railway industry'. Superficially, Mr Asquith was brave and uncompromising, insisting that if a stoppage ensued his Government would use all the civil and military force at its disposal to see that the commerce of the country was not interfered with. On 18 August, just one day after Asquith's declaration, the railway system suffered an attack of paralysis. The union telegrams calling the stoppage contained the words 'your liberty is at stake, strike at once.' With commendable speed the Liberals told the railway companies to grant the unions' wish for a round-table conference, and within forty-eight hours full trade-union recognition was granted. Although khaki uniforms and fixed bayonets were prominent in many railway centres, the railway workers gained in two days of action what they had been denied in three decades of requests and memorials.

The political acumen and advanced thinking of the railway journalists can be judged by the front-page article of the *Railway Review* for 18 August 1911. According to the all-grades journal the strike was for freedom and the dignity of labour. But how did the dramatic and often violent activity of the 1911 strike fit in with the theory of company loyalty?

RAILWAY WAR.

THE SITUATION LAST NIGHT.

PROTEST AGAINST MILITARY AT WOLVERHAMPTON.

NEGOTIATIONS.

CONSIDERING BOARD OF TRADE PROPOSALS.

COMPANIES TO STAND FIRM

Negotiations between the Government and the men were on Friday conducted with Mr. Ramsay Macdonald, M.P., chairman of the Labour party, as the chief intermediary. He was fetched from Unity House, Euston, where the men's executive met at 9 a.m., by Mr. Jones, Liberal Whip, and had consultations with Mr. Lloyd-George and Mr. Buxton.

"NO BRICKS OR BOTTLES."

ANOTHER MASS MEETING IN WOLVERHAMPTON

INDIGNATION AT MILITARY BEING CALLED

"I bless your movement—on one condition. Do nothing illegal. Your cause is too good for that."

This remark was made by the Rev. J. J. Darmody in addressing a very large meeting of railwaymen on the Wolverhampton Market-place on Friday night.

This meeting was called for seven o'clock, and by that time a great number of railwaymen

Fig. 2 Headline from the *Express and Star*, Saturday, August 19, 1911

The success of the 1911 strike was the sign of real change, and created a new confidence among the railway workers in their industrial relations. Political loyalties, however, underwent dramatic change. The old animosities between Conservative and Liberal trade unionists changed into a struggle between the socialists and the brash new theory of syndicalism. The syndicalists, who held the view that one big strike could topple capitalism, pointed to the railway strike of 1911 as a justification of their theory. The power of syndicalist theory was reflected in the growth of the National Union of Railwaymen, an all-grades union which reached at its peak a membership of around 500,000. But syndicalism could not sustain its momentum, and despite the influence of its ideas in the great struggle of 1911, socialism of the Labour Party variety captured the loyalty of the railway workers.

The events of 1911 gave company loyalty a surprising fillip, as trade-union emblems and company insignia were worn together on railway caps and jackets. Here was a new phenomenon, a novel marking-off, as companies and trade unions strove for and developed rival forms of corporate identity. After 1911, railway workers became servants of the company and the public and brothers aware of their collective rights rather than serfs within an industrial manor.

During the First World War, the railway workers, whether in company livery or military uniform, displayed a high degree of courage and loyalty to their nation. For example, in 1914, Mr Herbert Evans, a clerical officer of the Metropolitan Railway, was one of the 184,475 railway workers who went to war. Mr. Evans acted as a shunter-guard on the sector between Popperinge and Ypres. At night his train took men and supplies to the front line, returning with the dead and wounded men rescued from the mud. The engine tanks were filled by buckets and biscuit tins dipped into waterlogged shell holes. One night, Mr Evans took 300 men of the Middlesex Regiment 'up the line', where they suffered an intense bombardment. The men were caught in country without deep shell holes to give protection. Next morning Evans returned with five live soldiers.[31]

The London and North-Western sent 31,744 men and the Great Western 25,460—34 and 32·6 per cent of their staffs respectively. The Easingwold and Avonmouth Light sent two men each and the Southwold one man from its staff of ten. Some 40,000 served directly with the railway troops.

The first demand was for construction gangs, and these companies were composed mainly of plate-layers, of whom 7,000 went directly from the railways. During the war the railway companies constructed over 2,000 miles of new track and kept them in continuous repair and renovation. The Great Push of 1918 required the renovation of more than 1,500 track miles. This was in addition to the work on the 2 ft gauge light railway which ran from the railheads to the trenches. The battle of Passchendaele in October 1917 required 160 trains daily to the railheads plus another 100 to serve the transverse lines of communication; the motive power was usually a small 0–4–0T. The Great War claimed the lives of 21,522 railwaymen, and the monuments at British railway stations testify to their sacrifices.

While the Second World War was a war of roads, despite the important part played by railways and railway workers, the First World War was clearly a railway war, the last of its kind. But afterwards, however, in 1919, the railway workers again found themselves on picket duty. This time khaki uniforms clothed their antagonists, not their friends, and the army guarded not national, but railway interests.

The reasons for this new type of conflict were not hard to find. By August 1919, the engine-men had achieved a national standardized wage for their member grades. Norman McKillop, official historian of ASLEF, speaking as a locomotive-man concluded, 'We had proved that, properly organized within our own society, we could convince our employers that the days of serfdom must cease as far as we were concerned.'[32] After eight years' driving, a top engine-man was on 15s. per day. After five years' firing, the stoker achieved 11s. per day. Engine cleaners over the age of twenty enjoyed 7s. per day. The railway workers, apart from foot-platemen, understandably anticipated that they would benefit similarly. The companies did not agree, however, and their proposal that the special war wage be terminated—which meant wage cuts of 14s. for some grades—was greeted with something less than enthusiasm.

A national railway strike for standardized conditions of service began in September 1919. The engine-men, who had achieved a huge success with their own campaign, unhesitatingly placed their support behind the all-grades union, a move of almost unprecedented class loyalty. For nine days class and grade differences were lost in the pursuit of justice for the humblest as well as the best paid. The strike, fought out while tanks patrolled the railway centres, brought a temporary unity based on class and ideological loyalty and won for the men the eight-hour day and national conditions of service for all railway workers. But the spirit of 1919 was soon abandoned and never again regenerated in the railway unions. This lack of common policy was to cost the men dear in the next decade.

In 1923, in one of the largest amalgamations of money, men and machinery ever seen in Britain, 123 privately owned railways combined into four large groups. In reality, four new independent industrial kingdoms came into being, almost uncompetitive but with new identities to establish. At the moment of transfer of power few railway workers would admit that their own company had not been a viable and competitive concern. To have admitted the bankruptcy of their company was by implication a slur on their own competency. Sid Mosley, working as a goods guard, remembers how, before amalgamation saved the day, the Midland men of Wigan would taunt the staff of the North-Western with hints of the imminent demise of that company.[33] Twenty years after amalgamation, the overcoats issued by the Furness Railway Company were still being worn by men of the London Midland and Scottish Railway, the lapel of the coats still embellished with the red initials of a long-dead company. From Carlisle to Camden Town the railwaymen were reshuffled and rearranged until the senior men from the original railways were correctly marshalled to the satisfaction of the companies.

For the railway workers, a new and uncomfortable era opened as redundancies followed in the wake of reorganization and rationalization. After amalgamation, neither merit nor potential kept a railwayman in work. His only lifeline was his seniority date—the day he began in the parent company. If redundancy struck, home and family were uprooted to another area in order to retain a post. Many of the transferred men failed to make a successful transition from one subculture to another. Though the men retained some of the old instinctive loyalty to the companies for providing them with wages and a kind of shelter, an arbour of safety within a stormy economy, the uprooted man often found it hard to forgive those who had wrenched him from his home and deposited him in a strange and hostile territory. A man redundant in the area of mountains and hills could not take kindly to a new post in the flat and watery Fens, any more than a city-born and trained railway worker would welcome a shed poised half-way up a Pennine. These things happened frequently, and even in the 1950s many railway workers who had been uprooted three decades earlier would hot-foot it back to friendly territory as often as possible. Redundant men were rarely welcomed in any area. Whereas the old companies had always expected and got gratitude and loyalty for the smallest concession, the new companies found themselves facing agitation and militancy.

In the years of amalgamation and redundancy, sheds, depots and yards, once the stronghold of tradition, custom and vernacular speech, now became repositories of migrant cultures as the transferred men infused new behaviour patterns and contributed to a mosaic railway language. In newly badged uniforms, working in strange environments, separated from each other by rival traditions, the transferred men sought desperately for a fresh and corporate identity.

The companies viewed the General Strike of 1926 as the supreme disloyalty. Company authority suffered a severe body blow when the railway workers proved that an efficient railway system could not be operated without skilled and devoted men. After the strike, the record cards of men who continued working were marked in red ink—'remained loyal'. The Great Western Railway, the only railway to retain its original title after amalgamation, issued a special thank-you certificate to its loyalists, but at the same time these men never lost the label affixed to them by their colleagues—'blackleg 1926'.

Any organization, if it wishes to promote a corporate loyalty, must provide and maintain the status of its participants. Status can be based upon straight cash rewards, the respect and payment accruing to special skills, or the recognition of rank and degree within the hierarchy. The railway companies encouraged their staffs to think not as individuals but in a corporate way, and the ethic held for many years because railway workers in the years of steam enjoyed high status in the community.

The Second World War changed all that. In 1939, many railwaymen were veterans of the 1911 strike. Still more had taken part in the strikes of 1919 and 1926. Thousands of them had known redundancy, transfer and the constant threat of further rationalization. They now faced another era of long hours, domestic deprivation and the threat of enemy action against railway installations. All this they endured, but the greatest cost was to industrial loyalty. The immediate post-war years saw morale sink to an all-time low. Recruitment was on the basis of 'Anyone interested in railway work?'—a far cry from the rigorous selection procedures of the previous decades, when men adjudged themselves to be proud servants of a company, although servants without servility. By 1945 the status of railwaymen had gone, and for many railway work was the last resort. In the 1950s declining wage differentials with outside industry, public discontent with the services offered, and a slowness to institute modern equipment and methods led to strikes, go slows, 'putting on the big hammer' (working to rule), and sheer bloody-mindedness. The lineage which began with George Stephenson conquering Chat Moss Bog was clearly disintegrating, for traditional loyalties would not pay shopping bills.

The Transport Act of 1947 ended a century of private dominion over the railway system in Britain. It had been a century of furious activity, in which a host of rival companies had eventually created the most intensive railway system and some of the strongest corporate images in the world. Both new loyalties and new prejudices had been born and nurtured. Those who stood against the companies looked to public ownership as the only means to end the insecurity and bitterness of the past. But the past had its defenders also, men who felt that public ownership was the quickest means to anarchy. These men, like ex-stationmaster Francis Almond, looked back with pleasure on the days when railway work was carried out with military precision and no backchat from the staff. 'The unions, not the owners, run the industry today,' he believes.[34]

Nationalization created no new loyalties in the industry. The state and its representatives appeared as remote as the private managers had been in attendance. The railway workers who retired in the 1960s had seen the best and the worst of private enterprise, and they went out of the industry with the knowledge that no industry before or since had engendered and fostered the corporate spirit which characterized the private railway companies and marked them off so clearly from other complex organizations. When I joined the railways in 1946, the great loyalties were still to the private companies. An amalgam of tongues, an entrepôt of railway cultures, could not be welded into a united whole while memories of the Lanky and the Midland and the Maryport and Carlisle dominated the thinking processes. These men had lost something and they never retrieved it. British Rail has failed to give its workforce a specific, corporate identity.

3

Signalmen and Guards

Britain's railway signalman of the present day evolved from a group of early railway grades which included railway policemen, pointsmen, switchmen and crossing-gate keepers. From the beginning of the railways, legislation provided that signalmen should be nominated by three directors of the company and then be appointed by at least two Justices of the Peace. From such successful candidates, whose references had to be impeccable, the companies expected total loyalty; how the early pointsmen were treated is another matter.

Pointsmen were quickly classified into grades. Grade 1 men took the most important junctions, Grade 2 the less complex boxes and Grade 3 the ordinary sidings and minor posts. In the early days, railway premises were usually badly lit, the handlamp providing the main source of illumination. The telephone was non-existent and the telegraph office was often some distance from the signal cabin. The whistle of an approaching train was often the only indication the pointsman had as to the state of the traffic. Even when operating hand points for the shunter, the pointsman needed to calculate the state of the line and the signals for which he was responsible. The work of the pointsman separated him from other grades; not for him the joy of a relaxed moment, a 'fiver' for a smoke. Time was the enemy. The urgent early-morning tap on the switchman's window, the station clock, the driver's half-hunter, the printed circular and the inexorable sweep of the signal-box clock formed a ritual which passed from one generation of signallers to another like a burning brand.

The early pointsmen worked twelve-hour turns of duty and during this period they were often required to help out in the nearby shunting yard. O. S. Nock records, 'Their work involved running from one end of a shunting yard to the other, across sidings, over rough ballast, through pools of water. . . . His instructions were that no second train might follow an express under a margin of five minutes; an ordinary passenger train must have a start of ten, and a goods train fifteen.'[1] In freezing kennels and within the icy wastes of marshalling yards, these slaves to lamp and lever laboured a seventy-two hour week.

Mistakes meant fines, often imposed by men who must have known the weight of the injustice they were inflicting. Joseph Paxton, designer of Crystal Palace and Director of the Midland Railway, once fined a pointsman 5s. for a minor misdemeanour.[2] Fines could be inflicted for such offences as men being away from their telegraph instruments even though they were occupied with other duties. On the Great Western Railway in the 1870s, a fine disqualified a man for the customary bonus for good conduct. On this company in 1869, fines averaged 15s. 2d., almost a week's wages for the lower grades.[3]

For £1 per week pointsmen and signalmen regularly put in turns of sixteen consecutive hours. Changing turns at weekends meant that the men had only six hours' rest between turns. Men who worked on Sundays were often played off during the week, that is, given a day off without pay to prevent the earning of high sums of money. It never occurred to the companies that the signalman might grow resentful of such treatment; the sight of the few flowers signalmen occasionally grew outside their huts was taken as an indication that they were contented. The medical world, however, was a little uneasy, and in 1862 the *Lancet* published a report which commented that 'Signalmen, dazed by want of sleep, become confused, and in a moment the engines are pounding up humans between them.'

When fog occurred the pointsmen and signalmen were assisted by a fogman. Fog was the dread of all railway workers, especially of signalmen and engine-men, and these grades became dependent upon the fogman when nature went atwist. A fogman could be any railway person trained in the knowledge of signals and the use of detonators. 'Fogging' was an emergency; thus a man who had just completed a day's work could be retained for fogging duties or dragged from a cosy bed at a moment's notice. No refusal was acceptable. It was his duty and he was obliged to go.

The fogman, posted in the reeking air at the base of the signal post, was blinded by fog and choked by the fumes of his frost devil. This was a coke-burning brazier, whose heat kept the signal wires from icing up. On shift, the fogman often had to cross running lines to do his duty; many were knocked down and mutilated by trains. A moment's delay could lead to appalling consequences. Fogmen often stood at their posts for sixteen unfed and frozen hours. The maximum pay was 6d. per hour, but 2d. was a more general rate.

The early companies divided the working day into two elements: first, the overall working day, and, second, the actual working day. The overall working day was the time between signing on and signing off duty. The actual day was the period spent pulling, shoving, hoisting and slamming at the means of production. From the companies' point of view any time not spent in activity was a rest period, if not actually thumb-twiddling; thus a turn of eighteen consecutive hours could be calculated as a turn of only nine hours. For the early signalman excessive hours were the norm, part of an accepted system of exploitation. To protest was to invite dismissal. Overtime was unpaid; indeed so many hours of unpaid duty meant that the staff was paying for the privilege of working for the company.

Despite the low status afforded signalmen by the companies, Albert Williams, the Swindon blacksmith writer, saw these men as an elite, and he wrote: 'Good reliable men only are retained in the signal boxes, who have been tried and proved, who are unhampered with exterior business, able to concentrate on the signals and instruments. One lapse of memory would be sufficient to bring about calamity; they would be ruined as far as the railway was concerned.'[4]

The early signal huts which preceded signal boxes were often pivoted at the base so that they could be turned against the prevailing wind. These huts were replicas of Army sentry boxes. Later, when signal boxes were built complete with windows and stoves, the signalmen, still chafing under long hours and poor wages, were dubbed 'poor men in their glass houses'.[5]

Early uniforms had a military and police look and the promotion system of constable, sergeant, sub-inspector and inspector maintained that tradition. Signalmen's truncheons were as symbolic and as emblematic as the baton of a field marshal. The Great Western truncheon sported a golden crown, picked out in red, white and green, the letters GWR being emblazoned in gilt script.

The hours and conditions of signalmen in the golden age of railways give us some evidence of how the railway companies cared for the safety of the passengers or the personal needs of the men working in the boxes. The conditions were outlined in a letter to the journal of the ASRS:

Sir, No apology is required from me for addressing myself to you on the subject of the hours of duty, payment, etc. of a signalman. I myself am a signalman, and have been in the employ of the London, Chatham, and Dover Company for eleven years next June, during which time I have averaged eighty-four hours per week. As there are only *two* of us, we relieve each other on Sunday morning at 8.30 a.m. to enable us to change over from night to day. We remain on duty till 7.30 the following Monday, so as to enable one of us to have twenty-three hours off duty once a fortnight. In addition to the ordinary work on points, signals, block instruments, etc., we have to forward and receive all telegrams, and keep accounts for the post office, as well as the company, for which we do not receive a penny extra. Our pay is 23s. per week, with an annual bonus of £5, providing we give satisfaction to our superintendent and others, which at times is a very difficult matter, I can assure you, and to make things worse, if we are fortunate enough to get a week's leave of absence (say once in two years) they do not fail to stop the pay during such absence. There are two relieving signalmen kept for the London district for the purpose of giving us an occasional day off duty. But to enable you to form some idea of the frequency of our relief from this source, I will give you the dates of the days I have been so relieved—21 November 1870, one day; 12 March 1871, 30 August 1871 and 7 November 1871; and to render such relief almost useless, we never know when they are coming. Last year all the signalmen doing twelve hours' duty in the London division, to which I belong, petitioned the superintendent for one day's relief in fourteen. We suggested appointing a man to relieve so many stations as would enable us each to have twelve hours off duty in that time; but sir, even this moderate request was not granted.[6]

A switchman from the Black Country reported on similarly harsh conditions in 1873:

. . . We have above 100 trains passing here daily, and for every train or engine that passes, we have to make in a train book no fewer than eight different entries, besides attending to the single needle instrument and block telegraph. We are allowed one day off in every fourteen . . . we have to work, on an average seventy-five hours per week. . . . Our wages at this station are 3s. per day. . . .[7]

A South-Eastern Railwayman reported that at a box which incorporated level-crossing duties, in a basic twelve-hour turn of duty the men acted as gatemen, shunters, porters and ticket collectors. They are responsible also for cleaning offices, waiting rooms and fire grates. Their food was taken when the work permitted. 'For this,' he wrote, 'we receive the magnificent sum of 17s. per week.'[8]

Around this time a crippled gate-keeper at Raynes Park wrote to say that he had 'worked sixteen hours per day, for ten years, my wage being 16s. per week'. The signalman with overall responsibility for the crossing gates was regularly working shifts of eighteen hours. 'Who can tell', asked the all-grades journal, 'what hair's breadth escapes have occurred to trains flying past this box?' In October 1874, the Bristol District Secretary of the ASRS, Mr Evans, claimed that many Great Western signalmen were earning only 20s. for seventy-two hours' duty.[9] Some signalmen, at 16s. per week, were paid less than carriers.

Railways were often reluctant to supply staff with mechanical aids, arguing that such assistance could lead to a lessening of attentiveness with a consequential increase in accidents. Technical advance, however, was inevitable. In 1884, over the protests of Sir Richard Moon, Chairman of the London and North-Western, this company could boast that 90 per cent of its points and signals were interlocked.

In the 1870s, overwork and the constant strain led to many accidents, which of course meant unfavourable publicity. Usually it was the individual, not the company, who paid the penalty for lapses of regulations, despite the impossibility of following scrupulously all rules over such long hours. The signalmen, like other key grades, wished 'to belong' to their mini-state. Proud of their calling, all they asked was for fair dealing. The employer however was, to say the least, ambiguous in human relationships. As late as 1880 on the London and North-Western Railway, men working twelve-hour boxes were granted two Sundays in three free from duty—a huge step forward—yet this easement was withdrawn almost as quickly as it was suggested, the men being advised that the new method would be two Sundays of twelve-hour shifts with eight hours to work on the third Sunday. There was no recompense for the extra labour.

In 1874, George Hill, a signalman at Durham, was convicted of manslaughter and sentenced to one month's imprisonment by Baron Amphlett. The public reporting of the accident made no reference to the hours worked by signalmen, and this omission led to a furious letter in *The Times* which was reprinted in the all-grades journal:

Sir, The case of George Hill, railway signalman at Durham, who was lately convicted of manslaughter and sentenced by Baron Amphlett to one month's imprisonment, is doubtless still fresh in the public mind. I have before me as I write a copy of the *Durham Chronicle* of Friday 6 March, in which this case is reported, and it appears to me, as also to others whose attention I have drawn to it, that there is not one syllable respecting the number of hours that George Hill was on duty, though whether it was touched on or not at the trial I am, of course, unable to say, as I have only the report in the paper alluded to to go by in this instance. As the organization of duties of the railway signalmen is one that must necessarily have a great interest for the travelling public, permit me, sir, in their interest, through the medium of *The Times*, to place before them a few facts concerning the consecutive number of hours the railway signalmen are on duty, and with the details of which but few are conversant: these facts I can and will vouch for the accuracy of, and I shall be perfectly ready at any moment, should it be necessary in the public interest, to supply all details. I am informed, on most reliable authority, that in the main the system I am about to describe is that pursued on the large majority of our English railways, and therefore it may be considered a fairly correct illustration.

On one of our large and prosperous railways, at a junction not fifty miles from London, there is a signal box or cabin in which are nearly twenty levers (signals and point) and also the necessary telegraphic communication for the working of these. The duties in this box are performed by two men, who work as follows. Each signalman has the entire charge of these levers for the same number of hours every day or night in each week. One works the eleven day hours from 7.00 a.m. to 6.00 p.m. from one Monday to the following one; the other works the thirteen night hours from 6.00 p.m. to 7.00 a.m. during the same period. The signalman who has had the eleven day hours during the previous week changes to the thirteen night hours for the next week, that signalman taking for the same period the eleven day hours.[10]

How strong was the loyalty of the Caledonian Railway signalmen who in 1891 were working in boxes where a twelve-hour turn was the norm? This company argued that twelve hours on duty in a main-line box was reasonable and that longer hours could be imposed on branch-line signalmen, who were not so active.

In his evidence to a Parliamentary Select Committee in 1890–1, Mr James Thomas, signalman at Newtown on the Cambrian Railway, told how the company paid him 10s. for a week of eighty-two hours. He was sixteen years old.[11] Later, Mr Thomas, who had been disabled as a result of falling under a train but had been kept on by the company, explained that there was no limit to the hours a signalman was expected to work. There was no extra pay for Sunday work. On special occasions, if the Newtown men worked over eighteen consecutive hours, time and a quarter was paid after the twelfth hour. As an adult with the Cambrian Railway, Mr Thomas earned 16s. for eighty-four hours' duty. It was not hard to see from whence the capital came to provide signals which interlocked with points.

The glass and concrete consol-type signal boxes of the 1970s have little in common with the early structures, as H. A. Simmons discovered when he went on a tour of his section and commented:

> That afternoon I had an hour's practice with Bob in his signal box. In his signal box I say, but half in and half out I ought to say, for there was only room for one person. . . . The directors believed that the signal box should not be a source of comfort to the occupier. No door was provided, but the signalman was allowed to turn it round according to the direction of the wind. Bob had, however, stolen a march on the regulations, for he had grown two huge bushes of the tea plant, which met at the top, and formed a complete arch, and which, together with the signal box, a little brick paving, and a few odd pieces

of rusty sheet iron interlaced in the top of the tea trees to make it watertight, formed quite a little Robinson Crusoe dwelling. . . . The roofing in the little tea tree was, he told me, composed of old tea trays and tea kettles battered out, which had come down in the truckloads of London refuse. . . . [However] having got it a bit dry under foot, and built up a bit of a fireplace, kept going with coal he picked on the line and which had shaken off the trucks when they are shunting, it was not so bad now. Bob had put a seat in his signal box, and planted primroses and violets outside.

The whole structure was one of the most crucial combinations of nature and art, but there was a neatness and ingenuity that at once told you that Bob was a man who could adapt himself to circumstances and improve the opportunity with the best means to hand. The garden was part of the railway bank, and the soil was the vilest greasy clay . . . [but] Bob had got the ground to work so that he could grow vegetables to view with those who had the best of gardens. His French beans were prolific, and his potatoes immense, and he could always make up a bunch of flowers, which Bob boasted were the produce of a packet of seeds some lady had thrown him from a carriage window of a passing train.[12]

As late as 1890 the signalman at Quaker's Yard on the Taff Vale Railway achieved a reduction in hours, relief being afforded between the hours of 11.00 p.m. and 3.00 a.m. The man relieved was not allowed to remain in the box but had to prowl round the railway until it was time to return to duty. In the same period Mr Forbes, Chairman of the London, Chatham and Dover Railway, wrote, 'that the generality of railway servants have little or nothing to complain of, and that they are well paid and not overworked except in an emergency. . . . For instance, I sometimes work myself seventeen hours a day.'[13] The Railway Herald, in reply, asked Mr Forbes if his work compared with the seventeen hours a day worked too frequently by many of the servants of the companies over whose councils he presided: 'Is it as arduous, attended with as much discomfort, so much risk to life and limb as that of some of the lowest paid of the servants?' Mr Forbes did not respond to the challenge.[14] At this time there was a society for the prevention of cruelty to animals but none to rescue signalmen from overwork. There was more to signalling than the happy picture of shining floors, gleaming levers and polished bells. A signalman on the Chester and Shrewsbury reported that for eleven years he had worked an eighty-four-hour week and in that time he had never known a clear Sunday free.

In 1890, on the South-Eastern Railway, the signalmen had an agreement that six days' work would constitute a week's work and that

Sunday duty would be paid for at the ordinary rate. Some of the station-masters refused to put their signalmen on the paysheet for Sunday night duty, arguing that the South-Eastern Railway could not afford to pay for Sunday nights. What loyalty could be expected from the signalman who wrote in 1890: [15]

> I am classed as a signalman at a twelve-hour post; but, unfortunately, live in one of the company's huts (I really cannot call them houses) at the level crossing, which I have to attend to, besides attending to all work at the siding situated near it. I come on duty at 6.00 a.m. and, if all trains run to time, am off at 8.30 p.m. Of course this looks to anyone not acquainted with railways as if I get paid for two and a half hours per day overtime, but I must beg to state for their infor-mation I only get paid for half an hour, the other two hours being deducted for meal times, although I can get no stated times for meals. I have asked our district inspector to state the times I am allowed, but the only answer I can get is he cannot state them, and if I do not like it I can resign my post, and send in my clothes.
>
> No doubt there are others besides the few I can mention who are treated in the same shabby way. But what I should like to know is, if this is done by Mr Burlinson's instructions, or if it is done in the superintendent's office to keep down the overtime pay of the division.
>
> Perhaps some of your numerous readers can enlighten me on this point.
>
> PLACECRAIG
>
> Coalport, 4 February 1890

These may have been the 'Gay Nineties' for the 'stage-door johnnies', but that was hardly the case for signalmen. At a time when the map of the world glowed red with British imperial possession, the signalmen of the Cockermouth, Keswick and Penrith Railway were paid nothing for overtime. Signalmen at this time were among those classes of Weekly Paid Servants who were allowed to resume work with less than eight hours' rest after a previous shift of twelve hours' duration. The Gay Nineties for signalmen were less than ambrosial years.

During this period, signalmen had stirred sufficiently to promote a National Movement, and this led, in 1896, to a meeting of the Board of Trade.[16] There was plenty to discuss, but the signalmen, probably over-awed at their own success, did nothing except urge their colleagues to make use of the Hours Act, and to approach the Board of Trade in all cases when hours of duty were excessive.

The men in the glass houses had numerous complaints to ventilate. At Trent, in an ordinary shift, 120 trains were handled, 2,000 lever movements were made and 2,500 signals were sent; in one night a train register book could contain over 1,000 entries. Hand signalling was necessary when trains were shunted near the box. When otherwise unoccupied the signalman was required to keep a sharp lookout. Of conditions on the South-Eastern Railway one signalman wrote in desperation, 'at this station we signalmen work fourteen nights for the fortnight. . . . 168 hours . . . for which we receive £2. This is a signalman's pay—2s. and 10d. per day.'[17]

It is easy with hindsight to condemn signalmen for their lassitude in not fighting such conditions. Some were in fact criticized at the time. One militant whose courage failed him at the last moment was sent a white feather and a poem which read:

> Fit honour for a noble man
> Who had so much to say,
> And when the time for fighting came
> Why, cut, and ran away.[18]

This does not take into account the fact that the company's answer to the militant signalman was dismissal.

The Great Western Railway used the bonus system to ensure the good conduct of the early signalmen. Bonuses were by no means automatic. The Grade 1 men of this railway qualified for an annual bonus of £5 only if they were deemed free of any offence considered punishable by the company. Likewise on the Great Northern, a signalman at Laisterdyke who had been involved in an accident had his bonus cut by 50 per cent. At the time of the accident the man in the box was earning 8s. per week.

In the great railway strike in mid-August of 1911, a number of signalmen distinguished themselves in the eyes of the company by staying on duty until removed by furious pickets. At Whitland, one of the chief centres of dissatisfaction, the signalmen at Tenby and Pembroke Junctions were reluctant to leave their boxes, but were eventually persuaded to lock up and leave.[19] Relief signalmen were sent to those boxes but pickets forced them out, one of the signalmen having to ford a river in his escape. At Black Bridge the electric telegraph was immobilized. Outside York the points were jammed with stones and coal—a signalman's nightmare.

At nearby Goose Hill Junction a crowd of over 1,000, many miners included, set siege to the signal box. Goose Hill, a vital box on the Lancashire and Yorkshire Railway, was being operated by signalman Percy Maynard, who had gained access to the box by turning up in civilian clothes, a gross violation of railway rules, which demanded uniform at all times on duty.[20] Normanton Station was then opened, with thirty soldiers guarding signalman Proctor.[21] The young fry on the

demonstration climbed the barricade which protected the signal box
from the clamour of the highway and made the night horrendous for
Proctor by kicking the advertisement tablets. Colonel Harding, in
charge of the soldiers, was howled down by the crowd. In spite of the
tenseness of the moment, signalman Proctor retained control of his
bailiwick, a remarkable story of one man's loyalty to his task. The box
at Newton, near Stafford, was attacked at midnight, after the signalman
had withstood two hours of derisory chanting from a large crowd. Only
a baton charge by the police cleared the bridge. As a precaution the
Chief Constable of Stafford ordered the closure of seven public houses
in the town.[22] At Bradford, the signalmen of the town were advised that
a gang of 100 men were stalking the tracks, bent on mischief; this
force of men was halted only by a line-up of police. By 18 August 1911,
thirty-seven miles of sidings in the Derby area were blocked with
trains. In Cumberland twenty collieries and thirteen furnaces were
closed, putting 12,000 men out of work.[23]

In 1919, the signalmen, now within the ranks of a powerful union,
the National Union of Railwaymen, achieved the eight-hour day, the
six-day week and many other valuable concessions. Eighty-one years of
slow and grinding hardship in which the railway workers, signalmen
included, had made our home railways the centre of national and international acclaim. There was little problem in finding men to staff signal
boxes after 1919, for railway work still had a high status, despite the
massive stoppages of 1911 and 1919.

Alex Waterman, who started as a sixteen-year-old at Crystal Palace
Tunnel Box in 1923, was glad to get such a job at 16s. per week. Mr
Waterman has recalled that the men at Crystal Palace were elderly men
of 'Brighton stock', and very particular.[24] They would tell the box boy
not to sit on the cabin lockers when trains were passing, but to stand
by the train register book. The boy was forbidden to touch the telephones. At Tunnel Box, as it was called, all was ritual. The early-morning
boy did the chores. Monday and Friday were brass mornings; Tuesday
was windows and on Wednesday the box floor was scrubbed. The signal
lad had to keep at the register book from 7.00 a.m. until 10.00 a.m. and
from 4.30 p.m. until 7.30 p.m. The signal-box boy was always considered part of the team at Tunnel Box, and remained on the same shift
with his seniors. This was fine if the lad got on well with the bobbies,
but bad luck for the boy who was rostered with a 'toe-the-line' type of
signalman.

The signalmen always had 'coal starvation'. Taking coal from railway wagons meant instant dismissal, so engine-men shunting coal
wagons would 'bang-up' the wagons to create spillage, and this was
dutifully collected in the signal-box scuttle by the signal-box boy. News-

papers of the day were delivered to the box by the drivers and guards of empty, sidings-bound stock.

Mr Alex Young worked on the London and North-Eastern Railway at Newburn in 1924, and he has recalled: 'I washed the cabin floor, my portion of the window glass, and all the brasswork. The levers and the block instruments I cleaned with paraffin, pumice stone and emery cloth. I trimmed all signal-box lamps, fetched coal and cleaned grates.'[25] Mr Young was responsible for large, cosy fires in the grate, for burnishing the steel fender and fire irons and for whitestoning the hearth. As a train register boy, he was forbidden to work signals, points, bells or gongs. A good register boy was a great help to a signalman, but a poor or unwilling lad hindered the work, whether he was a green schoolleaver or a mature eighteen-year-old. Yet signalling was a vocation, a task calling for calmness and judgment, a job which isolated a man from his neighbours.

The signalman was given a cabin labelled 'private'. No one entered without his permission. The care lavished on brass, glass and bells testified to his pride. It was 'my box, my levers, my junction'—the classic territorialism. The signalman was a creature apart. His grade was conscious of a particular separatism, based upon special responsibility. Should the signalman, by stupid or misguided action, precipitate a calamity, the responsibility could not be avoided. The position of the needles in the signal indicator boxes would bear silent and damning witness to his transgression. This singularity edged signalmen away from their contemporaries, leading to a breakaway union and later demands for independent negotiating rights.

One man who tried signalling in the 1950s was Mr J. Lyon of Edinburgh, who occupied a box in his native city for a number of years. Mr Lyon soon found out the reason for the signalman's dictum, 'If you are unmarried when you take over a box, chances are you will never marry.' The sheer isolation of a quiet signal box eventually drove Mr Lyon to fields where his intelligence could be put to better use. As he has written, 'It was at night that I became aware of the isolation. After 11.00 p.m., when the city is silent, and no matter how much sleep has been taken during the day, 2.00 a.m. brings its own fatigue.'[26]

In his first few weeks Mr Lyon talked endless nonsense on the phone to other cabins in the area, or hung out of his box windows, listening to owls and bats. He has a verified IQ of 147 on the Cattell Scale, and so felt compelled to use the long monotonous hours to his advantage. Tied to his silent bells by invisible cords, he set about painting, modelling, working out chess games and playing solitaire. In the Morningside Road signal cabin he completed nine correspondence courses in English, art, politics, geography and natural history.

Although the district is now built up, in Mr Lyon's time cattle and sheep grazed in the fields behind the signal box and along the nearby canal. In the 1950s the box had no gas, electricity, or water. The canal served as a toilet for the station staff and the men who operated the level crossing gates.

Almost every signalman can tell a particular story about visitors to his box, and Mr Lyon is no exception, his tale being particularly bizarre: 'One winter, about 4.00 a.m., a young man in pyjamas knocked on the cabin door, his bare feet rattling on the hard frost which covered the cabin steps.' Mr Lyon let him in and made him some tea. The young man told him that he was of royal blood, his mother being Queen of South Africa. As Mr Lyon continued to signal trains, the visitor signed a cheque for £250,000 on a railway telegraph form as a reward to Mr Lyon for helping him to reach South Africa. After an hour of such nonsense the nocturnal meanderer was led away by the Edinburgh police.[27]

In the days of steam, signal boxes appeared in many strange places. They could sit alone on the tops of mountains, such as the boxes at Ais Gill and Beattock. They could be buried under city streets like Holborn Low Level, open to little but smoke and sulphur fumes from passing locomotives preparing to attack the inclined tunnels at King's Cross which led to Finsbury Park or Kentish Town sidings. The Midland box at the North London Incline was an eyrie high up on the wall of St Pancras goods depot, and reached by a flight of extremely steep stairs. Another high flyer was the box at Clapham Junction, which stretched across the tracks like an elongated crab. On starlit, frosty nights, boxes often resembled an amber pendant on a diamond necklace. On softer, warmer nights, they glowed snug and yellow against backgrounds as diverse as fields and fish docks. The more isolated the box, the more pernickety the signalman, the more welcome was the assistance afforded in moments of need.

For a century and a half the watchwords of signalmen have been reliability, service and coolness, As a youngster, Alan Butler, who became a signalman on the Great Western, was imbued with the spirit of community service, and he has recorded:

> I was brought up in an orphanage, and given an education which stressed the value of service and responsibility to others. Inside the orphanage the high walls denied the boys most of the sights and sounds of the outside world, but the railway connected us with outside society.
>
> From the centre of Bath, this line climbed around the hill on which the orphanage stood, before it struck out for Gloucester and the Severn Bridge. Unable to see the tracks, we were yet totally aware of

its presence, for the engines bellowed and hissed as they struggled to breast the hill with their heavy loads. We boys never tired of imitating the noises of the monsters we never saw, for their sounds fed our imaginations in a way that vision could not.

The dark evenings of winter added a new dimension to our lives, for the sparks from the funnels of the engines and the wide arc of orange illumination from the firebox spoke of a warmth and power of which we had little comprehension.[28]

At Pill, in Somerset, Butler was not overworked, but he soon learned about the stamina and dexterity needed by the 'bobbies', the nickname for signalmen which goes right back to the days of the constable-signalman. The signals at Pill were $1\frac{1}{2}$–$1\frac{3}{4}$ miles from his box, and out of his vision. To move these signals required great strength as well as skill because of the immense weight of cable and pulleys which had to be moved. The usual movement to pull off a signal was for a bobby to stand facing the signal lever frame in which the levers sloped away from him. He would brace himself with one foot on the frame, release the catch which held the lever secure in the frame and with an immense heave and backwards swing pull the lever towards him. If the signal failed to respond fully to his first swing the movement had to be repeated. Replacing a signal involved a pushing movement of the levers which was no less demanding of strength.

London Midland Railway signalling frames were raised about a foot above the floor whereas GWR ones were arched only an inch or so above floor level. In addition, the point at which the levers were connected below floor level was different so the arc covered by the top of the levers in their swing was about 3–$3\frac{1}{2}$ ft in the case of the LMR and only 2–$2\frac{1}{2}$ ft on the GWR. The shorter swing was harder but safer in the narrow confines of the signal box.

Of the relationship between the key grades of railway workers, Alan Butler has commented:

Before joining the railways I had assumed like many non-railwaymen that a train driver actually drove the train wherever he chose, selecting a line and turning the engine into it. But as a signalman it was made clear to me that in spite of the massive power at his fingertips the driver has to follow the route set up by the signalman, who dictates whether a train should stop, go, change routes, etc., by operating signals and switching points. Some drivers seemed to have an almost blind faith in signalmen and would go anywhere a signal directed them, when in fact they had a joint responsibility with the signalman to ensure that they operated on lines over which they had been passed as competent to work trains.[29]

Signalmen generally disputed the drivers' claim to be 'Kings of the Road', and in the days of steam believed that drivers and firemen were chosen mainly for their physical ability to stoke, and control their engines. They had to have sufficient responsibility to operate at safe speeds and obey signals, but the bulk of the safety burden lay on signalmen who were stationed wherever track layout became more complicated. The signalman's life is governed by a set of complex rules and regulations in which he has to pass an examination before entry to the grade and annually thereafter. The rules and regulations for railway work cover both normal and emergency working. Normally the driver would make the major decisions on the movement of his trains, but in emergencies he would accept the ruling and direction of the signalman. Signalmen of course had good local knowledge whereas drivers needed total knowledge of signals and routes over a large part of their region. Generally, however, signalmen and drivers were good friends, for they relied a great deal upon each other.

Engine-men and signalmen could be strongly contrasted when they met in a signal box. Signalmen, long known as an extremely neat group of men, did not take kindly to their box being sullied by heavy-booted engine-men. At a signal box, the engine-men who wished entry would tap on the door and await an invitation to enter. Inside the box, the visitor stood on the doormat and did not transgress the highly polished cabin floor, complete with its protective newspapers, until invited. Lonely or not, the signalman was rightly suspicious of any visitor, no matter how cheerful, who crossed his floor. In work-stained overalls and shifting uneasily from boot to boot, engine-men looked completely out of place in a signal box. If they had committed an indiscretion, such as running a few yards past a danger signal when the rails were wet and slippery, then the fireman might bring a small peace offering to the signalman. This could take the form of a driver's hand cloth, much prized by the box-proud signalman who disliked handling polished levers with bare hands in case rust appeared. At other times, handfuls of cotton might be offered; a big prize was when large lumps of coal were shovelled from the engine to the line-side to be collected later by the signalman.

The job was not without its humorous aspects, however, as Alan Butler discovered on busy bank holidays at Pill. Owing to a signal failure, trains could only pass Pill on the written authority of signalman Butler. Traffic was heavy and the forms ran out long before the end of the emergency. Butler used the box toilet rolls. Passengers leaning out of the carriage windows to query the delay had the delicious experience of watching the signalman hand to the driver a modest piece of toilet paper, on receipt of which the throttle was opened and the train sent speeding.

Railway workers are not immune to travelling difficulties, and when required for early turn or to open up a service on a branch line they have to rely often upon the assistance of others to get them to work. A 6.00 a.m. start often means rising at 4.30 a.m. to ensure a punctual arrival, and adventure often catches the shift worker at the most inconvenient time. Once, Alan Butler decided to cycle the five miles from his house to Shirehampton, where a ferry could carry him over to Pill. On arrival at the ferry, however, the motor would not start on the regular boat. To help Butler open his box on time, the ferryboatman offered to row him across to Pill, in a boat half full of muddy water. The River Avon was at flood tide, but with the ferryman at the oars and Butler bailing water with an old tin, the water level was kept under control and landfall was effected on the southern shore in sufficient time for the determined signalman to open his box. This was the true spirit of loyalty to the task and to the industry of which the Great Western was so proud.

Butler mixed with all types of railway worker and was continuously surprised by the wit and intelligence he encountered. In his signalling days he learned to assume nothing about his fellows, no matter how menial the task at observation. In his travels Butler met a lengthman who was an expert on opera and a driver and shunter who had exhibited paintings at London galleries. Despite these colourful moments, however, the work, if the signalman did nothing to overcome the problem, was repetitive and monotonous. The telephone, the means of overcoming the man-made isolation, created friendships among men who never saw each other. In order to enliven the conversation, signalmen created and developed a special language of bell codes which eliminated eavesdroppers and also gave advance warning of the arrival of officials and inspectors.

While many railwaymen had the ability to describe their work and aspirations in slangy speech and secret bell codes, signalman Walter Sinkinson possessed poetic vision. As a young signalman Sinkinson marvelled at the sights and sounds of the Tyneside coast; his early memories were 'ship-masted, ship-funnelled to the eye, fog-warning to the ear.' Tyne Dock piped, 'whistled and blared at the North Sea, while Marsden Rock steamed and Roker warmed its beach in the sun.' He earned 24s. weekly, with a little extra for night work, but his heart was full of railway poetry. Who better to employ in a signal box than a cheeky youngster with a passion for drawing signals and totting up train mileages? Handicapped by the three-shift system, Sinkinson still found time to study English composition, music, history and art. The box boy could speak French, translate Ovid and break in a new horse. In Sinkinson we see and hear William Morris's dream of socialist man, an ideal creature possessed of a high degree of both efficiency and literacy.

With Sinkinson we enter another world, where signal boxes never shut but 'close their eyes'. Men who laboured in three-shift boxes were 'continuous men', never divorced from their job. Of these complex men, Sinkinson has written: [30]

The Signalman

His mind a schedule
Serving the public hours
Route gradient, distance
Adept in speed and power

Hand implementing
The permits of the brain
A common carrier
But proud of track and train

Men who were masters of their trade
Dream, vision, wonder, all in flower
This track, this train, these signals made
Gave strength to beauty, grace to power.

According to Sinkinson, early-morning duty was the 'sours' of the service. A 6.00 a.m. start meant rising at 4.00 or 5.00 a.m. Signalmen always dreaded opening a cold signal box in winter; it inevitably meant lifeless signals, points held rigid with cold, a fireless grate, water cans iced into a block and even the ink solid in the wells. Of this season he wrote:

The frenzied rain, driven hard,
Against the track,
Streaming the shunter's cheek
The tapper's back

The raw and bitter blast
That seeks the bone
Numbing the lengthman's grip,
His feet of stone.

It was the very devil to work through any one of winter's variants, ranging from black damp to polar white, sometimes with a choking fog seeping into every corner of the freezing box. Fog brought out the 'railway artillery', the filthy darkness was punctuated by the roar, flash and smell of the rail-placed detonator. Fog turned the smiling embankments into barricades; the line-side was a forward position where a fogman manned a strategic post in the battle against the weather. These company servants put duty before personal safety—their loyalty to employer, industry, public and fellow workers 'glowed like a virtue'.

> The smoking brazier glows,
> Beside the smothered track,
> Only a glimmer shows,
> Of signals tall and black.
>
> As ear gives vision aid,
> When veiling mists obscure,
> A detonation's made,
> Safe running to ensure.

The signalmen, as with all other grades, soon established a special hierarchy of working places. Distinctions in cabins were a matter of size and number of levers, telephones and block instruments. According to Sinkinson, the smaller boxes were fog huts, and ground frames were dog kennels. The fog huts and ground frames were usually termed 'hell holes' by the occupants. Instead of sprinting down a long line of levers, the signalmen in these small places operated in a small circle, with rapid movements between lever frame, instruments, telephones and desks.

Walter Sinkinson was one of a breed of men which the railways will never see again. He joined the service at a time when railway work meant status in the community. In May 1967, after forty-two years' service to industry and community, Sinkinson was made redundant with a final payment of £427. In his railway career, he was sustained by a powerful religiosity. He described his role as working on 'God's Railway'. His religion was no transient piety, no donning of special clothes to suit the mood and the place; it was as real as the metals in the road bed. He was aware of a guiding hand warding off the evils of carelessness, error, mischance, and he ends his writing to me with:

> God! there are busy lines to cross
> And many rapid lines to run
> And laggard wheels are public loss
> And lives are precious every one.
> Before we turn to start our day
> To put head and heart to good employ
> Uplift us Lord to trust, to pray
> A good shift worked, our pride, our joy!

Sinkinson brings us a firm stride, a fresh lustre, a special vision to the world of wheel and rail. We should be grateful for his perception.

The grade of pointsman developed in the rumbustious marshalling yard, a maelstrom of labourers, number-takers, wagon examiners and repairers, axle-box greasers and shunters. A marshalling yard was a nightmare of thumping, crashing wagon buffers, interspersed with the wristy snick of steel-tipped hickory poles taming rusting and reluctant couplings. One way out of this situation was promotion to goods guard, a catapaulting from the multiplicity of grades into the singularity of life in a rattling wheeled box at the end of a train. Rare in the days of steam was the man who transferred from the 'goods' to the dizzy heights of passenger guard.

On the earliest goods trains, the guard was termed a breakesman. His job was to break the speed of loose-coupled wagons by use of the hand-operated iron rods on the side of the wagons. Before the use of brake vans, such men lay on top of the contents of the wagons. In icy weather more than one guard was lifted dead from wagons of frozen bricks or vegetables.

When trains were descending inclines the guard had to jump from wagon to wagon in order to pin down the primitive brakes, and many of them were killed when they misjudged the jumping distance. For many years the railway companies were under no statutory obligation to initiate safe working conditions, to inquire into accidents or to provide compensation for injury and death.

On the North Union Railway in the 1840s, any guard who failed to account for damage or neglect to equipment or goods in his care would be called upon to pay compensation. Guards on this line could be fined when their trains ran past signals—something beyond their control— and also if proven truculent to passengers.

A goods brake van was a weighted four-wheeled vehicle about sixteen feet long. Its furnishings were a number of lockers which doubled as seats and a small coal-burning stove. There was no lighting except for the glare from the fire and the guard's handlamp. In the centre of most vans was the brake wheel. Screwed down, it applied the brake shoes to the van wheels. On falling gradients, or on 'switchback' routes, the guard showed his skill by applying and releasing the brake in order to keep the wagons 'buffered up'. Without the use of the van brake, loose-coupled trains would simply snap couplings when the train was negotiating a number of different curves simultaneously. Many brake vans had the wheel positioned on a verandah—a platform extension of the van—to encourage guards to take the air, as the fumes and stuffiness of the van interior might overcome the occupant. Not all railways provided heat for the guard. As late as 1895 the Great Northern Railway of Scotland had brake vans operating without stoves.

James Greenwood tabulated the weekly roster of a guard in the *Daily Telegraph* in 1871: [31]

Monday: Left home quarter-to five in the morning. Home, half-past one Tuesday morning.

Tuesday: Left home quarter-past twelve noon. Home, half-past eight Wednesday morning.

Wednesday: Left home twelve noon. Home, quarter-past five.

Thursday: Left home quarter-to five in the morning; got home quarter-past one Friday morning.

Friday: Left home twelve noon, got home twenty minutes to eight Saturday morning.

Saturday: Left station eight o'clock at night—got home quarter-to twelve.

In the early days, any guard who complained about his wages or working conditions was pointedly asked, 'Have you brought your clothes?' The Derby goods guard who spent 168 hours at work in two consecutive weeks knew the meaning of the railway term 'a lonesome pine'. Another Midland goods guard suffering these appalling hours asked, 'Why doesn't the Midland provide us with line-side huts labelled Midland slaves?' On the Taff Vale Railway, guard Hurcombe was dismissed for protesting about his miserable existence. At Bordesley in 1895, goods guards were allowed to work one train the whole week, causing them to be on duty for eighty hours.

Of all the qualities necessary in the make-up of a goods guard the most important was the ability to sit alone and calm on his seat, his head turned to stare into the night through the side or gusset windows of the van. A brake van could be a nerve-racking place. Apart from screwing on his hand-brake or exhibiting a hand signal from his gusseted dungeon, the guard faced a shift broken only by fleeting glimpses of signal arms and the smack of wheel flanges across points and junctions.

On loose-coupled trains every touch of the engine brake sent a vicious snaking action down the length of the train as the wagons buffered up. If the guard was slow in observing the response of the driver to a lineside signal, the brake van would feel the full force of the concertina effect and the guard would be hurled from one end of the brake van to the other. The engine crew, forty or fifty wagons in front, would feel nothing.

Most goods traffic was carried during the 'dead hours'—between midnight and 5.00 a.m. The goods guard was therefore working 'Australian days'. Throughout the night hours, his body was buffeted and banged by every wrinkle in the rail, his ears were tuned to the early screech or groan of tortured axles, and his eyes grew red and strained looking for the ugly glow of an axle-box running red and hot. In the light of such conditions a goods guard might be expected to watch out for any unusual creature comforts that might turn up. Mr Sid Mosley, whose father was a goods guard on the London and North-Western Railway, has told how his father once found a mattress in the locker of a 'Wessy' brake van; such information imparted to the truculent engine-men helped them justify the allegation that goods guards got their living like prostitutes, 'lying on their backs'.[32] The allegation was never true, but the phrase passed with well-oiled precision into railway lore.

Nevertheless, goods guards usually got on well with the engine-men —especially if the men crewed together regularly. When travelling on the engine to pick up a train, the goods guard would often share the contents of a tea can with the engine-men. If the guard was young enough he might try his hand at keeping up the steam pressure while the fireman passed acidulous comments on such attempts to 'play the banjo'. The guard was forbidden to touch brake or throttle—these instruments were understood to be reserved for the 'driver only'.

Until the 1920s, goods guards on the North-Eastern Railway had the distinction of 'owning' their own van. These North-Eastern vans were kept spotlessly clean by their users, who often decorated the utilitarian interiors with railway posters of the locality. At the end of each turn of duty the brake van was shunted out, locked up by the guard and not used again until he returned to duty.

In 1906, the London and North-Western Railway instituted the hated 'trip system', a system of bonus payments which depended on the ability of the guard and the engine crew to 'beat the clock' in the moving of goods trains between blocks of sidings. A goods guard from Wigan wrote at the time:

> I am one of the chaps who works on the trip system, and I should think that a blessing had fallen on us if the trip system was abolished at this very moment. One of the first things to happen would be a reduction in accidents.
>
> When I book on duty the first thing I think about is the trip rate, and all the while I am on duty I can take little interest in my work. While we are running around like madmen we are liable to give the driver the wrong signal or to turn the wrong points and find we are on the ground with a wagon on top of us. Many foul words are spoken —we are like mad dogs snapping at each other.[33]

The trip guard had to nag at signalmen, beg oil from engine-men and plead with shunters to get him a brake van which was fit for the road. All the wagons were privately owned and had to be recorded on a duty sheet. Once the train was coupled up and the seething driver pacified, the battle began over reaching the destination before being overtaken by the clock. If the day's duty was performed according to schedule, the pushing, swearing and agitation produced the sum of 9d. extra. As late as 1968, the railways of Britain attempted via pay and efficiency talks to introduce a modern version of the trip system. The railway unions found the proposition unacceptable and the scheme was abandoned. Although dominated by the clock, railways are not clockwork mechanisms. Tripping and trip rates stand out as one of the most iniquitous schemes ever inflicted upon railway workers.

Life in the brake van had few compensations, but Mr Alex Young, who was a guard on North-Eastern goods trains, has recorded:

> One of the most pleasant runs was that from Durham to Whitby, across the rolling moors and through the Cleveland Hills, past the neat stations and the neater farms. The friendly Yorkshire people would often ply the crews of ballast trains with eggs and fresh milk. In response, a few slabs of coal would roll from the engine tender to the isolated cottages near the embankments. Station staffs on the London and North-Eastern were often presented with a freshly killed rabbit or a pat of fresh butter.[34]

Standing in superb contrast to the heavy-booted and accoutrement-laden goods guard was the polished personage of the passenger guard. These guards were the face of the company during the passage of the train. Buttoned and burnished, decked with carnation or rose, this gentleman, with watch, whistle and flag, exemplified tradition, service and assurance. The passenger guard was at the apex of a career, but his duties marked him off quite clearly from his distant relation on the goods train. Passenger guards had a direct link with the guards of the mail coaches, whose duties had included the responsibility for the timepieces which would regulate the running of the coach plus the guardianship of public and private valuables. The manifold dangers of marshalling yards, knowledge of far-away sidings and running loops, the wristy swing of the shunting pole, were aspects of railway work unknown to passenger guards. Track peculiarities and the humouring of truculent engine-men were likewise the bailiwick of goods guards.

Generally, passenger guards had high status in working-class life. Moving up and down their line acting as guide, friend and philosopher, such men were the potentates of the railway system. What happened in the van of a passenger train was determined by the mood of the guard, but any misdemeanour by a passenger guard was dealt with most severely. In 1842, a passenger guard on the London and South-Western

Railway was fined 40s.—two weeks' earnings—because his train failed to stop at Gosport, Hampshire; the fine was lenient because the van brake was working in a contrary direction.

By 1870, although passenger guards were, in common with other railway workers, tormented by long hours, it seemed that once they had achieved their goal of being paid for each day separately, they lapsed into languor. In this period the guards dare not sign their names to letters or articles in their union journals for fear of dismissal. Discipline was maintained with fearful penalties for miscreants. In 1880, a passenger guard on the London and South-Western Railway who helped himself to half a sovereign from a mailbag was sentenced to seven years' penal servitude.

The London and South-Western Railway was always keen to separate its guards into sharply defined groups. In 1841, guards on this line were designated first and second class, the former being distinguished by a belt. By 1847, the original scarlet coats had been replaced by a quieter blue, although the scarlet collar was a reminder of earlier sartorial elegance. Trousers were blue with a double row of scarlet piping. In 1885, the uniform had altered to dark blue cloth with silver collar badges, plus pouched belts for storage of detonators. In 1863, the South-Western returned to tradition when it issued scarlet coats to the guards of royal trains. Guards on the London and North-Western Railway, elegantly attired in frock coats plus red bandolier, must have looked very formidable to raw recruits.

In 1865, two passenger guards paraded before a joint committee of the Edinburgh and Glasgow and North British Railway companies. As the North British was taking over the Edinburgh and Glasgow it was decided that its uniform for passenger guards would be retained after the merger. The guards wore a navy blue overcoat piped in red with 'North British' on one side of the collar. The word 'Guard' was quatrefoiled in gold thread on the other collar. Trousers were made of Oxford doeskin —as made for Sandhurst—and a Zouave-style cap completed the ensemble. Guards of mixed trains got pilot jackets, as on the London and North-Western Railway. Pointsmen got indigo jackets with red collars and caps with red bands. Porters were provided with red cotton neckcloths.

The London and South-Western retained its liking for sartorial display among passenger guards well into the twentieth century. Many were like the grandfather of Mr W. Bishop of Portsmouth, who has written:

My grandfather's principles were unwavering—Tory. He never went on duty without highly polished boots, gleaming buttons and a flower in his buttonhole. In the early 1920s, just before amalgamation, the company issued red ties to passenger guards; the old stickler refused to wear his because it was the colour of the local socialists. He got away with his refusal.[35]

As might be expected, the uniforms of goods guards in the days of steam were far more functional. Just before 1900, goods guards on the London and North-Western wore corduroy trousers with a large drop-flap at the front, waistcoat and cap. In summer months the guards were issued with large linen sun hats.

In the 1960s, after years of unsuccessful pleading, passenger guards were awarded mileage payments on the same basis as engine-men. The goods guard did not share in the sudden bonanza. The reaction of engine-men to mileage payments for passenger guards retains its unprintable quality.

Despite his beautiful appearance, his air of authority and his un-doubted responsibilities, the passenger guard was the lesser mortal of the two types of guard. The goods guard could perform both tasks efficiently, but the passenger guard was totally unable to work any kind of goods train.

4

Ashpits and Offices: The Engine Shed

Without formal opportunities for isolation and contemplation, opportunities that require enclosed space, free from prying eyes and extraneous stimuli and secular interruptions, even the most externalized and extraverted life must eventually suffer.

—LEWIS MUMFORD,
The Culture of Cities

In the age of steam, the engine shed was the pounding and romantic heart of the railway industry. Like a coal mine, it dominated the area and the lives of those who worked in or near it, attending to its gargantuan appetite for people and supplies. The engine shed took in rested, clean and willing people; at the end of a shift it spewed out its exhausted oil- and coal-stained rejects.

There was neither night nor day in an engine shed, just different hours at which men and boys presented themselves to the unrelenting task of servicing the leviathans of steam. The diverse elements of railway work from timetabling to train time crystallized at the moment the engine, throbbing with quiet anticipation, emerged from the confines of the shed. What had, an hour earlier, been an inanimate assemblage was now a giant of the track, an admixture of steel, iron, copper, brass and white metal ready to tackle moor or mountain, valley or viaduct.

Engine sheds were usually built well away from the urban centres, but as trade increased so did urban encroachment. At the end of the steam age most engine sheds were hemmed in by factories, shops, offices and houses, and gave much offence by the daily emission of sulphurous smoke and flying ash.

Kingmoor shed at Carlisle was in its later years a concrete box squatting in the damp fields north of the city which swung wetly away to the Solway Firth. Its near neighbour, Upperby, was pinched between the North-Western main line and the arterial road to the south. On the old Midland main line, Millhouses (Sheffield) and Rowsley belched indelicately on Pennine slopes, while Hellifield nestled securely at the southern aspect of the descent from Ais Gill. The doyen of the north Midland was Leeds (Holbeck), a walled fortress among a complex of working-class houses and shops.

In the first century of railway operation, the engine sheds achieved enviable reputations for cleanliness, but in the closing decades of steam power this process was reversed, and engine sheds became known for their filth, grease and smoke. For many years, the creation of smoke by engines was punishable by company fines, and although engine-men and inspectors alike attempted to minimize smoke nuisance, the issue was never completely resolved. The lighting up of dead engines made the engine sheds an inferno.

Few steam engine sheds enjoyed internal lighting; no electric bulb system could pierce the blackness of engine smoke. Lighting was 'personal', individual; that is, by handlamp or flare torch. A personal flare torch was made by tying a paraffin-soaked rag to one end of a large spanner, igniting it and then balancing the torch on a suitable ledge in the cab.

Albert Williams, a railway blacksmith at Swindon, has left us his memories of life in a railway forge, which, in the early days when sheds were reputed to have been airy and spotless, was one of the exceptions:

> Railway sheds now resemble contract premises. Piece-work rates are cut to the lowest possible point, it is all push, drive and hustle. One part of the shed is often working at breakneck speed, while another is working but three or four days a week and men are in a half-starved condition. One would think that the various divisions of the works were owned by separate firms or people of separate nationalities, such formidable barriers appear between them. There is no freedom, just the same coming and going year after year. The workmen lose interest in all life beyond their own smoky walls and dwellings.

For an intelligent man, the harshness of the life, the bone-wearying labour performed in restricted, sulphurous surroundings, and the know-ledge that all around him men were treated little better than slaves, created an especial form of alienation. We can see how unfamiliar were the new methods of work by the reactions of early Victorian artisans who found themselves doing skilled work for the new railway com-panies. In a letter to the *Railway Times*, Joseph Alexander, a fitter in the Derby locomotive works in 1844, complained of the work expected of him:

> ... I was ordered to repair a firebox. ... I had all the old stays to drill out from both ends (and they were in a very awkward situation to get at). ... I had all the holes to rimmer out from three-quarters of

an inch to an inch, and tap them afresh; I had likewise to screw sixteen of the new stays myself by hand, and put the whole of them in
and rivet them. I was about six days in completing the job, and I
appeal to the judgement of any person who is at all acquainted with
the nature of the work to say whether there was anything unreasonable in the time. . . .[1]

Mr Kirtley, the Works Superintendent, told Alexander that the job
should have taken only two days and that was all the time for which he
would authorize payment, take it or leave it. Alexander, with commendable spirit, left it, and his brave letter shows that his pride and professional skill had been impugned; furthermore, he did not think that he
could repair even a pair of shoes for Mr Kirtley in the future, let alone
a firebox. This was the true spirit of the artisan reacting to unfairness
and Victorian industrial tyranny.

The engine shed had many moods, and even more faces. On wild
windswept winter nights, with the atmosphere fouled with billows of
filthy smoke, sulphur fumes and ash particles, the engine shed was hell
on earth. On a still spring morning, with the smoke rising straight to
the heavens and the sun bouncing from the walls, an engine shed could
beam at the world, especially if it was freshly whitewashed on its prominent parts. Sunday mornings brought the guided parties, the railway
enthusiasts, the model builders, even railway historians. Little interest
was evinced in the work of the shed staff—the engines were the stars.
When the tourists left, the real work began—getting ready for the
Monday morning rush.

On busy days, with the sun ablaze outside, men worked a full shift,
punctuating the gloom within with lamp and torch. An engine shed in
full flow was no place for jay walking or rubber necking. Every fume-
filled yard contained its own hazard—an open hydrant, a patch of oil,
rushes of scalding steam. Heaps of brick, ash or clinker lay in silent
wait for the careless step or the ungarded moment.

The engines were the focal point of the shed. They were given femi-
nine gender from the earliest days, and their individual foibles were the
stock-in trade of shedmen, foremen and drivers. When an engine arrived
on shed from a day's work, it was freshly coaled, its tank filled and it
was then sent to join the queue of engines on the pit. Here they stood
like a line of elephants, awaiting the attentions of the shed engine-men.
There now began the process known as engine disposal. Two men were
needed to dispose of an engine—one worked in the cab and the other
in the ashpit. On opening the firehole door, a blast of heat radiated round
the cab, starting up an immediate and uncomfortable sweating. If the
firebox was full there was no alternative to using a nine-foot-long

clinker shovel, with which the top layer of hot coals was removed. In the confines of the cab, great strength and dexterity were needed to draw out the hot coals, stand up, manoeuvre the long shovel and tip the coals over the side of the cab into the skip drawn up alongside the engine.

The clinker shovel soon got very hot and was dangerous if mishandled. The cab filled with dust and fumes from which there was no escape. When the top layer of coal was cleared, a long, heavy steel bar with a sharp end was then used to smash into the heavy clinker, which stuck stubbornly to the firebars. These heavy lumps of clinker were removed with the clinker shovel, and a tool known as a slice was inserted between the clinker and the firebars, a very difficult and strenuous task. Once an area of five or six firebars had been bared it was the turn of the tongs. The tongs were actually long-handled nippers which were inserted into the firebox to grip each bar individually. To use the tongs, a man bent double and put his face right up to the firehole door in order to drop the nipping head of the tongs onto the selected firebar. The heat from the firebox started sweat streaming down a man's face, searing his eyes with salt. Once the nippers had gripped, the man stood up and, with a mighty heave and twist, dragged the heavy firebar from its socket and pulled it onto the floor of the cab. This man was now ready to start work on clearing the firebox, while for the man in the pit below the firebox a nightmare was about to begin. While the man in the cab was drawing the firebars, his mate descended into the pit and pushed a heavy steel skip into position beneath the bottom damper door. This skip ran on rails embedded in the pit bottom. Into the skip he directed a short water pipe, which, once turned on, helped to keep down the flying dust. These, however, rarely worked.

The pit, which was about four feet deep, was usually kept swept and tidy by the shed labourer, but in busy periods he was unable to gain access. The result was that the pit floor was usually ankle-deep in clinker and ash, often hot enough to burn the soles of a man's boots.

For pit duties the men used old sets of overalls, which they kept in their lockers. These overalls were never washed as neither laundry nor self-respecting housewife would attempt to clear from them the oil, grease and perspiration with which they were saturated. When the stench of them became totally unbearable they were burned in engine fireboxes. The outfit was completed by a pair of goggles, a handkerchief tied round the mouth and a pair of leather gloves.

With the skip in position, the raker-out then eased into position across the brake stretchers and inserted into the ashpan a springy ten-foot ashpan rake, with a broad round-toothed head. As he bent double and squeezed into position for raking out, tiny spots of boiling water and red-hot globules of engine oil fell on his cap, overalls, shoulders and arms. Only the grease on his clothes prevented the boiling oil and water penetrating to his skin. He then called for his mate in the cab to open the damper and start 'pushing through'.

Suddenly the damper door would wrench open, exposing the wide pitted floor of the ashpan. A cloud of hot sulphurous air and dust would envelop the raker-out. The firebars having been removed, he could see up into the firebox, which contained great heaps of clinker stacked along the sides.

The business end of the rake lanced into the ashpan and then all hell was let loose. Into the ashpan were pushed great chunks of heavy clinker, live coals, showers of sparks and clouds of choking white ash. As the evil mixture thudded into the ashpan from above, the raker-out dragged it forward frantically into the metal skip positioned below the ashpan. Foul perspiration streamed from the raker-out, across his back, between his legs, and water gushed from his eyes. There was no escape from the heat, the dust, the smoke or the sparks. The men worked like maniacs, the one above pushing, the one below pulling, the rakes snaking and reddening like creatures demented. This was an inferno even Dante could not describe.

Suddenly it was over. The firebox rake was withdrawn and pitched, angrily distorted, onto the adjacent heap of ash and clinker. The raker-out manoeuvred his red-hot implement across the stretcher bars and placed it in the pit-drain to cool. Shaking, sweating and gasping, he extricated himself from his doubled-up position and ran beneath the engine until he reached dust-free air. All along the ashpit the air was filled with almighty blasphemies from sweating, frustrated men as they slammed into the brutalizing work.

The fireman had not yet completed his duties. Another dangerous and filthy task awaited him—the clearing of the engine smoke-box. In order to do this job a man had to climb onto the narrow framing at the front of the engine and swing open the huge round door which guarded the boiler tube ends and the blast pipe. This huge cylindrical box contained fine black ash from the boiler tubes which was hot and restless from being continuously subjected to a stream of hot air from the steam-controlled blower. Balanced on a narrow ledge, blinded by flying black dust, facing a constant threat that the heavy door would slam him off his perch into the pit, the disposer shovelled out three or four or more barrowloads of the filthy black muck into another skip. That done, the engine was then trundled into the shed. All of this work was a race against time, for the steam pressure in the boiler fell rapidly once the fire was drawn.

The ashpit was no place for people with delicate feelings. It was the

14. The Vigilants: Jim Swain carrying banner; Bob Lunniss marching behind raincoat over shoulder. Note size of policemen.

15. New faces at King's Cross, 1965: Bob Lunniss and a new recruit.

18. Mrs. Pat Forward working as a tube cleaner at Kentish Town engine sheds, 1942.

17. Women engine cleaners, 1941 Notice the scraper.

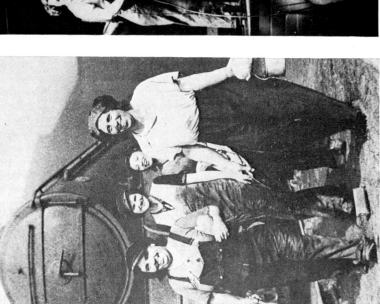

16. Jim Swain (*centre*) with two other engine cleaners, King's Cross, 1933.

19. 'The Binch', Polmadie, Glasgow, 1947.

20. Locomotive for lodging: LNER express locomotive type A.4., fitted with corridor tender, enabling east coast enginemen to pass from the train to the cab of the locomotive, thus eliminating special stops for the relief of train crews.

21. Banbury Lodge, Great Western Railway: the corridor is typical of an old-style lodge. Notice how partitions do not reach the ceiling.

22. Facing the future: part of the Old Oak Common Hostel, London, 1949.

23. North Road Lodge, Plymouth Great Western Railway.
Wooden hut 1941; stone hut 1957.

24. Crewe Lodge, Mill Street, 1845.

25. Rugby Lodge.

26. Immingham Lodge.

27. Mallaig Lodge.

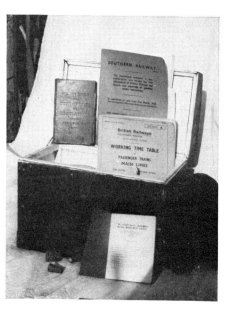

28. A lodging basket.

29. Mrs. E. Maillard at the keyboard of 'The Nunnery', Sheffield.

30. The Midland Pullman.

31. A Kentish Town driver and second man ready to take out the Midland Pullman in the mid-1960s. These men were met by taxi and taken to the lodge at Longsight, Manchester.

most brutal place on the railways, a spot for hard muscles and no nonsense. These conditions, which appertained on the most modern of engine sheds until the end of steam, were a great advance on conditions at the turn of the century, for as one railway historian has written of the year 1904, 'It was no uncommon thing for me in one day to have to crawl on my stomach beneath several locomotives to clean the ash-pans.'[2] In my own time on the railway sixteen- and seventeen-year-olds were allowed to do this type of work. The ashpits were known as 'dust holes' in England and in Scotland as 'binches'.

What happened to all the clinker which was cleared from locomotive fireboxes in the years of steam? Much of it is now doing sterling service as hard core on the new motorways and roads of Britain. For many years the clinker from Midland routes was deposited on the marshy ground at Scratchwood, near Elstree, Hertfordshire. The motorway at Mill Hill, Hertfordshire, is built over and drained by the clinker dragged and raked from countless thousands of fireboxes.

At Southall engine sheds in the 1950s the situation had improved only slightly, and Ron Smith, who worked there, has left a description of how, as a youngster, he stoked the two stationary boilers which provided the steam power which dried the sand and powered the radiators and tube-blowing equipment. He has recorded:

> On these stationary boilers, the firehole was about three feet above ground level, so once again blisters and physical exhaustion were my lot.
>
> On a windy black winter night this was strenuous, dirty and dangerous work with ash flying in your eyes and face. Having finished one engine I would dash round to attend to the boilers that used steam far quicker than any main-line express, I'm sure. By 6.00 a.m. I must have been a pitiful sight for a mere sixteen-year-old.[3]

Accommodation for the men working on the ashpits was usually a small hut with forms for seating and a central coal-burning stove. At Edge Hill, Liverpool, the hut was built with a urinal right outside the door. In slack periods on night duty the men would sit round the cabin in their evil-smelling overalls, red-eyed and filthy beings from a world of railways unknown to enthusiasts.[4]

The minutiae of tasks, and the separateness they bred, were responsible for the rash of small buildings seen in and around engine sheds. These consisted of messrooms, cabins, small sheds, shanties, shacks and old railway coaches. The tighter the division of labour the greater was the demand for separate premises. These cabins and huts abounded with characters who, within a more open system, may have left a greater mark on society than they did in the ladderwork promotion system of the railway world; nevertheless, they were the power in their own bailiwick.

According to Mr Jimmy Hulme, who was a fireman at Edge Hill, Liverpool, in the 1950s:

> The sand furnace was the place where the boiler washout men had their meals. This place was literally a cavern. The seats were the men's own lockers, the table was an old work bench; it was lit by one naked lightbulb, one could never see into any of the four corners day or night.[5]

At Polmadie shed, Glasgow, two characters, Charlie and Barney, had a hideout in the sand kiln. When old Charlie, whose job it was to hump pails of sand onto the engines, took a holiday, it took four hefty cleaners to do his job. Charlie would often start his work two hours before his rostered time, working like a Trojan to keep his engine sandboxes filled.

Old Barney, who was of Irish extraction and with little or no education, designed and built all manner of gadgets for the efficient drying of sand, which was used to prevent wheel-slip. His work was generally approved by management, who gave him financial rewards.

Personal hygiene was a late-starter in the engine sheds; men were expected to look smart on duty, but in the case of shed workers this was an impossibility and there were plenty of places such as that at Polmadie, described by Mr William McLagan:

> The bothy [as the messroom was called] was a small homely place with seating around the walls, a huge fire in the fireplace and a sink for washing. Working clothes were stored in lockers under the seats and shift clothes were hung on pegs on the walls. Drying round the fire were vests, shirts, socks and dungarees and the whole place was stinking with sweat and food. There the lads gossiped, argued, slept, played cards, ate their food and washed up before going home.[6]

A small army of workers in the shed attended to repairs to the engines. If the fire had been drawn in order to facilitate repairs, it was first given a stringent mechanical examination by fitters and its main defects repaired. The brick-arch repairman was one of the first to effect repairs. His job was to get into the firebox and replaster into position the large firebricks of the arch which protected the boiler tubes at the firebox end of the engine. These men, like the ashpit workers, rarely changed their clothes, which were coated with yellowish white dust, matching the colour of their faces. They usually worked alone in the confines of the firebox, their faces masked to avoid excessive inhalation of the firebrick dust. The brick-arch man was a human mole, burrowing and working in splendid isolation. Next came the firebar setter, usually a labourer who had been promoted for this important job. His equipment consisted of a long steel bar with a hook at the end. Pushing the long firebars through the firehole door and onto the firegrate, he skilfully turned them on end and slotted them into the firegrate slots. Next came the 'chippy', the shed carpenter, who effected repairs to broken floorboards in the cabs and to cab seating.

On the front of the engine worked the boiler tube cleaner, using a long steel blow pipe attached to a flexible hose powered by compressed air. He inserted the business end of the pipe into each boiler tube in turn and blew out the scale which had accumulated during the journey. These tasks completed, it was the turn of the boiler-washer to ply his particular trade. His task was to empty the engine boiler by removing a number of vital washout plugs, thus draining the life-blood of the engine. Once the boiler water was drained, he then refilled the boiler from a long hose attached to a water hydrant set in the floor of the shed. He wore black waterproof clothing and was always soaking wet. His wetness contrasted oddly with the yellow-grey dustiness of the brick-arch man, especially when they were working or talking together, like the sand meeting the sea. Lastly came the fire kindlers to restore the firebox with new life. The fire freshly lit and the cab redolent with the smell of paraffin firelighters, the engine was ready for the onset of the engine cleaners. William McLagan, who worked as fireman and driver at Polmadie, remembers the fire lighters of his day:

> The tools of the trade consisted of a large firing shovel and a naked paraffin lamp to examine the boiler water gauge glasses. Along with the constant hard labour there was the stink of firelighters and the acrid smoke and fumes from the fireboxes and chimnies, which made eyes smart and water. These lads never had much time to sit around bothies or messrooms but went constantly on their rounds attending to the engines.[7]

In the railway hierarchy, firebox repairing was classified as semi-skilled work. The enormous responsibility attached to it in the avoidance of accidents has been described by Mr W. Bishop, who performed his task at Fratton, Portsmouth, on the Southern Railway:

> When fireboxes leaked it was necessary for me to work in warm or even hot boxes. It was impossible to stay inside the boxes for more than a few minutes owing to the terrific heat. You entered the firebox through the firehole door, an aperture of eighteen inches. For a tall man all kinds of problems existed, from squeezing through the hole to arranging one's limbs inside the firebox in order to do the work. The Southern Railway dock engines had fireboxes only four feet in dia-

meter. The work of drilling, riveting, caulking and chipping was all done by hand.

I was proud of my work and would never take chances. Only once was I in trouble, due to the collapse of a firebox while an engine was in traffic. The brick arch, firebars and ashpan were blown onto the track by the blast. The engine-driver never again followed his occupation; after a full enquiry I was cleared of all responsibility.[8]

The masculine world of an engine shed, with its smoke, grime, grease and colourful language, was not a typical place for women to earn a living, but the Second World War brought a number of them into the engine sheds as replacements for men called to the forces. Mrs Pat Foreman, who worked in the Kentish Town engine sheds in 1942, has written:

During the war I worked as an engine tuber, being one of the first women to replace the absent men. The shed was a dismal place to earn a living and despite the friendliness of the engine-men and the shed staff it was obvious that the shed had been for many years a miserable place to work. As a tube cleaner my equipment was a long flexible hose which ended in a rigid metal tube about five feet long. The pipe was fixed at one end to a steam valve on the floor of the shed. The steam valve created a stream of compressed air in the rigid section of the pipe, and this air was blown into the boiler tube ends at the smoke-box end of the engine. I stood on the framing at the front of the engine, swung open the heavy door, and balanced myself on the often greasy and grit-strewn platform. Soot and grease would enter any cut on the surface of the skin. As temporary workers we were given little in the way of protective clothing. Once, taking one of the greatest steps of my life, I led a deputation to the local management to ask for protective clothing or boiler suits for the women working in the sheds; we did eventually get trousers, jackets and mob caps. Our messing facilities comprised a small lean-to shed built against the shed retaining wall. At Kentish Town the engine-men's messroom was a dark and dreary place, cheered only by a large coal fire, over which men boiled their tea. Most of the drivers were elderly men and had obviously been firemen for many years. The messroom steward was an ex-express-train driver who had been crippled in a train smash. His fireman that night perished by being knocked head-first into the firebox by the force of the collision.

Tube sweepers were given a number of engines to do and we would pair up and share each other's engine to work on and natter while we worked. You would never have seen two men standing on the front of the smoke-box—they would have got in each other's way—but the women managed and would not work any other way, though I preferred to work alone. We had no fixed tea break either, but would work like mad for an hour or two then spend a good hour sitting in the cab nattering and smoking, keeping a watchful eye for the charge hand who would 'chase us up'. I even had a party on my birthday. The 'girls' had clubbed together and bought me a flower vase. As no one else had had a present on their birthday, I was so touched that I slipped out and bought a cake and a bottle of sherry. We worked to get our jobs done in advance and all met in the messroom. I started off the singing, then the charge hand banged on the door and yelled to us to come out to work. I went out with the bottle and glass and with a lovely smile I offered him a drink. I thought he was going to have a heart attack! He said it was the cardinal sin to have drink on the railway; it meant instant dismissal. He rushed away saying he hadn't seen anything but for God's sake send some of the women out to work as we were conspicuous by our absence if the manager took a walk round the sheds, as he often did. I must have been very naive, but I really did think it didn't matter so long as we did our work.

Sometimes we were taken off sweeping duties and put on 'coaling', a job hitherto banned to the women. Some were sent to Cricklewood depot to 'shovel up'. I was detailed to a full wagon of coal on the shunting lines outside the sheds with three or four other women. On an adjoining line an empty wagon stood and more women stood in this. The purpose was for my crowd to throw the lumps of coal across to those in the empty wagon. It was very difficult work, as the coal we were standing on was shifty and sharp and cut our ankles as our shoes were not made for such treatment. The coal lumps were also very heavy and hard to heave the necessary distance. We were not on that job long however as a lump of coal caught one of the women and she was taken to hospital with a broken pelvis. We never did that work again but we had to do one day a month on 'manual' work. This was clearing piles of clinkers with a large shovel. I refused to do this as I really felt it degrading and on grounds that I was taken on as a tube sweeper. (I had a 'thing' about women with shovels.) During the war there were two or three weeks of feverish activity on a couple of engines when royalty was going to travel by train. I was told that other sheds were working just as hard on spit and polish for engines, and as only one engine was needed—with a standby—I thought it was a terrible waste of manpower.

As it was strictly a wartime temporary job for women, it was not worthwhile for the railway to make things better for us—other jobs had the edge on ours—buses, fire service, etc. Why did we stick it? We could not get our release, but in any case, there is something about railway work that gets you. It is a way of life rather than a job. There was a lot of singing and laughing among the women on the railway; they worked hard, they shared the hazards of the men. They also shared their pastimes, a drink, a smoke, and a game of darts in the pub across the way.

I felt that peacetime must have been a very worrying time for railwaymen, they must have had many fears, for breaking the many little rules could lead to a day or two of suspension without pay, and for a family man with poor wages that could be a real hardship.

When I did leave it and went into a cosy little factory for awhile, I was not a factory worker, but an ex-railway worker working in a factory—that is how I felt, and in spite of the comfort I was miserable.[9]

Another lady who worked in Kentish Town sheds during the war was Mrs Tansley, who as a widow knew that railway work would give her extra cash from Sunday work, and that she could enjoy cheaper rail travel for her children and herself. She saw:

> ... three sheds with cobbled floors; these were always greasy, but two women were employed to clean the shed floors—with hand scrapers. In the shed, ashes from the engines were often dumped by the side of the inspection pits. On Sundays some of the women workers would sign in to shovel these ashes from ground level into trucks which had been shunted into the shed. I did coal humping also, which meant travelling from Kentish Town to Cricklewood sidings, unloading coal wagons by hand, and stacking it by the trackside. I also painted the smoke-boxes of engines and did some engine cleaning. All this was heavy, dirty work which made our hands horrible, but we still managed to enjoy ourselves.[10]

However, there are few deserts which do not possess at least one oasis. In the case of the general hurly-burly, bangs and smashings of the running shed, the fitting shop was a haven of cleanliness and quietness. Fitters would not allow engines in steam to enter their shop. Engines for repair would be cleaned of all fire, towed into the fitting shop, and, once repaired, would be shunted out again. Except for the noise of hand hammers, all was stillness and hush in a railway fitting shop. No smoke, no fumes, no undisciplined blowing off at the safety valves was tolerated. Compared with the Stygian gloom and lurking dangers of the running shed, the fitting shop was a cottage hospital, its white-washed walls usually displaying a pristine glory, the silence demonstrating the power of the railway fitters over their particular bailiwick.

In my time on the railways a night-time visit to a main-line shed would reveal a number of men 'deep in the arms of Morpheus'; these were the 'overnight men'. At large sheds a percentage of the work was early-morning duties, with trains starting the journeys between 1.00 a.m. and 6.00 a.m., involving the engine-men and guards in great problems of getting to work for the early trains. By the 1950s the insistence on living in call had long been abandoned. Men lived where they could, but many elected to live as far away as possible from the gloom and grime of their workplace. Until the mid-1960s the motor car and the motor cycle were rarities on an engine shed. In wintertime especially, fog-, ice- or snow-bound roads and the problems of starting up combustion engines put the train services in jeopardy. No early-morning men meant few or no trains until mid-morning. Men who could not get to work simply lost a day's pay. For this reason many men utilized public transport and joined the ranks of the overnight men.

The last trains would carry men who would appear at the shed two, three or four hours before they were due to start work. Strictly speaking, these men were trespassing, but the foreman turned a blind eye to their arrival because their presence ensured that the morning trains would be crewed.

Awaiting duty, the men developed a variety of ways of spending the waiting hours. Some would drift through the hours in the numerous card games the messroom offered. Others would shake down in warm corners of the shed, and be wakened in good time by a friendly nudge. Some would curl up on a cab seat, back to the boiler, for a fitful hour or two. Another group would do it in greater style; these were the hard-ened overnight men. These men would hang around the train board until an engine was allocated to their train. They would take to the engine, get up steam and oil it ready for the road. After a cup of tea, they would fill up the engine bucket with hot fire and then, wrapping an old over-coat round themselves, they would sleep on the engine floorboards until the other crewmen arrived at the appropriate time, bearing hot sustenance in a tea can. After a wash the engine-man was ready for his day's work.

A shift plus overnighting could mean thirteen or fourteen hours away from his home. I never once heard a man complain about overnight-ing; if he didn't like his job he could resign, for it was never a responsi-bility of the railways to provide individuals with the means of getting to work. Staff trains had been provided on a limited scale for a number of years in the London area, but the vast spread of shift duties made a full all-night service totally uneconomic.

The London Midland and Scottish Railway, even at the height of its power, was not too anxious to provide the type of messing facilities which would encourage men to sit and drink tea while on the job. Len

Housden, who spent a lifetime working trains out of Euston, has in-effaceable memories of the messroom at the Old Camden shed in the 1920s and 30s. He has written:

> With just an open firegrate and two or three long stools, the mess-room had no facilities for washing or cooking. The labourers and cleaners who used the messroom made their tea by dangling a metal tea can full of water into the open firegrate. Tea, sugar and condensed milk were then scraped from a paper wrapping into the boiling water. If this operation took place outside the official break, a look-out man was posted. Culprits were reported and disciplined. Except for cold water the only means of washing was from a bucket filled with hot water from an engine. Dirty overalls were washed in buckets and hung in the sand furnace to dry. The entrance to the toilets had no door, but was shielded by a wooden partition. Between 8.00 and 8.30 a.m. the three seats provided were fully occupied, the occupants gaining privacy by shielding themselves behind newspapers. No chang-ing rooms or lockers were provided; most men travelled to and from work in their working clothes.[11]

On the Southern Railway men often fared worse. Mr W. Bishop, who worked at Eastleigh as a boilersmith, remembers that in the 1920s and 30s the boilermakers rarely had a cabin of their own. At Eastleigh, men managed as best as they could in the shed; as boilermakers they were everywhere outcasts.

Twenty years after Len Housden's experiences at Camden, the situ-ation had changed but little in the messrooms, as Mr F. Higson dis-covered when he was employed as a railway fireman on the London Midland Region. Describing the engine-men's messrooms at Crewe north and south depots he wrote:

> The messrooms at both sheds were . . . abominable. Open-vaulted roofs, dirty dishevelled walls and high dingy windows made them op-pressively gloomy. Furniture was reminiscent of a junk shop—long battered benches and greasy-topped tables set on a cracked flagstone flooring. In one corner of the north shed messroom stood a veteran gas cooker, by the side of which on a gas ring sat an almost per-petually boiling kettle—a vast black iron example, laden with scale within and cloaked with accumulated grime without.[12]

As late as 1953, when I arrived to work at Kentish Town shed, one of the crack depots on the Midland route from St Pancras, there was a large messroom for drivers and firemen which had been doubled into use as a locker and changing-room for ashpit workers and labourers. The room was centrally divided by a wall of small lockers; the seating round a coal stove consisted of backless benches. The tables were deal tops, scrubbed daily by the messroom attendant. Each shift of shedmen changed into their shed clothes in full view of the drivers taking their meals. The stench, especially in the winter months with the stove going full blast, was appalling. Mice, attracted by the scraps of food falling from the tables and the lockers, played happily around the stove.

Within the engine shed walls could be seen the startling contrast between engine-men and shed staff and clerical officers. Bound together in time and space, the grades were united yet strangely separated. The grime, frustration and colourful language of the operating staff was at odds with the cleanliness and muted instructions which characterized the railway office.

Controlling and guiding the multifarious activities of the steam engine shed were two vital but hugely contrasting administrative offices, the foreman's office and the general office. In the days of steam, the foreman's office was usually a small, drab, dusty and draughty affair in the heart of the shed. The main furniture was the shift foreman's desk and the bank of telephones. The walls were decorated with little but sheafs of clip-boarded instructions, the floor covered with the eternal railway brown linoleum. At the main desk, the man 'in the chair', by a combination of good humour and hectoring, kept the service going until he handed over his baton after eight hours' struggle with men, machines and weather. Day and night the foreman's office was a din of telephone calls and shouted messages. The telephone operator was often an ex-foot-plateman demoted by reason of physical or eyesight failure. His generic nickname was 'Marconi'.

For the railway workers time was the great enemy. Every clock was a hostile agent, an opponent of foremen, engine-men, fitters and shedmen alike. It was the job of the shift foreman to co-ordinate all the efforts and present the train service to a public almost totally unaware of the organization required to get the 8.15 on the road. Foremen varied from the type known as 'The Whip', to that of 'The Balloon', whose plea was always, 'Don't let me down boys'. Both types were in evidence and successful in their different ways. The assistant foreman, who occupied the chair on Sundays and during holiday periods, was based in the foreman's office, but his job entailed roaming the shed and relating to the relevant staff the orders issued by the often desk-bound foreman. The assistant foreman was known to all as 'His Master's Voice' or 'the foreman's half-back'.

Life in the railway clerical grades was never easy. As we have seen, the prospective railway clerk had from the earliest times to be not only a person of sharp intelligence, but one who was often expected to provide financial security for his employment. In the 1860s a prospective railway clerk needed to provide testimonials before he could even appear before the board of directors. Once appointed, however, like all young men they demanded relaxation and they were not afraid to risk departmental wrath in their search for diversion. Their dress was often loud, and included chains, rings and studs as part of their *tout ensemble*. They were, according to one observer, patrons of the theatre, the concert halls and other public places. They were great admirers of the fair sex.

There was, however, little time for such relaxation. H. A. Simmons, who became a station-master on the Great Western, has given us the following description of working conditions on that railway about 1879:

> I was never more astonished than when I opened the door to this office. It was like an immense schoolroom, only that the boys had whiskers and most of them were out at elbows, and all looked miserably thin; moreover, they were all standing to write, and the bundles of papers before each were enough to turn each poor fellow's heart sick. At the head of the table sat a deformed gentleman of about fifty years of age, who I afterwards learned was Mr Fretsum, the chief accountant. He had gained his position by steady application, had worked himself up from being an ordinary clerk, and had joined the railway from its commencement. He always came to business at 8.45 a.m. and never left until 6 p.m. and invariably subsisted on a biscuit and a glass of water during the day, ridiculing the idea of waste of time for dinner. Poor man, the outside world had no charms for him, so he had devoted his life to his office, and was then in receipt of an income much in excess of his requirements. Many of the poorest of the clerks, from necessity's sake, followed his example, and when the clock struck one they quietly pulled out their drawer and ate a piece of dry bread and cheese; but the majority hurried off to a cheap dining-room in the neighbourhood.[13]

In 1863, on the North British Railway, when the chief clerk of the Edinburgh office was told to increase the office hours of the staff without increasing their pay, he reported that:

> . . . the existing hours of 9.15 to 6.00 are merely nominal because it is frequently 7.00 p.m. before they leave the office. In some cases it is even later, and one of the directors at least has found them at work between 9.00 and 10.00 p.m. They also take papers and documents home with them when necessary to keep up the work of the office. No extra pay is allowed for that work.[14]

In this Victorian haven twenty minutes were allowed at 1.00 p.m. for refreshment. Mr Walker, the keeper of the head office of the North

British in Edinburgh, enjoyed a salary of £130 per year and out of that he paid the wages and board of two women cleaners. Whether a keeper of the head office, a chief clerk at Edinburgh or a humble clerk at a wayside station, the work was exclusive, demanding and largely badly paid. In a letter to the *Railway Service Gazette*, in 1872, one clerk recorded:

> One of your correspondents asks what hours a clerk is expected to work for his 15s., 18s. or 20s. a week. I will give you my experience. At our station (which shall be nameless) we are obliged to work ten, twelve, and sometimes fourteen hours a day, and when asked for extra pay our managers coolly refer us to rule one of our *Rules and Regulations*: 'Every servant must devote himself exclusively to the service of the company, attend during the appointed hours, reside and do duty *where and when required, Sundays included.*'
>
> Bearing in mind that, with the exception of an hour for dinner, and sometimes a few minutes for tea, our work is constantly at the desk, I put it to the mind of every sensible man, if anyone is fit to bear this drudgery, this slavery for any length of time? His health must ere long give way, and the only door which will open for the admittance of himself and family is that of the workhouse, for even when in health it is but a thin partition that divides us.[15]

The answer of this clerk to such conditions was the foundation of a union, after which their hard taskmasters would be forced to admit that clerks 'are human like themselves'.

Another kingpin in the foreman's office was the list or roster clerk, a man with the power to create misery and delight at the stroke of his pen or the swish of his india-rubber. The task of the list clerk was to fit men into their appropriate time slot, to match man with train. Tightly bound by national and local agreements on the movement of men according to an agreed rostered time, the list clerk was the nearest thing to a computer any shed could provide.

The list clerk virtually ran the train service. He knew every train allocated to the depot and he could provide the route knowledge of the entire driving staff. He could recite national and local agreements until complainants retreated under the barrage. In the days when men 'hung up behind the door' awaiting the call of duty, the job of such a man was easy, but the restrictions placed upon him by union-negotiated agreements called for great skill in complicated situations. It was said of list clerks that each Christmas the most important present they could receive was a new car tyre, which could be cut up into india-rubbers by the thousand.

By comparison, the general office was usually large, airy and quiet. The air of calmness, however, belied the battle for status, which was continuous, only the actors changing as promotions and transfers altered the mix. In the general office the chief clerk ran the place like a ship, his bridge being the table which gave him strategic and tactical dominance. When he stood up at his desk to call a subordinate even the office clock reduced its tick. Occupying the humblest rung was the office junior. In between were the 'needlenoses', the various clerks who ensured that no blue-collar man received a penny more than his entitlement. There was a 'pencil halver' at most depots, a man looking for promotion to the ranks of the 'razor gang', and travelling clerks who checked at irregular intervals the log books of the various offices in their districts.

A common but erroneous view of the railway is that because of its size, the industry is wasteful of resources. The truth is very different. The railway, like the army, issues little of value without the presentation of a printed form. In the days of steam, oils of all description were severely rationed commodities; hand cleaning rags had to be returned before another was issued. On the shed all scrap from big end brasses to tiny screws were saved and sorted into scrap wagons, old sleepers were lifted and sold for walling and garden fencing. The railway offices were also not immune from the continuous desire to save invaluable material. As late as 1920 the Great Western was issuing the following instructions to staff:

Economies: Instructions to Staff

1. Cover inkwells not in use.
2. Use reverse side of blotting paper.
3. Clean electric lightbulbs when light on. When cold the wire is brittle and liable to break.
4. On moonlit nights adequate lighting may be secured at many places by lighting only alternate lamps on approach roads and at the end of platforms.
5. Straw. Collect straw from inward trucks and store for future use.

Any observer could consider these instructions as parsimonious. Yet use of materials always made sense in the harbouring of resources. On the Great Western Railway looking after pennies meant saving many pounds. Even in the 1970s recycling was practised in the industry. The redundant assets of the steam age were zealously retrieved and often sold at high prices to a public hungry for railway relics. In the late 1960s bricks stamped London and North-Western Railway were fetching 50p each at public sales. Mr J. Davis, who began firing on the Southern Railway in the 1930s, has noted that shed officials and stores issuers of those days make our present economizers look like degenerate wasters. Mr Davis has tales of storekeepers who issued oil as though they bought it, and of others who would split a fireman's hand brush down the centre, and who would upon complaint demonstrate the efficiency of this truncated implement by sprinkling sand upon the ground and intoning, while sweeping it into a heap, 'Nothing wrong with the brush, it's a new back you need.'[16]

For many years deference to authority was one of the accepted ingredients of railway service. The hierarchical system worked because each grade except the lowest had upward and downward reference groups with which to compare status. The arrival of railway officers for site visits was a time for such comparisons and forelock touching. In 1914, when Mr Francis Almond was working in Dewsbury for the Great Northern Railway, he found that the local agent was always addressed as 'Guv'nor'. According to Mr Almond:

> The agent was always upon his dignity, and spoke to no one unless first addressed. His walk, the unhurried gait of a man in command, commanded respect. His well-cut lounge suit and the umbrella carried like a foil added to this aura. The agent was a man who looked at everything and missed nothing; the humble and ill-educated wages grades viewed such men with great deference, to them he was 'the company—in the flesh'.[17]

In general, however, across the years of steam, the clerical grades were usually better educated, more sophisticated and more confident than the wages grades. Although many of the clerical officers, even after long service, still earned less than a main-line fireman, the confidence born of superior education combined with the collar and the status gave them an air of superiority when they paraded for lunch, or met the uncomfortable oil-stained artisan across a shiny-topped desk. In the presence of a clerical officer on duty, the practice of removing hats was always demanded.

Although clerks were often regarded as conservative and reluctant to identify with manual organizations, office workers on the railways broke this stereotype when in 1897 in Sheffield the Railway Clerks' Association was founded. In 1889, this association registered not as a friendly society, but as a trade union. The history of the union shows not only its working-class origins but its sense of loyalty to the labour movement. By 1904, out of a possible membership of 60,000, the young RCA had enrolled 4,000.

Before 1914, the clerks were unable to achieve recognition from the companies; approaches to the employer were by petitions and memorials. The desirability of joining with the national union was well debated, but fears of being submerged and the chronic railway disease of differentiated interests kept the clerks independent.

The prospect of trade unionism among railway clerks was anathema to most railway companies. The North-Eastern Railway penalized men who joined the union against the advice of the company's office. The Midland Railway 'red inked' the records of clerks who were trade unionists. These early struggles demonstrated the wisdom of political and industrial affiliation, for without such associations the union might have foundered.

The aims of the union were gained by political, not industrial action. It affiliated with the Trades Union Congress in 1903 and to the Labour Party in 1909, the year in which only 10 per cent of railway clerks were earning more than £160 per year. Working through these bodies, the union was able to hold up railway bills until the grievances of railway clerks were brought within the Workmen's Compensation Bill. In 1907 a Board of Trade committee embarrassed the companies by illuminating deficient responsibility in relation to superannuation funds.

On the eve of the 1919 railway strike the union was awarded recognition by the companies. It broke another mould in 1926 when it stopped work in support of the miners. At the end of the General Strike the membership of the union had increased by 3,000. After the Trade Disputes Act of 1927, when the law on political levies was altered, 83 per cent of the membership volunteered or 'contracted in' to pay the political levy to the Labour Party.

Unlike his counterpart in private industry, the railway clerk was usually of working-class origin. In order to get his job he was spoken for by members of his family or other near acquaintances. Clerical work was, on the railway, a masculine preserve, retaining until the end of steam a black-coated rather than white-bloused image. The railway clerk had special skills, but, like those of engine-driver or signalman, they were relatively unmarketable outside the industry. Although the tenure of a railway clerk was relatively secure, the grade never achieved high material status. Between 1939 and 1954, the salary rate of railway clerks increased by 80 per cent among class 1 clerks and over 100 per cent for class 5 clerks. The only other groups with comparable increases were the grades of driver and motorman. After the second railway mania, job opportunities and employment prospects for railway clerks were clouded by the recruitment of top-rank personnel from outside the industry. To move ahead, a railway clerk had to make his presence felt very quickly, and for most this was simply impossible. There was a ladder of promotion, but to scale it meant transferring from one area to another within his own railway.

Like the great mass of railway workers the railway clerk was propertyless, contractual labour. He was not, however, lumpen proletariat. He had a job for life, and even though it paid poorly, it was regular; this gave him status in the community, and an organization with which he could identify. The railway clerk may have been alienated from other grades of clerks but he never suffered from false class consciousness—his views were determined by a common economic position.

When Herbert Evans started work on the Metropolitan Railway in 1908 at £20 per year, he replaced a clerk who had been earning £100. Mr Evans obtained this post largely because his brother was personal clerk to Mr William Holt, Traffic Manager of the Metropolitan Railway. At Portland Street Station, the staff consisted of the station-master, who was usually patrolling the platform, the clerk in charge and young Evans. The station-master earned £105 annually and the clerk in charge, who was a little tin god, £100. The Metropolitan would employ no one whose father was employed by the rival District Line. Metropolitan clerks were not allowed to consume liquor within a quarter of a mile of Metropolitan premises. Between 1908 and 1912 such clerks were not allowed second-class privilege tickets when third class was available. When on duty the clerks were not allowed to converse with other grades. According to Mr Evans, 'Our little office on the platform was warmed by coal and lit electrically, but as the office had large doors on two walls the office heat was lost to howling gales and the light fittings swung crazily from the ceiling.'[18] The Metropolitan was short of staff toilets, the clerks using the public facilities on the platform.

In those early days, Mr Evans became a member of the Railway Clerks Association, a move which could lead to staff blacklisting. In the great railway strike of 1911 Mr Evans had to stand by helplessly while his elder brother paid men off with the Army looking on. Although Mr Evans had some bad moments on the 'Met', such as the long hours before the 1919 settlement, he loved the line and its passengers, some of whom at Christmas time would pay extra for their tickets as a bonus to the booking clerk. Loose cash, or 'extras', was also claimed by the junior clerk. As a clerical officer Mr Evans was reported once in fifty-one years' service—over an animal. One day a lady arrived with a dog, for which she refused to buy a ticket. Because the clerk refused to let the woman travel, her husband demanded in writing the immediate dismissal of Mr Evans. Later, after the Railway Clerks Association became respectable, the accused were allowed to see the home addresses of those who had reported the offence.

In 1914 Evans went to war with the Twelfth Light Railway Corps, as discussed in Chapter 2. By 1923, Mr Evans was a £200 per year relief clerk between Surrey Docks and the Metropolitan-Great Central Joint Railway. In his capacity as roving clerk, Mr Evans lodged out at 3s. per night at towns right across the Middlesex Weald. He was responsible for finding his own accommodation, and often lodged in haylofts in Chalfont St Giles and Wendover.

Mr Evans discovered that the Metropolitan scrupulously observed its moral duties. He recalled the auditor visiting the stations on Fridays to catch any sign of weekend insobriety. On the Met all stations closed for church time—11.00 a.m. until 1.00 p.m.—a break for the clerks who were, until 1919, putting in a fifteen-hour shift for which they were paid for only eight hours.

Best of all Mr Evans loved the trains of the Met, with their brown, white-lined coaches and chocolate-painted engines. Though a bit short on second- and third-class comfort, the Met provided a nice first-class coach. After all, Raphael Tuck, the picture-postcard tycoon, was a regular on the Met, and the line had eight miles of track right across the estate of the Duke of Buckinghamshire. With the railways owned by people of this calibre, it was little wonder that fees to the Railway Clerks Association were paid after 10.00 p.m., and then only after a special knock on the office door.

Mr Evans had no time for the District Line, which he viewed as a shabby undertaking. The District did not belong to the Railway Clearing House and always wore the cognomen 'light railway'. At the Monument, where the Met shared with the District, the latter scored a distinct victory when all the staff of the 'Joint' wore District livery. It took the big guns of Baker Street to stop that rot.

In 1933, the Metropolitan was incorporated into the London Underground. It had become king of Joint Railways. In 1939 Mr Evans was appointed Senior Clerk at Old Street, City and South London Metropolitan and Great Northern City Railway—a title fit for a potentate. Mr Evans was a lover of the Met and an opponent of railway nationalization. His main argument against state control was that private ownership would have kept the branch lines open—and who is to say he was **wrong?**

5

Engine Cleaners and Firemen

In the heyday of steam, before the amalgamations of 1923, the engine cleaner was a popular and versatile member of the running shed staff. Despite his humble status, he was suitable for and utilized in a vast number of tasks on and off the shed. The duties of engine cleaners ranged from cleaning engines to sweeping ashpits and helping to rerail wagons.

Engine cleaning demanded young men—sixteen was an ideal age to start and the promotion sequence was as follows:

Step 1 Engine cleaning and shed duties.

Step 2 Passed Cleaner. A passed cleaner had qualified for firing duties by virtue of examination in *Rules and Regulations* and one trip on the foot-plate, where under the eye of the driver and inspector he was adjudged capable of stoking a moving boiler.

Step 3 Red Ink Fireman. A red ink fireman was a passed cleaner marked up on the shed roster to a regular firing job for the summer period only.

Step 4 Black Ink Fireman. Full grade status. Starting with shed and shunting work, the fireman now began his slow rise on the ladder of promotion. This period was often twenty years.

Step 5 Passed Fireman. The passed fireman was an engine-man who had passed technical and practical as well as oral tests; he was now adjudged capable of driving any train at his depot.

Step 6 Red Ink Driver. A red ink driver, like a red ink fireman, was marked to regular driving duties during long holiday periods.

Step 7 Black Ink Driver. Full status. For many years even the black ink driver was circumscribed financially by classification; ie, the payment for work was based on managerial assumptions about the importance of work.

Until 1903, engine cleaners were not members of the foot-plate union. Cleaners were unorganized and at the mercy of foremen. Despite this, engine cleaning could be the beginning of a long association with engines and engine-men. Long before the turn of the nineteenth century a visitor to an engine shed could come across a motley crew of youngsters distributed over, under and around a travel-stained engine. Some were busy with scrapers and rags, speedily and effectively removing the dirt, while others were daubing the engine with a greasy concoction just to create a pleasing complexion. This was the surface impression. The reality, as we shall see, was rather different. The happy scene was underlaid by a complex system of role relationships based on seniority, merit, experience and often brute force. H. A. Simmons attempted to show the class of men from whom engine-drivers were promoted in the 1860s:

> A lad seeking to drive an engine had to commence work as a night cleaner of engines. If he got on pretty well, he had others under him in time; and a very great promotion was to be 'lighter-up', in which capacity he had the responsibility of putting fire into an engine four hours before she was wanted. . . . As to education, I won't venture to make a remark about it, as the pay and the occupation altogether abolished the idea; but I will go so far as to say that some of those engaged were too dissolute and too lazy for the farmers to employ them. . . . I never attended the cleaning shed without both hearing and seeing scenes that impressed me most unfavourably.[1]

This is a far cry from the demand of the Great Western Railway for literate, obedient men. The pay for a night cleaner in the 1860s was between 10s. and 14s. per week. The penalty on the Highland Railway for poorly cleaned engines was dismissal. Cleaners had ample time to clean engines for the working shift was twelve hours minimum. Engine cleaners had little bargaining power over hours, wages and conditions of labour. The lack of protection for cleaners was highlighted by the death of a fourteen-year-old cleaner at the Great Western engine depot, Westbourne Park, London. The case was described in the all-grades journal:

> John Harris worked his regular time (thirteen or fourteen hours per day) until Wednesday, when, on leaving the shed in the evening, he was told to come again at ten o'clock. He went back to work at the time specified (having been at home three hours), and continued occupied in the locomotive cleaning works until Thursday evening, making thirty-two or thirty-three hours. He then had a fair night's rest, and went to work again on Friday morning; and he was actually kept employed for that time until six o'clock on Saturday evening—thirty-six hours—when, feeling very cold, he got into the firebox, or furnace, of an empty, or 'dead' engine, to warm himself previous to going home; and while there, being so extremely fatigued with his long term of duty, he quickly fell asleep. Shortly afterwards a stoker came to prepare the engine for service, and, in order to get up steam (not

suspecting, of course, that the youth was there), he put a large shovelful of blazing coals into the furnace on top of the boy, which burnt him so terribly that he died at St Mary's Hospital soon after being admitted.[2]

The Great Western regretted this unfortunate accident but argued that the conduct of the foreman in allowing such a state of affairs was in express and direct contravention of the laws of the company. At the time of his death John Harris was under the age for such work, as laid down in the Factories Acts, At the inquest on 14 February 1873, a verdict of accidental death was returned.

Seven years after the accident to John Harris the London and North-Western Railway was allowing young engine cleaners to work shifts of twenty-six hours' duration and one of the tasks was to assist in the repair of engine fireboxes.[3] To repair a firebox a man had to climb through the firebox door and squat on the firebars, taking care not to smash his head on the mighty brick arch which protected the boiler tube ends. On a steam engine the firebox was the scorching heart of the machine, but once the fire was drawn, the firebox became an icy terrifying tomb, certainly no place for a petrified youngster. Jim Swain recalls:

> In the days when the Gresley Pacifics were the toast of technologists, not a finger was raised against the inhuman practice of putting an adolescent into the firebox of a boiler still containing steam, where he sweated to replace burnt-out firebars while the heat of the grate burned the soles of his boots. Due to constant sweating, many boys were reduced to skin and bone.[4]

For Jim Walker, in Stoke-on-Trent, the situation was similar: 'As the youngest cleaner on the shift I was used as "bar boy". This vile job meant climbing into the firebox and sweeping the dust from the top of the brick arch which protected the ends of the boiler tubes.'[5] In sweeping, the white dust could find only two outlets—the one through the firegrate bars, the other into the lungs of the sweeper. As soon as a firebox had cooled sufficiently to allow air to circulate, the more daring engine cleaners at Stoke would clamber inside and play cards by the light of a paraffin lamp.

The job of repairing fireboxes and sweeping brick arches should have been performed when the firebox was cold, but a quick turn round of the engine often meant that the repairer needed to enter the firebox while the engine was still in steam. Adam Bradshaw, who worked as an engine cleaner for the Lancashire and Yorkshire Railway, has recorded that bar boys at Fleetwood shed worked in fireboxes with steam pressure of 100 pounds per square inch in the boiler. These boys could not argue—they were 'the busy bodies of the shed'.[6] The use of young cleaners on firebox duties continued until the 1940s.

William McLagan remembers that the dust in that small space, plus the hard work that went with it, led him to his first trade-union meeting to protest at the use of young engine cleaners on firebox repair duties. 'A wee boy among movers and seconders, his argument was that such work was injurious to the eyesight of future engine-drivers.'[7] After a year of such agitation, engine cleaners at Polmadie shed, Glasgow, were forbidden to do such work.

At the turn of the century, cleaners at Gorton shed on the Great Central earned 17s. for seventy-two hours' work. Twopence of this was deducted for canteen facilities. The cleaners were called to tea break by a bell, and to the rhythm of this bell arose the Gortonian chant, 'Work and clem for sixteen and ten', 'clem' being Lancashirese for hunger.

From the earliest days, engine cleaners sent out on emergency firing duties faced hostility from the regular drivers. A Lancashire and York-shire driver complained:

> Just fancy, a driver having a mere lad with him to do a man's work! This boy, when he is not out firing, will be cleaning in the shed at 8–10s. a week. . . . The driver is the man. If he allows the boy to put coal on the fire, it is as a rule put on to waste. . . . There are hundreds of tons of coal wasted in this way. . . . The driver invariably puts on the coal when it is safest, and not when he actually wants it on.[8]

The objection to cleaners by drivers continued into the late 1930s. Many drivers were terrified of paper work involved in answering ques-tions relevant to lost time or engine failure. Some refused to take engine cleaners who had limited firing experience. Inexperience could mean trouble on the line, and trouble meant writing. The elite of the line did not always run to craftsmanship with a pen.

Engine cleaning was basically the same wherever one went, but there were some regional variations. The Great Western at Bristol had, on the eve of the First World War, two sets of cleaners—one set on piece-work, the other on day work.[9] The piece-workers had their 'own' engines, in which each gang of four took special pride. Side and connecting rods were polished bright and covered with a film of petroleum jelly for pro-tection against the weather. The brass work was scoured and then rubbed over with dry soot from a smoke-box to give a high finish. Boilers, tenders and tanks were all washed with cleaning oil, and then wavy patterns were made in the oil by applying tallow fat. On com-pletion, the leading cleaner would 'pass' the engine as cleaned by rub-bing his hand between the axle spokes or under the foot-plate. Men were paid four hours for top of boiler, four hours for the tender, four hours for the side, and four hours for gears and motions. The cleaners at Bristol rejoiced in such names as Bulldog, Farmer, Little Barton Hill and Big Barton Hill.

In 1916, Anthony Sperdutti started work as a cleaner in the Millbay sheds at Plymouth.[10] At fifteen and a half years of age he earned 13s. for a week of seventy-two hours. There was no payment for overtime and no overalls were provided. Although boys of his own age were earning £3 weekly in the local munitions factory, Sperdutti stuck it out in the hope that the money would improve when he became a fireman. Because he was under eighteen, young Sperdutti was given only half the war bonus, although he was employed on such exhausting and filthy jobs as boiler-washing and fire-dropping, jobs to test the strength and endurance of the toughest man.

The Midland Railway had, before amalgamation, claimed it had the cleanest engines in the world. According to Charles Brooks, who was a Midland foot-plateman at Cricklewood and Kentish Town depots in London, 'If ever a railway believed in cleanliness, it was the Midland.'[11] He was amazed on his first day as a cleaner at Cricklewood at the spotlessly clean shed floors, and pits scrubbed daily with boiling water, and the turntable woodwork scrubbed white. Engines standing in the shed had trays containing sawdust placed beneath the tender axle boxes to prevent oil dripping to the shed floor. In those days, cleaning at Cricklewood was done by gangs of four boys, the oldest boy being known as the captain and the youngest as 'the board boy' or 'chummy'.

The job of the board boy was to place a 'Not to be moved' board on the engine to be cleaned, and then to draw the necessary cleaning material from the stores. Returning, he would divide the cotton waste into four parts, which were shared between the gang, the captain taking the largest share, followed by gang members one and two, leaving the smallest amount for the 'chummy'. Cleaning was done on a piece-work system; usually sixteen hours were allowed to clean an engine, that is, a gang of four men working four hours each per engine. The captain and the board boy worked together. Now and again the captain would call out 'Slog in, chum' as a reminder that the sooner the job was finished the sooner the next engine would be brought in for cleaning.

The method of cleaning was to dip an oily 'soccer' into water and draw letter 'S's over the paint work, then rub it all over with a clean soccer. The brass and copper work was cleaned with brick dust and oil and brought to a brilliance by rubbing it with a soot-covered piece of dry waste. Compared to the Western, the Midland was very generous with cleaning material. The ration for one man in the Cricklewood gang would have served a gang of four at Southall. The foreman cleaner at Cricklewood always cleared the cleaning gang away from the engine before his inspection, which he did with a flare lamp. This was punctuated with acid comments such as, 'Do you call that left fore eccentric clean?' The cleaners were sacked regularly each day by the shed superintendent. When a royal train was passing all cleaners were under orders to leave the shed; it would not do for royalty to see such low forms of life as engine cleaners.

At Camden on the London and North-Western there were more variations. In the 1920s, when cleaners were abundant, the engines were kept scrupulously clean. On big passenger engines the senior cleaner was 'ganger'. The senior four cleaners did the boiler barrel, this being the easiest task and the one to which all lowly placed cleaners aspired. An allowance of twenty-four new cleaning cloths was made, cleaning being done with hot water, black oil, a thin clear oil called 'longlight', and a petroleum jelly.

The usual leg-pulling was inflicted on new starters; the more gullible were sent to the stores for a bucket of steam, a packet of big ends or side rods, an umbrella if rain was entering the shed. Awaiting delivery of a 'long stand' has sent many a young cleaner fleeing from the store, red-faced and embarrassed, after the hoax was explained. Camden had about 100 cleaners in the 1920s and '30s and they did almost every job in the shed: tubing boilers, steam raising, fire-dropping and sand-box filling.[12]

In theory, discipline was very strict. Swearing was forbidden and could merit six days' suspension, the names of the culprits being posted in the office window. Men were sent home for being ten minutes late, and were often carpeted before the shed superintendent, grave warnings being issued to the offender. However, the 'japper' fights, messy affairs of throwing clods of oily waste at each other, still went on. On night shift fun and games were abundant. There was a resident bookmaker and a friendly money-lender. Jim Barry, a boiler washer, sold sweets and cigarettes on credit, doing a roaring trade. If the management knew about such goings-on they never interfered.

In the 1930s, passed cleaners had a special status. As 'permanent' staff they were exempted from paying unemployment insurance contributions. It was almost impossible for the railways to terminate their employment, but the reverse meant that cleaners had to accept almost any kind of work available, inside or outside their grade. The surplus cleaners at Sheffield Midland were sent out as temporary platform porters at the passenger station where some of them learned the gentle art of weezling, the process of extracting tips from passengers.

After 1919, when the great gaps in the staff consequent upon the First World War had been plugged, promotion simply dried up in many areas. Sheds such as Kingmoor in Carlisle started only a handful of men between 1919 and 1939. Vacancies on the train-crew rosters were simply filled by senior redundant men who had been farmed out as porters, waiting to re-enter the ranks from which they had been declared redundant after the 1923 amalgamation. Meanwhile, many station porters were dismissed to make way for the permanent passed cleaners. In the engine sheds cleaners were put to labouring tasks, cleaning fire hydrants and lavatories.

On shed, the cleaners rarely had any accommodation of their own. At Plymouth in 1916, Anthony Sperdutti found that 'the cleaners' cabin was a dull place, with a wooden seat running round the wall. There was one long table and a steel box to house the fire. There were no washing facilities, a bucket was used as a basin. We were "allowed" into the cabin used by the drivers and firemen and sometimes, if the steward was missing, we would enter the cabin for a wash and warm.'[13] Likewise, at Kentish Town in the 1930s, the cleaners were not encouraged to be forward; everyone knew their place in a way reminiscent of work in Victorian England.

An engine cleaner could be asked to assist in the oil stores, issuing rape oil, paraffin and drivers' hand cloths. The hand cloths, which were simply squares of a highly absorbent wool and cotton mixture, were always in great demand by drivers. The storemen divided the cloths into three categories: 'white' (new), 'dirty' (greasy, oil-stained) and 'half-dirty', the latter being cloths which had been through a washing process which left them brown and harsh to the hand. Ex-foot-plateman Frank Mason came up against the strange ritual early in his career:

Before a man was given a 'white' cloth he had to give in a soiled white cloth, and his weekly ration had to be recorded in a register.

My 'high priest' had issued an edict: 'Thou shalt not have a white cloth until careful examination proveth thy returned cloth to be of the same ilk.' Consequently, we tied a knot in the corner of each new cloth as it was issued and, when the 'dirty' was returned, the store boy picked at the knot to establish the chastity of that errant return.

The operation of tying the knot, and subsequently undoing same, was irksome in the extreme: a travesty of the penny-pinching economy of the time. You can imagine the reactions from both sides of the counter!

One day a massive fireman, late of the Royal Navy, chided me, in good-natured banter, as I tied the sacred knot; 'Make it a bowline.' I promptly tied a bowline (not very easy on a 12 by 9 inch cloth). He stared, smiling. 'A pound if you make it a bowline on the bight!' I commenced to perform that task when my tall tormentor grabbed the cloth and fled, to keep his wager intact. On the following parade night I told my Scouts, with big-headed satisfaction, of the encounter.

On the Lancashire and Yorkshire the cleaners had by 1911 achieved a week of sixty hours divided into six shifts, and their rate of pay was classified as follows:

CLEANERS—RATES OF WAGES

18 years of age and over	17s. per week of 60 hours
17 years and under 18 years	15s.
16 years and under 17 years	13s.

The following rates were paid for cleaning each class of engine by piece-work:

Four-wheeled coupled Bogied Engines (1400 Class)	3s. for engine only
Eight-wheeled coupled Coal Engines	3s. for engine only

On above classes of engine, 2s. 6d. was paid for cleaning three tenders:

Shunting Tanks	2s. 0d.
Pug Engines	1s. 6d.

In the years of rationalization, 1920–35, the adult engine cleaners had little hope of promotion. They married and brought up children on a cleaner's wages, which, in 1931, were classified as follows: [14]

Age in years	
16 years and under	4s. per day
17 years	5s.
18 and 19 years	6s.
20 and 21 years	7s.
22 years and over	8s.

A prospective engine cleaner would not be taken on unless he possessed perfect eyesight and this had to be maintained throughout a main-line career. Different companies employed different methods of ascertaining acuity, some bordering on the ludicrous. Norman McKillop, the official historian of the foot-platemen, has written of the 'dot and wool test' on the London and North-Eastern Railway at the turn of the century:

The dot and wool test as a humorous performance had its merits, but as a gauge of a man's eyesight it left something to be desired. The test, usually carried out by an inspector, required the victim to count the correct number of square quarter-inch dots displayed on a card at a given distance . . . when the eye missed out one or two in the frenzied attempt to keep track of thirty dots, it became somewhat confusing, especially if the inspector came by a different number each time he checked up on the unfortunate examinee. The wool test was even funnier. Up to a dozen skeins of wool were suspended from a wooden bar, and the examinee had to pick up a hank of wool from an assorted bundle and solemnly match it with one of those hanging from the bar. The fun started when certain of the colours presented varying names to the inspector and his victim, and hot debates ranged around hues like amber and orange, salmon and salmon pink.

The engine cleaner, having passed the rigorous colour test, was then exposed to the smoke and sulphurous fumes of the engine shed, the ash and char of the fire-dropping pits, and the doubtful delights of night duty, oil lamps and flare torches. It was a minor miracle how any engine cleaner ever retained his eyesight at the standards required to become an engine-driver. All through his driving career an engine-man was subjected to eyesight tests at regular intervals, and the disappointment of many men was total when, after years of waiting for a main-line post, their eyesight failed at the moment of success. The shunting yards and sidings of British railways became the eventual workplace of thousands of men who three decades earlier had set off on the road which they hoped would lead them to the very top of their chosen career. These were the luckier ones. Other drivers, whose eyesight failure was total, ended their days as messroom stewards; some were offered jobs as shed sweepers, and others had to settle as latrine attendants in the shed where once they aspired to be kings of the iron road.

When I first began my engine cleaning career at Kingmoor in Carlisle, my first impression was one of dirt, dust, grease and decay. There was a chronic shortage and huge turnover of the men who in the past had kept the shed in apple-pie order—the engine cleaners. In 1946, other jobs with better pay and better prospects were opening up, even to those with minimal education. An age had passed since men had pleaded for their sons to be given a start, since the polishing of fire hydrants and scrubbing of the turntables and the request at Durran Hill that spent matchsticks should not be thrown onto the shed floor. The older railwaymen were now advising youngsters to stay away from the engine sheds. Many came to test the situation, but most left.

The engine cleaners I found at Carlisle were a mixed lot, ranging from bright-eyed teenagers to hard-bitten and cynical ex-servicemen.

Some of the youngsters were fugitives from the compressed atmospheres of local shops and factories, some had come into town from the outlying districts, others had drifted in from other towns.

Starting on the cleaning gang I was politely informed by the foreman cleaner that as a junior I was as worthless as three rows of crow's droppings, and that I had as much chance of ever becoming a fireman as a snowflake had in Hades. Cleaning at Kingmoor was usually done on dead engines in two back roads at the shed. I soon discovered the joys of wiping over the inside big ends of a Stanier streamliner. I was given a bucket of oil, a wedge-shaped scraper, a heap of waste, a flare lamp, and told to 'get underneath'. Down into the pit I went and looked up into the mighty entrails of a passenger engine. By the light of my spluttering flare lamp I could see little but festoons of dirt hanging in mute evidence of the counties the engine had travelled.

Sweating with fear as well as activity I climbed up into the belly of the engine across brake hangers, stretchers and slide bars. I sat across a brake stretcher, the filth oozing through my overalls and trousers, trapped in space. For more than an hour I perched there in the darkness broken only by the spluttering of the flare lamp, almost overpowered by the sense of isolation and danger. The dankness of the cotton waste, the sickly smell of the cleaning oil and the menacing black underbelly of the boiler petrified me. The fear and the terror were compounded: I was gripped by both the horror of the task itself and the fear that I would be forgotten by the men outside and mangled to death in an unwise shunting operation. I had now discovered the daily ritual of the junior cleaner on the shift.

When fifteen-year-old Dave Bush began cleaning at Gloucester engine shed in 1952, he was put through a series of initiation ceremonies. Soon after he arrived for his cleaning duties he was overpowered by his cleaning gang mates, and dragged to a high interior wall. Here his jacket was removed and fitted with a strong coat hanger. With the assistance of a shunter's pole he was made airborne and simply hung by the coat hanger, twelve feet above ground level, until the gang felt he had passed his 'preliminaries'. Later, he was captured and forced into the tender of a locomotive where in the dark wetness he shivered the imprisonment away while his captors performed their ritual dance on and about the tender. Finally, he was locked into a stinking ash-filled smoke-box, and with no hope of escape was tormented by handfuls of smouldering cleaning waste being dropped down the engine chimney.

In Scotland, things were done a little differently, as William McLagan found in joining the London, Midland and Scottish Railway in August 1939:

All one's senses were shocked on entering this new environment, the sense of smell being choked with a mixture of sulphurous smoke, hot lubricating oil, paraffin oil wash, ash, coal dust and grease. Eyes smarted and watered, throats were irritated, and lungs had to be constantly cleared of sooty deposits. There had to be a strong wind blowing before you could see through an engine shed. An engine shed in action was an awesome sight as the shiny passenger engines and the filthy freight engines belched black and yellow smoke and fumes. Heaps of clinker and smoke-box ash dotted the area and what you did not see you would either bang into, fall across or trip over.

I now found myself among a squad of engine cleaners, the junior member of the squad, all dressed in dungarees, a uniform glazed cap, and a tackety pair of boots, the essential apparel for cleaning engines.

When an engine was given to us we tossed a coin to see which pair out of the eight-strong gang would do the work while the other sat in and around the engine arguing about politics, sport, religion and railways.[15]

When I was firing between Carlisle and Glasgow in the late 1940s, there was a chronic shortage of essential equipment for locomotives. Many firemen would report early for duty and spend an unpaid hour searching the sheds and robbing dead engines of essential parts such as boiler gauge glass protectors and coal slaking pipes. This activity was strictly forbidden but if trains were to run the policy of robbing Peter to pay Paul was the only possible alternative. We at Kingmoor shed were forced into this situation, but woe betide any foreigner who stepped into the cab of a dead engine at Polmadie with the intention of removing anything.

At that time, Polmadie was a grim area of factories, railways and tenements, and the cleaners at that shed were a product of that environment. Hardy and independent, they were treated with a healthy respect by foremen and foreign engine-men alike. Card schools in the cabs of engines were a regular feature of Polmadie shed. These games, known to but unmolested by the foremen, kept many Scottish trains on the road, for any English fireman brash enough to attempt the removal of boiler, gauge lamp, slaking pipe or fire irons would soon be surrounded by a group of Glasgow engine cleaners whose manner said simply, 'Pit it doon, or else'. The engine cleaners soon adopted their own definition of territorialism, based on 'what is at Polmadie, is Scottish, keep off'. From these young cleaners would come the firemen who worked the run from Glasgow to Crewe, 250 miles of track taking in the ascent of Beattock Summit and Shap Fell each way, a gruelling run equalling anything else performed by a man with a shovel on any foot-plate in Britain.

The ordinary shift times for an engine cleaner were 6.00 a.m. until 2.00 p.m., 2.00 p.m. until 10.00 p.m. and 10.00 p.m. until 6.00 a.m. When his seniority took him to the apex of the cleaning gang, the youngster faced a rigorous test of his ambition to become a foot-plateman: he was placed on split shifts. Cleaning on split shift gave him a roster of 11.00 p.m. to 7.00 a.m., 7.00 p.m. to 3.00 a.m. and 3.00 a.m. to 11.00 a.m. Split-shift working put a youngster into the legion of the damned and effectively removed him from the hours of normal people. He now worked railway hours, and his life took on the aspects of a real railway worker.

To begin work at 7.00 p.m. was harsh enough as it immediately removed him from the social whirl; there was also the problem of getting home at 3.00 a.m., especially in the winter months. The 11.00 p.m. to 7.00 a.m. shift at least gave the young cleaner the opportunity to sleep all day and to prepare for the night hours. It was the 3.00 a.m. start which tested the mettle of an engine cleaner. It was a constant battle against the natural desire to sleep. In steam days men required for such duties were called by the railway knocker-up. Many of the private companies insisted that foot-plate staff had to live within reasonable walking distance from the shed or yard. One mile was the usual radius. Men who had to be on duty between one o'clock and six o'clock in the morning were always knocked up to ensure that they would be at work on time. The task of the knocker-up was to bang on the front door until he got a reply; only when he was satisfied that the young cleaner was awake would the knocker-up leave the door. In houses occupied by large families, the clashing of the front-door knocker would set up an orchestra of protest from upset children.

For the 3.00 a.m. shift, the engine cleaner rose at 1.30 a.m. and after the engine cleaner's breakfast of one cup of tea and a Woodbine he set off on his freezing journey to the shed by bicycle or on foot. The dark, clear frozen stillness of these mornings was in direct contrast to what he found when he arrived at the engine shed. At 3.00 a.m., a large engine shed was a bustle of activity. Always poorly lit, the engine shed was in those hours before dawn a black smoky hole punctuated with hand lamps and flare torches. The air was rank with the smell of paraffin-soaked firelighters, sulphuric smoke and the curses of men whose tempers at 3.00 a.m. were delicately balanced. At 3.00 a.m. the night shift of shed drivers and shed workers such as boilersmiths and fire-raisers were working at high tempo preparing the engines for the early-morning services. The heat generated by the engines rose quickly to the roof of the shed, leaving the ground level a mass of swirling draughts.

At 3.00 a.m. the youngster signed on for duty and at 3.05 a.m. he was given a bucket of freezing cold engine cleaning oil, a metal scraper and a bundle of damp-smelling cotton waste which had to be examined most carefully as it often contained sharp pieces of metal picked up when the waste was swept from the factory floor.

On joining the engine-cleaning crew the early morning man discovered a group of black-faced, red-eyed youngsters whose main ambition was to see the hands of a shed clock pointing to 5.55 a.m. A winter night of cleaning a cold engine left many of them literally frozen. The younger members of the gang had not qualified for overalls and wore only what old clothes the family could provide in lieu of protective gear. The oily shed floor and the oil spluttering from bucket and waste was fatal to shoe leather, a pair of boots often lasting only two weeks. To the jeers of 'Who got you up, your ma?' the young cleaner plunged the ice-cold waste into the freezing cleaning oil and started work. At 6.00 a.m. his companions left him and in front of him stretched an eternity of five more freezing black and oil-stained hours.

At this point the day-shift cleaners arrived to find him at his labours, already blackened and stiffened by the activities of the past three hours. He worked with both day and night shifts, but was a member of neither. His life was spent in no man's land: neither night nor day existed for the split-shift cleaner. His great ambition was to get back on his 'own' shift where he could regain his original identity. This, however, was impossible. He was now a shift worker, a real railwayman in a world where night and day had lost their meaning and where his personal relationships were centred on his working rather than his leisure hours.

The cleaning gang had no time for social deviants; the norms were sex, railway, sport and entertainment, in that order. The propagator of singular views was ostracized. A persistent offender against group morality would have his jacket removed from the messroom peg, strapped to the buffers of the yard shunting engine and after it had been smashed to a pulp it was returned to its peg or nail, often full of dirty cotton waste. The language of these young men was a fearful combination of blue jokes, military jargon, Americanizations and railway slang, the latter a sub-language in its own right.

The leading cleaner or shift foreman on my shift had a specific sanction against cleaners who upset him. He banished the offender to the cabin at the top of the hundred-foot-high coal elevator to clean the machinery when it was not pouring its black dust-laden contents into the tenders below. A lad adopted the rationale of his shift or got out. But the cleaning gang trained the youngster for the life of the foot-plate, and the hard-swearing cleaners developed eventually into capable and responsible foot-platemen.

During his cleaning days, Mr McLagan was transferred to the Glasgow engine shed at Corkerhill. This was a former Glasgow and South-Western Railway shed and, according to Mr McLagan, it was hard to believe that it was in the same country let alone the same city as Polmadie. The cleaners at Corkerhill seemed much more reserved than their counterparts at Polmadie. The cleaners, firemen and drivers spoke mainly with the soft accents of Ayrshire, Dumfriesshire and Galloway. The ex-Caledonian men nicknamed the Sou'west route the 'Hornby Railway' because of its restricted route mileage and its light trains. Mr McLagan has a special memory of Corkerhill shed which sums up the complex industrial, political and religious patterns of Glasgow. ' "What are you?" asked the Corkerhill driver of the young man stoking the firebox. "I'm a cleaner," was the reply. "I know you are a cleaner," said the driver, "but are you a Catholic or Protestant?" '[16] To be a Protestant by birth and upbringing was an advantage at Corkerhill, but it was cancelled out by being a Catholic cleaner at Polmadie.

In the 1950s, despite staff shortages, many sheds attempted to retain the pre-war atmosphere of company pride and discipline. Ron Smith, a keen Great Western Railway engine spotter in his schooldays, decided that he would become an engine-driver, and he started at Southall after an introduction to the shed superintendent by Inspector Ball, a friend of Ron Smith's father. It was later pointed out to engine cleaner Smith that to start at Southall in the great days of the GWR, a cleaner needed references from such people as clergymen, doctors or police officers before one could be considered for employment.[17] Discipline in the 1950s was still tight. Each man was given a brass disc on 'signing on' which was stamped with his pay number. If a foreman wished to discipline a man he would ask for his 'brass' and then send him home. Instant dismissal was meted out by the shed superintendent for petty theft or for any serious breach of the rules. The GWR approach was well summed up by the man who wrote: 'Civilization is founded on the Ten Commandments—ten wise rules of conduct, in defiance of which man may know no peace or happiness . . . from the Ten Commandments have sprung a multitude of lesser laws or rules, written or unwritten.'[18] In 1950, when Ron Smith presented himself for his first shift as an engine cleaner at Southall, he found a world far away from the bookish world of the railway enthusiast, and he has written:

I was a very proud but shy lad in my new overalls when I presented myself at Southall sheds. The little Dickens-type office was crammed with sheaves of paper. Booking and roster clerks sat on high stools. Engine-men were coming and going, checking their turns and engines on the duty sheets. Shed men were booking on, chatting among themselves. Fresh from school, this was, to me, a mad whirl. A clerk told me to report to the superintendent's office, where Mr Shepstone lectured me on my future behaviour, conduct, duties and general shed rules. Although a strict man, he would always address everyone by their first name, which I thought was rather nice after being 'Smith' at school. I was given check number 375.[19]

Young Ron was soon to find that the work of an engine cleaner entailed more than that of trainee locomotive-man. He was, at sixteen years of age, expected to do the heaviest work in the shed, and there was plenty of it. He has given us a picture of some of his activities:

Owing to a shortage of staff I was to go shed labouring; I was bitterly disappointed but at least I was soon made a little happier when I was told that I would be paid at the adult rate of 2s. 3d. per hour.

Our first job was to clean the shed up; this we did, Mike and I, with big heavy brooms with which we swept down the roads and between the tracks, right down into the shed itself. We then started again at the other end, sweeping down into the sheds again; having done this we would sweep all the dirt, clinker and coal into the inspection pits and shovel it out into large metal wheelbarrows. I found this very exhausting, especially throwing the rubbish up from the pits into the barrow; by the time I had finished the first morning my hands were covered with blisters. How I remember wheeling that heavily laden barrow to the rubbish tip over several sets of rails; every now and again I would hit a sleeper or oil and upset my barrow! Coupled with the pain of the blisters I was very near tears by the time we had finished—but there was more to come. After a tea break, Mike and I would return to the rubbish tip and sort all the coal out and wheel it down to the coal stages.

This would take us to lunchtime and by now I was just about whacked. Following lunch there would be a variety of odd jobs to do. Sometimes I had to off-load a wagon full of wet sand into the sand-drying plant, or firelighters had to be off-loaded. This was real heavy manual work and by the end of my first week I literally had blisters on my blisters; the parts of my hands that did not have blisters had splinters from the firelighters; my knuckles were grazed and cut; my back and arms ached like hell.

My duties at night were varied but most of the time I would be in the lamp room. This was a corrugated iron hut where all the engine lamps were kept. The firemen would collect their lamps from here when preparing an engine and return them on bringing an engine into shed. You would always get rough old lamps in from engines working in another depot. I came on at 10.00 p.m. and there would be about 100 lamps to clean; the lamps were quite heavy and you could only lift four at a time onto the cleaning table. Out with the cotton waste and paraffin can, open the lamps and out with the reservoirs, pinch the crust off the wicks (this was a hard deposit that formed while the lamps were burning), take the wick holder out, fit new wicks if needed and then fill the reservoir. Clean the reflector on the door and the big bullseye lens. Take the 'plums' out, clean them and put them in separate trays. The 'plums' were red glass slides that were slid down behind the bullseye lens to convert a white light to a red one; that is, a head lamp to a tail lamp or danger signal.

Another duty I had to do on nights was to meet the stores train at Southall station at midnight. This train, as its name implies, runs from Swindon to Paddington every day, dropping stores at all the stations. The train was called the *Punch*, why I don't know, unless it is a corruption of the word 'punctual', as she was rarely more than a couple of minutes late. I well remember one night having to wheel an engine safety valve down to the sheds from the station on a two-wheeled sack trolley. The valve weight was about 8 cwt and getting it over all the tracks to the shed single-handed was no mean task. Despite the coldness of the winter night I was exhausted and the sweat was running off me by the time I had finished.

I would then finish the rest of the lamps, have a cup of tea by the pot-bellied stove and sign off duty at 6.00 a.m.[20]

The days of scrub and shine disappeared in 1939, never to reappear; those of us who started as engine cleaners in the 1940s and 50s knew nothing of gleaming boilers and polished brasswork. We wanted to be firemen, not engine cleaners. We could think of a thousand reasons why we should not be standing in a howling gale at three o'clock in the morning, scraping great swaths of dirt from the wheels of a steam engine by the light of a flare lamp.

On every shift there would be a Valentino, a cleaner who despite every provocation would keep his overalls a spotless duck-egg blue. In contrast there was usually another who could survive the foreman's wrath despite appearing for a dozen shifts without wiping a wheel.

The record of one dozen non-cleaning shifts is held, we believe, by Johnny Ralph of Dairycoates, Hull.

When Noel Cox was cleaning at Scunthorpe in the 1950s, the 'old hand' cleaner usurped the title of foreman cleaner, and when called for firing duties handed the baton over to the next senior lad.[21] New starters were introduced to the art of cleaning by the foreman, George Harrison, who demonstrated the art of cleaning and polishing metal with great skill, promising them an early finish if the lads showed willing. The lads polished their first machine with great enthusiasm—it was Harrison's push bike.

At Edge Hill, a shed on the old LNWR—or 'lean and narrow-waisted' as the men called it—senior cleaners were allowed the warmth and protection of warm boilers while the new men did the scraping of wheels and motions.[22] The youngsters were given the heart-breaking task of cleaning engines which had undergone major surgery and had been freshly lit up—a rhapsody in grease, soot, oil, brick dust and sulphurous fumes. At Edge Hill the cleaners would often abscond to the 'Mystery', a large open space bequeathed by an unknown Merseyside benefactor, or to the nearby Magnet Cinema, where it was rumoured missing cleaners were called back to the shed by a slide placed in the projector during the performance.

Another task which befell the engine cleaners was that of knocking up. Regular knockers-up were employed, but if one was ill, the ubiquitous cleaner was pressed into the breach. In the 1920s few homes had doorbells—it was the heavy knocker or a bang on the window. Many cleaners dreaded the task of wandering the streets by night and thrashing the door knockers of strange and sleeping houses in unfamiliar parts of their own town. For young cleaners this job had few compensations. Often they would knock at the wrong house and be chased off by irate householders. In Carlisle in 1946–8, when I did knocking up, I found many of the door knockers muffled to prevent the household being awakened by my hammering. Often terrified stray dogs would attach themselves to me, and quite often a vicious stray would bar my way into a road or street.

In Glasgow the young men on knocking up had recourse to the heat of a Kippering store, where they sometimes received free samples. Bakeries would be the donors of hot morning rolls for the young cleaner on his rounds. William McLagan once fell asleep on the doormat of the house he was knocking up, to be kicked off by an irate driver on his way to work. In Manchester, Jim Walker was supplied with a bicycle to call the men of Patricroft, a bicycle which had seen sterling service for it came with two oil lamps and a box of matches with which to light them. In Hull, the basis of emergency calling up was the 'ticket system'. If the signing-on time of a driver or fireman had to be changed, a cleaner with a special ticket carrying the information might be sent to the house. This advice note could only be accepted by the person to whom it was addressed, and many pantomimes resulted from their attempted delivery—often it was akin to serving a writ. Men would refuse to answer the door, or they would send another member of the family to say: 'Dad's not in—we don't know when he will be back.' According to Peter Bell, who was calling up at Dairycoates, Hull, in the early 1950s, the best refusal was when the driver or fireman pressed a couple of shillings into the caller's palm with a quiet injunction as to what the shift foreman could do with his note. At Worcester, Harry Core didn't mind the job in the early mornings 'when the fruit was about', and as a youngster he knew the whereabouts of the most succulent varieties and delicacies in the Evesham Valley. It was not without truth or humour that a Manchester knocker-up claimed that he 'had parted more married couples than a divorce court judge'.

The system of rank and degree persisted until the end of the steam era. One man who wrote about it was Ramon D'Onion (a pun on Damon Runyon—the American humorist) who told us in a series of articles in the *Locomotive Journal*:

In the good old days of steam, when I am nothing but a young cleaner-boy at the Big Freight Depot, it is well known to one and all that young cleaner-boys such as myself are apt to engage in certain practices that are not strictly in keeping with the provisions of the *Rule Book* on this man's railway—or the provisions of any other rule book for the matter of that.

In these days of which I speak it is quite customary for young cleaner-boys to have differences of opinion about this and that, and one thing and another, and these young characters have their own special code of practice for dealing with any conflicts that might ensue. This code of practice is a most odd code that grows up, like little Topsy, over the years, and its disciplinary powers are often terrible to behold. It is by no means unusual for drastic physical discomfort and pain to result from the retribution meted out to some erring young cleaner-boy—and this is something that is recognized by all concerned within all locomotive depots up and down the system.

It is naturally the job of all young cleaner-boys to deal with the large steam locomotives that are assigned to their particular depot and it is quite incredible how much dirt and grease and filth will accumulate on all parts of a steam locomotive during the course of a run each day. So the young cleaner-boys are issued with such implements as metal scrapers and cans of cleaning oil and cotton waste and sponge cloths and I do not know what-all, and they set to work on a great 100-ton lump of mud as though they are nothing but young chambermaids dusting the lounge of the rectory with a feather-duster.

The size of a cleaning gang on a shift can vary from just a mere handful of young cleaner-boys to as many as thirty or forty, according to how many cleaner-boys happen to be rostered out on firing turns of duty on each particular day. The senior member of such a gang is known as the Gink and this character is all-powerful within his gang. In fact, the Gink of any gang is widely considered to be a very powerful guy indeed, and is held in great awe by all concerned at all times.

I once heard it said by a reliable authority on the subject that, compared with this code of practice operating in a locomotive depot in the good old days of steam, the well-known Prefect-and-Fag system adopted in English public schools is really kindergarten stuff. In fact, I also heard it said at this time that the Prime Minister of Great Britain and Generalissimo Joseph Stalin are considered very small fry in this field of operation—and gangsters in Chicago like little old Al Capone are mere babes-in-the-wood alongside the Gink of the Cocoa Gang at the Big Freight Depot.

In circumstances of such power it is understandable that the Gink is most unlikely to soil his hands or muss up his overalls on such things as filthy engine wheels and gears when he commands a company of junior members of his gang who can be detailed to perform such tasks. It is commonly understood that the Gink will take up his position in the driving cab and, from this position of advantage and comfort, he will conduct the whole cleaning operation exactly as the conductor of a great symphony orchestra will operate from his rostrum. In fact, I once heard it said a young lad from a place called Manchester known as John Barbirolli often looks in at the local engine sheds to get a few tips before he goes on stage to lead the Hallé ensemble.

On bitterly cold nights it is by no means unusual for all such cleaning gangs to buckle into the work with great gusto for maybe three or four hours—polishing off three or four locomotives before the meal break at, say, two o'clock in the morning. In the meantime it is the job of the Gink to select a nice, warm locomotive tucked somewhere out of sight of the night foreman and this locomotive becomes the dormitory or dosshouse of the gang for the rest of the shift.

It is commonly regarded as proper, when young cleaner-boys are taking their rest on a locomotive in these circumstances, that the

Gink will take his forty winks in the driving seat, which he has been keeping warm all along until now, and the remainder of the gang will occupy places of vantage and diminishing comfort—in strict seniority order of course. In this way there will be young cleaner-boys stretched out in the most odd places all around and about the locomotive, and the junior members of the gang will no doubt be situated underneath the boiler, lying along the big end with maybe an eccentric rod or two handy to keep them from falling off the big end and into the pit below.

Personally, in the wintertime when the snow is on the ground and old Jack Frost creeps up around the engine framings, I consider this position on the big ends by no means a loser as it is always nice and warm and snug, being right beneath the hot boiler and with the firebox just in rear. Furthermore, when the night foreman's indigestion keeps him awake and more ornery than usual, he is apt to get out on the prowl after sleeping young cleaner-boys, and it is usually possible to escape detection in this position on the big ends, especially if the big end is on the top-back centre—way out of sight and reach.

Naturally it is most essential that a young cleaner-boy who sleeps in this place on a live locomotive shall always keep one ear open for sounds of the vacuum brake ejector being blown up, or the hand brake being released, because if a driver should come round and absent-mindedly happen to move a locomotive with a young cleaner-boy stretched out along a big end, the result will be very messy indeed, although I personally never worry about this because any mess in the gears will naturally have to be cleaned up by the gang and it is most unlikely that the Gink will allow the gears to be all mussed up in this way especially if his gang cleans the gears beforehand, anyway. In fact, it is part of the code of honour within a locomotive depot that the Gink will protect his flock at all times against any danger that may threaten from any source whatsoever.

I mention these reminiscences merely to give some idea of the rigid code of practice accepted by all cleaner-boy staff who are regarded as mere beginners in the long process of education. It is a tough existence and truly a survival of the fittest—with many a young cleaner-boy member of the staff falling out along the way.

Despite their special status and problems, engine cleaners never achieved independent recognition from companies and trade unions, leaving them with little defence against company discipline and trade-union inertia. Even long-service cleaners, men with families had to rely upon the higher echelons of the unions to present their case.

In the years before the First World War the shed foreman often possessed the right to hire and fire the young men who aspired to become engine-drivers. In 1913, when engine cleaners were being used as firemen on passenger trains for 3s. 9d. per day on the Lancashire and Yorkshire Railway, there were strikes at Bolton, Blackburn and Bury, but no details have survived of the actions. In the 1920s there was further agitation among cleaners for a special conference of their own, but the campaign could not achieve official trade-union backing.

This early agitation was at a period when men could be dismissed if caught reading a newspaper in their employer's time[23] and when an engine cleaner on the Lancashire and Yorkshire Railway, after shovelling fifty-four and a half tons of coal during his twelve-hour shift, was reported and cautioned about his future behaviour for having the temerity to wash his face and hands after eleven hours and forty-five minutes on duty.[24] In the mid-1920s, however, a group of mature engine cleaners decided to campaign independently of the trade-union machinery, which was fully committed to a defensive posture after the amalgamations of 1923. Mr Bob Lunniss, who was active in the minority movement, has recalled:

> Over the decade from 1923 to 1933 the full effects of the amalgamation of the old railway companies into four main groups were being felt more and more by the railway staff.
>
> The apathetic attitude of railwaymen towards their trade union in the early 1930s was brought about by the stagnation of rates of pay and conditions in the fifteen years since 1919 and the infamous $2\frac{1}{2}$ per cent plus reduction of wages forced upon the trade unions. This $2\frac{1}{2}$ per cent levy on the wages of railwaymen to assist the companies was an outstanding example of the fallacy that sacrifices by employees can solve the economic problems of employers in big industries.[25]

In this sort of situation it is not surprising that apathy prevailed among railwaymen. Those engine cleaners who realized this dangerous trend set up the Railway Vigilance Movement in 1934 as an organization to combat this drift away from active interest. The old cliché that 'the price of freedom is eternal vigilance' was as necessary in 1934 as it ever had been. Many little, local, managerial despots were reading all sorts of interpretations into agreements and receiving approbation from their superiors if they got away with it. The function of the Vigilants was to see that they did not get away with it. They matched the ardour of the old-time religious evangelists with a constant watchfulness over the policies of the trade unions and employers alike. This inevitably led to clashes with both. An irritant was being introduced into the placid, flabby area of relations between trade unions and employers which had existed in the railway industry since 1919 when the great gain of the National Conditions of Service had been obtained and which the employers constantly tried to erode. Only twice had this calm been disturbed: by the strike by ASLEF in 1924 and the Great Strike of 1926, both of which left railwaymen worse off than before.

There was no more fertile area of staffing for rendering men redundant and for instituting general rationalization than the locomotive departments. The four companies went to work with a will on the project. Its thoroughness was only matched by the heartlessness shown to staff affected. Engine cleaners with fifteen years' service, and married with families, suddenly found themselves confronted with an ultimatum which in the present day and age would only be regarded as impermissible. They were told to report to a depot which in some cases was 400 miles away. The alternative was discharge and the queue at the labour exchange, which at this time was 2½ million. The companies offered no lodging allowance, no allowances, nothing at all. Even a ticket to visit a man's family was difficult to get and depended largely on the whim of the local chief clerk. Two examples of closures will suffice to explain what was going on all over the country. At Cambridge, the London and North-Western, the Great Northern and the Great Eastern all had depots. Both the GNR and the LNWR were closed. At York the North-Eastern, the GNR, the Lancashire and Yorkshire and the Midland all had depots. Only the NER remained open. (See Fig. 3.)

Out of this attack by the companies arose the London Engine Cleaners' Vigilance Committee. Some drivers and firemen helped in the organization. Among those dispatched to the London area were Charles Lackie from Edinburgh, William Nelson from Glasgow, Archibald Manuel from Stranraer, Adam Bradshaw from Blackpool, Henry Doyle from Hurlford, and William Clarke from Wigan. These, along with engine cleaners in the London area, formed the committee. Francis Gates, Robert Lunniss and James Swain of King's Cross, and George Taylor of Neasden organized and spoke at cleaners' meetings all over London and as far as Tilbury. This upsurge of militancy among the oppressed soon had its effect throughout the country. Vigilance Committees sprang up everywhere. Carriage cleaners at Stratford and Hornsey were soon organized with their own committee. The Willesden Empire was packed at several meetings as was Stratford Town Hall and the Caledonian Road Baths.

Discussions were arranged in working hours, and Jim Swain of King's Cross eventually visited the Soviet Union as a delegate from St Pancras Trades Council. He was so overcome by the reception at the dockside that he flung his bourgeois bowler hat into the Neva.

The Vigilance Movement spread rapidly. Every stage of the trade-

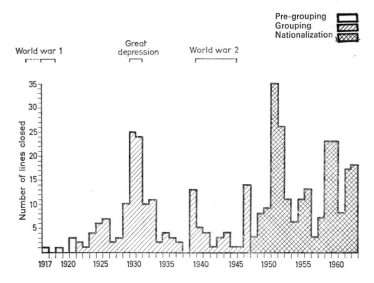

Fig. 3 Graph of lines (or part lines) closed between 1917 and 1963. Compiled from *Passengers No More* by G. Daniels and L. Dench. Ian Allan publication. (Graph redrawn by Peter Hudson)

union organization was infiltrated by its representatives—local departmental committees, branch committees, district councils, trades councils, sectional councils, annual general meetings and even executive committees. Every agenda was scrutinized and its resolutions analysed minutely. Resolutions for annual general meetings were formulated and placed before branch meetings for adoption. Many local victories were won by local departmental committees packed with Vigilance members.

The movement was formed on a strictly depot basis. Each depot had its own Vigilance committee working inside the local trade-union branch and local departmental committees responsible for local negotiations. There was no national executive committee of the Vigilants as such. Almost every grade in the depot had a committee working with the depot Vigilance committee, including engine cleaners and foot-plate staff, guards, carriage cleaners, examiners, goods workers and clerical staff. The national co-ordination point was the annual conferences of the movement, held at Stratford Town Hall. To these came representatives of the Vigilance Movement from all over the country at their own expense or financed by fellow workers making collections back in the depot. One recalls Alfred Clifford, later to become Area Organizer for ASLEF, cycling all the way from Derby to London and being given lodgings by London friends. At these conferences ideas were exchanged and attitudes taken to pending trade-union annual conferences.

A feature of the Vigilance Movement was the intellectual standard of those taking a leading part in the depots. This was a 'workshop floor' leadership emerging not as an alternative to the official leadership of the time but as a supplementary group of knowledgeable local representatives. Around those local committees revolved most of the active members of the trade-union branches. In this situation, inter-union rivalry was markedly absent. Such an atmosphere was created by the determination of the grade Vigilance committees to deal only with the problems of their own grades.

The period of the Vigilants was the period of the mechanization of the railway depots. It was with the effects of the mechanization and rationalization programmes that they had to deal. Mechanical coal hoppers and hoists took the place of the old manual coaling stage, carriage washing plants replaced hand washing, and larger locomotives did away with double-heading of the ever-increasing weight and length of trains. Diesel shunting locomotives operated by one man were used for the first time on the London, Midland and Scottish. All these things and many others brought about the stalemate on the issue of redundancy. Into the fight for the preservation of jobs went the full force of the Vigilance Movement. Many a man's livelihood was saved by Vigilant local departmental representatives refusing to agree to staff reductions, often against trade-union advice and stubborn local management. The King's Cross depot was often blocked for a week by work-to-rule in the movement of locomotives around the new coaling plant. Only when the threatened redundancies were withdrawn would representatives agree to discuss anything. The traffic in the loading and unloading bays of the goods shed often piled up to unmanageable proportions when a similar thing happened there. Urgent appeals were often made by management to trade-union head offices to calm down these Vigilance committee members.

At depot level the management was being challenged by weekend strikes, work-to-rule and general refusals to agree anything locally until an open meeting of the men in the depot had the opportunity to decide for themselves. This was a new departure. Until then the local staff representatives agreed something with the management and then told the men afterwards. Between 1935 and 1939 there were more spasmodic stoppages and work-to-rule than in all the years up to the General Strike. It is significant too that ASLEF was on the verge of a strike when the war started in 1939. The organizing secretaries were being constantly brought to depots to endeavour to settle local disputes. There were frequent scenes of goods loading workers conducting a mass meeting in the yards at King's Cross and Nine Elms using an empty wagon as a platform. All this sort of thing was a new departure in the years after 1926. The pressures on the trade unions were becoming as heavy as they were for the managements. Gone was the day when the organizer of the trade union appeared occasionally to advocate for a member on a disciplinary charge. His head office now more often sent him to a depot at the request of the management to intervene in a local dispute.

This whole atmosphere was the creation of the active leadership of the local Vigilance committees. Managements no longer approached staff negotiations with indifference and the old attitude of half-listening to staff grumbles and supplications so as to dispose of them before lunch. Local negotiation meetings now lasted two or three days and sometimes four. It was in this set of conditions that local agreements were first set up covering every aspect of depot working arrangements. This was a tremendous step forward from the old managerial insistence on its own interpretations of the national conditions of service. A new, more knowledgeable type of local representative, who had studied his rights in the manner of a law student, was now confronting local managements, who in many cases were sadly lacking in this particular training. In response, higher management eventually set up its own specially taught departments to advise ignorant local managers faced with new problems with which they had no ability to deal.

At this juncture the *Railway Vigilant* was published nationally. The little back room in St Paul's Road, Highbury, where this paper first saw the light of day, was soon to become a hive of industry. Into it poured letters and articles from all over Britain. Its pages were open to any railwayman who cared to write to it. Many a budding writer on trade-union affairs in the railway industry made his effort in the *Railway Vigilant*. From a crudely printed collection of sheets sewn together on an ordinary sewing machine it became a proper newspaper. Its distribution and sale reached most depots up and down the country.

It is interesting to follow the subsequent path in life that many of these young Vigilants took. Forced in their early years in industry to take steps to protect themselves and their fellows by methods that would not have been necessary in a more prosperous era, they became a living testimony to the theory of Karl Marx that man becomes a creature of the environment in which he lives. The Vigilants began as an expression of industrial discontent, but developed rapidly into a political movement of the Left. Harry Doyle served for years as Staff Representative on the LMS sectional council until his service ended. Archie Manuel became Member of Parliament for Ayr. Another became Assistant General Secretary of the NUR. Francis Gates spent a lifetime as a representative in one form or another. Robert Lunniss served the London district council of ASLEF for twenty-five years as Assistant Secretary, Secretary and Chairman and ended his service as National Trustee. James Swain was a representative for years and delegate to the Trades Union Congress.[26] Many others outside the London area could be mentioned, such as Richard Shaw at Burnley, who never let up until the day he finished. These facts need to be mentioned so that it may be understood how the seed of progress really takes root in an organization and eventually promulgates ideas that take over from the old order. Today the work-to-rule, the one-day strike and the open refusal to accept anything that is prejudicial to its members are the accepted weapons which stiffen the actions of railway trade unionists. For the Vigilants the period of co-operation was over. In the 1960s and 70s the tactics of the Vigilance Movement have been shown as the right course at the right time.

Events on the railway took place within a context of national and international turmoil. Progressives on the railway were quick to recognize the dangerous doctrines of Sir Oswald Mosley when he founded his Blackshirt Movement in 1930. Vigilants were active in anti-Fascist groups, supported the anti-Fascist marches in east London and were among the great anti-Fascist demonstrators in Hyde Park who shook the Blackshirt army. It was morally impossible to wage war against injustice on the railway and to ignore the wide international struggle. The environment created a political understanding which remained with us all our lives. The Spanish Civil War saw a continuous effort by a section of the British trade-union movement to assist those fighting to preserve the life of Republican Spain against the Moroccan mercenaries of General Franco. Vigilants attempted to explain the rise of Nazism, the conquest of Austria and Czechoslovakia, the calamity of 3 September 1939, and the overrunning of Europe which was the logical consequence of the policies of the Chamberlain Government. Vigilants were found marching behind the famous black coffin[27] of the Unemployed Workers' Movement when it was paraded through the West End of London on 31 December 1938.

The policies and methods of the Vigilants are accepted practices of trade unions in all industries today. What were revolutionary ideas in 1934 now have the rubber stamp of official policy on them. Trade-union executives now discuss the putting into operation of these actions as freely today as Vigilance committees did clandestinely behind branch room doors over thirty-five years ago.

Throughout the years of steam, the engine cleaner walked in the shadow of the fireman; once promoted, however, the newly appointed fireman found that the same held true of his reationship with the driver. The driver was king, the fireman vassal. On the foot-plate of a leaping, bucking locomotive, there could be one boss only, and every fireman who aspired to driving duties was acutely conscious that when he achieved the status of throttle-puller, he too would demand immediate obedience from the man with the shovel. Although the foot-platemen were double-harnessed by tradition and necessity, when the moment of decision struck, the driver of the train took the weight of responsibility. This was the relationship throughout the years of steam, and rarely was the principle contested, for dismissal from the service was the penalty for insubordination on the foot-plate.

But what was life really like for a fireman of steam locomotives? In the 1840s it was a totally new profession. There was no precedent—no written instructions to follow. The early firemen had to discover for themselves the finer points of the new art. This process, which began in 1830, was finished by 1960, and the skill of the fireman became a lost knack, an activity born of north-eastern mechanical ability pushed unceremoniously aside by the force of science. In his time, the railway fireman was a popular figure in literature, epitomizing cheerfulness and a capacity for loyalty and hard work.

From the earliest times, firemen were paid according to a strict system of classification. Here the job performed, rather than the worker, had the status. A fireman on express passenger trains earned more than a man firing express goods trains. The stoker on short trips earned slightly more than the shed fireman, who was on the lowest rate of pay. Progress through these scales could be long and frustrating.

In the 1880s, when the system was in full swing, it was often complicated by the ruse of using lower-graded men on higher paid duties. According to one source, 'Firemen, scarcely attained to manhood, are promoted to drivers. . . . These young drivers receive 5s. and 5s. 6d. wages per day for doing work which once upon a time entitled the performer to 7s. and 7s. 6d. per day.'[28]

Wilf Turner, who in 1919 was a fireman on the Great Western Railway, has written about classification in that company:

I was at this time a third-class fireman and promotion went like this. There were 15 per cent first class, 35 per cent second class and 50 per cent third class. A fireman started at 3s. 6d. per day, rising to 3s. 9d. after five years, rising again after a further waiting period to 4s. 3d., or if he had worked his way up to second or first class by then he received 4s. 9d. per day. This same system applied to the driver. He started at 5s. 6d. per day, rising to 6s. and again if he came in the top percentage a first-class driver received 8s. per day. This was classification and in my own opinion was a good thing as it kept a tight rein on all trains and all staff, it was not a free-for-all as now.[29]

Classification, the industrial perpetuation of rank and degree in feudal society, continued until the end of the steam era.

Side by side with these forms of classification imposed by the companies, there developed on the foot-plate a special form of ranking. Tradition on the foot-plate meant that the driver was 'the governor' and the fireman was 'the boy'. In the promotion of firemen from lower to higher tasks the drivers enjoyed great authority. They could spot the likeliest lads in the shed and were often able to invite such youngsters to join them on foot-plate duties. Mr A. J. Street, who was firing at Old Oak Common shed on the Great Western at the turn of the century, has recorded: 'When starting my express goods period I had been approached by engine-man Sam Heard to know if I would go with him as his fireman. In fact he went so far as to come down the shed the first Monday morning to interview the foreman.'[30]

Once established as a fireman, however, the prospective engine-man soon found that the time-honoured distinctions between driver and fireman were strictly enforced. In many messrooms the seating and eating accommodation was divided into 'drivers'' and 'firemen's' tables, the men parting company and gravitating to the table and conversation of their peers. When lodging away from home, the driver reserved the right to determine when the fireman should retire for rest. It was rare for such rituals to be questioned—antagonizing one driver was tantamount to antagonizing the entire grade.

An important sign of rank was the driver's box and tea can. Although there was nothing official, a fireman might buy himself a tea can, but he would never be so presumptuous as to buy a driver's box. In the days of steam, if the driver and fireman were out walking anywhere, the fireman, complete with ex-gas mask bag containing sandwiches, would be carrying the driver's tea tin while the driver strode along with his own black box containing time sheets, boiler gauge glasses, spare corks for big end and eccentric rods, sandwiches and his 'Bible'—the railway Rule Book. Status could not be questioned—if it was, the driver could make life very rough for the fireman.

The companies acknowledged and strengthened rank and degree by the provision of protective clothing. Ron Smith, who was firing in the 1950s at Southall on the Western Region, has observed: 'There existed a feudal system based on discrimination by rank. An engine cleaner was issued only with overalls. Promoted to fireman he gained a short serge jacket. As a driver he was entitled to a serge overcoat.'[31]

The driver's word was law, and as Ron Smith discovered, there was no pleasing some of them. Orders to the young fireman would come with bewildering speed and complexity: 'Watch that water, look at that steam gauge, sweep up the foot-plate, is that signal off?' In Smith's time at Southall, a driver attacked a fireman with a shovel because of non-compliance with an order.

At one end of the scale you had a situation where the two men fitted like 'hand and glove' and at the other was the problem of clashing personalities, where the atmosphere in the cabin could be morose and sullen. In my own time on express trains I had to work for two years with a driver who refused to speak a word to me because I had questioned his knowledge and experience. The management of all companies and later the regions were unable to cope with this problem. I never knew of a case when management intervened between men on the foot-plate, even though it was common knowledge that each day was torment for men put together by seniority who were poles apart temperamentally. The foot-plate was teamwork all the way. The only way to survive on the foot-plate when the daggers were out was to walk off and delay the train, a circumstance which led to much paperwork between driver, fireman and management.

Between the grades of fireman and driver was a hybrid status known as 'passed fireman'. The passed firemen were the senior firemen at the depot and they were used for driving duties on an emergency basis. A passed fireman suffered from the twin iniquities of cheap labour and unofficial classification. When driving, the passed fireman shouldered all the responsibilities of the regular driver, but he was paid according to the number of driving turns he had completed. In the 1950s and 60s it took three years' driving to achieve top-driver's rate; in practice, especially at small depots, the period could be much longer. In the 1950s there existed plenty of fifty-year-old passed firemen who would not uproot home and family in order to achieve driver status.

Both drivers and firemen came under the strict discipline of the motive power department, and many of the locomotive superintendents were strait-laced martinets, not the least being Mr John Armstrong, boss of Old Oak Common, of whom A. J. Street writes in his autobiography:

During Mr John Armstrong's time as Superintendent, if a man was a minute late, he was reported, and the third time meant dismissal.

Such were the hard rules under which the engine-men and firemen worked, for we never booked on at the same time for more than two days running. It was a serious crime to be caught smoking in the shed, the locomotive yard or on the foot-plate. Mr Armstrong was also very severe on anyone he saw entering or coming out of a public house, even if the men were off-duty. In my days, discipline and punishment for the smallest thing was carried out in the London Division.[32]

Street's company had a reputation second to none for paternalism, reflected in its housebuilding and insurance societies. But the company image is flawed when one considers the pettifogging restrictions it placed on its staff. The Great Western conciliation minutes of June 1917 contain two examples of these unnecessary restrictions. One was a protest from fireman B. Mathias of Neath, who was penalized for not being at home when sent for, although he had worked a week of seventy hours.[33] When fireman H. Pearce of Didcot protested that he had been refused a privilege ticket order on 24 March 1917, despite the fact that he was free from duty for fifty-four hours, the local management defended the decision not to issue the cheap ticket order. Cheap tickets were in wage negotiations a form of income; in quieter times they were issued as a concession.

By 1871, an average wage for an engine fireman was 21s. per week. The hours were unlimited, overtime generally being paid after sixty hours had been worked. In the early days the engines were small and usually coke burners, the fireboxes tiny and fuel consumption unexceptional; it was long hours rather than heavy shovelling which exhausted the men. The fireman usually lived 'within call', which meant within a one-mile radius of the engine house. He reported for duty when so advised and left duty not after a shift, but after a 'turn of duty', a period determined by foremen, men who used concepts of time and energy very different from those of today.

Nearly half a century later Wilf Turner found his hours of labour excessive, his firing turns being of ten hours' duration. When he was 'spare', and awaiting a call to duty, 'no call' meant no pay. If he worked on a Sunday, he was given a day off during the week, so that there was no monetary gain. If he worked overtime one day, he could be sent home under time on another. The GWR did not believe in lining the pockets of its firemen.

In the days of steam, the locomotive fireman probably donated more hours of unpaid labour to his company than any other grade. On mainline engines a high proportion of firemen would be at their engines long before the appointed time; this early start enabled them to take their time in the preparation of the engine and often to begin the duties of the drivers. If injured during this unpaid, unofficial work, the fireman could turn to neither authority nor trade union for recompense. He was, for all purposes, trespassing on railway property. According to J. Thomas, the historian of the North British Railway, the fireman on that line

> . . . had to be at the station at the hour appointed by the superin-
> tendent of locomotives or his assistant, but at least two hours before
> the time of starting, to light up the fire, and he shall, before kindling
> it, examine that all the firebars are in good order and the responsi-
> bility for any delay arising from the firebars being misplaced will rest
> with the fireman unless he reports same . . . at least one and three-
> quarter hours before starting. In cases where trains are due to start
> before 6.00 a.m., the fireman may, with the consent of the superin-
> tendent of locomotives, be at the station only one hour before start-
> ing, but in those cases, he shall, on the previous night, have all the
> firebars straightened and placed on the engine platform ready for
> use.

When preparing the engine the fireman would move into quick and purposeful action, the first job being to wipe the wooden seat which the driver would occupy 'on the road'. Boiler pressure and water level were his next concern, then the firebox with its tube ends and firebrick arch received minute scrutiny for cracks and leaks. Satisfied that pressure could be raised in the allotted time, the fireman then spread the contents of the firebox across the firegrate and applied a draught of air via the engine blower to encourage combustion. Any minor problem would send the fireman scurrying for assistance to one of the many shanties that abounded in the running sheds. A fitter might be needed to repair a sticking damper handle, or the boiler tubes might need blowing out. Worse, the brick arch might be cracked, requiring the opinion of the brick-arch specialist. A fitter's labourer might be needed to replace bent, burnt or broken firegrate bars. A small army of specialist, semi-skilled men hurried night and day across the shed ensuring that the engines were fully equipped for the task ahead.

Foot-plate work has long occupied a high status in British literature but a wide gulf separated the romance from the reality. The fireman of the 1860s would have made little of Ballantyne's rhetoric, which declaimed:

> Will Garvie . . . then opened the iron door of the furnace in order to
> throw in more coal. The effect would have stirred the heart of Rem-
> brandt. The instantaneous blinding glare of the intense fire shot

through the surrounding darkness, lighting up the two men and the tender as if all were made of red-hot metal; flooding the smoke and steam clouds overhead with round masses and curling lines of more subdued light.[34]

Despite this impression of heat, an engine-cab could be one of the coldest places imaginable. Cabs were never draught-proof, and once the firehole door was closed on a cold night the only heat in the cab was that which escaped the heavy boiler lagging or radiated from the copper water pipes. The slightest breeze on a cold night would set a thousand draughts swirling round the feet and legs of the engine-men. Out on the track snow and sleet would pile up in the far corners of the cab only a few feet from the boiler facings. It was quite impossible to keep warm even if the engine was standing in a siding. One half of the man would be roasted while the other half was exposed to the elements.

For many years engine-men stored small straw-filled sacks for use on such nights.[35] Newspapers were placed in men's boots and tied round their legs in order to obviate the myriad draughts. Hot weather was a startling contrast, when any piece of metal on an engine could scorch the bare flesh of thoughtless engine-men.

On the London and North-Western it rapidly became customary for the fireman to oil up the inside motion, but on the Midland Railway it was a bold fireman who usurped the duties of the driver with 'oil can and bottle'. On the Midland the fireman knew his place and kept it. Amateur work on the driver's duties could lead to unpleasant results, as young Frank Mason discovered when first handed the driver's oil can :

> I experienced for myself the other side of the story—getting an engine ready in trying circumstances with the measly drop of oil which was issued. Balancing on the side framing of an engine trying to fill a steam-fed lubricator on the side of the smoke-box. Rain lashing down, wind making balance precarious, numb-cold fingers operating a spanner which would not grip on the brass filling plug and then becoming burned when the hot plug suddenly released in a burst of scalding steam. Trying to pour oil through the narrow aperture as the wind jostled the flow and blew out the smoky duck-lamp. The build-up of steam inside suddenly vomiting boiling oil up into face and eyes while the driver shouts. 'Haven't you filled those sand boxes yet?'

In the 1920s and '30s a change in executive strategy affected the work style of the locomotive fireman. Faced with brash competition from the roads the companies adopted 'the big-engine policy', a move which gave them the dominant place in British land transport. The companies doubled the size of their main-line locomotives, allowing longer, heavier and faster trains.

The big-engine policy developed slowly. George Stephenson's Locomotion No. 1 of 1825 weighed 8·4 tons, and Ramsbottom's *Lady of the Lake*, 1859, 31·35 tons. After the death of the broad gauge in 1892 large engines settled in weight between the 73-ton pride of the Caledonian, *Cardean*, built by J. F. McIntosh, and G. Churchward's *Great Bear*, at 97 tons the wonder of the Great Western.

By the early 1900s all this had altered. In 1927, the Great Western introduced the 'King' class locomotive. It weighed 135·7 tons, carried 6 tons of coal, 4,000 gallons of water and had a firegrate area of 34·3 square feet, creating a boiler pressure of 250 pounds per square inch. In 1937 there appeared the London, Midland and Scottish 'Princess' class, a colossus of 161 tons. This class carried 10 tons of coal, and 4,000 gallons of water; it had a firegrate area of 50 square feet. The pride of the Eastern routes at this period were the Gresley Pacifics, green giants of 152·55 tons. Ready for action, these engines carried 9 tons of coal and 5,000 gallons of water. The firegrate area was 142·5 square feet. Although the engines doubled in size, hand shovelling was still the means of feeding the furnace, and these engines were probably the ultimate in what a man could do with a shovel. Only men who worked on these engines in full flight can appreciate the awesome power of steam locomotion. A main-line fireman had to keep in tip-top physical condition. He needed hard muscles, a supple back and no fear of hard work, for on a long-distance run there could be no escape from the toil and strain.

For the locomotive fireman these were furious days. The pride of being associated with such machines was modified by the back-breaking work required. Jack Morgan, who was firing on the Midland when Stanier's 5XP's came out, told me that such was the speed of the shovel in his hand that his cal_louses broke and blood flowed onto the handle of his shovel.[36]

Anthony Sperdutti, who was firing into Paddington from the West Country, remembers the drivers of those days as heavy lifters. 'They would keep time,' records Sperdutti, 'even if the fireman was prostrate with exhaustion on the floor of the cab.'[37] The history of Anthony Sperdutti typifies the dilemma of a fireman in those times. According to Sperdutti, 'Promotion at Millbay shed, Plymouth, was very slow. For a number of years I was trapped on the suburban "push and pull" trains on bare money. I had four children, and my pocket money was 4s. one week and 6s. the next, depending on whether the clubs were due or not.'[38] Sperdutti was firing for twelve years before he reached his goal of a 'twelve and six a day' man. When he got on the London mileage runs in 1938, Sperdutti could earn between £6–7 per week as a top-grade fireman. But for this he was shovelling six tons of coal per day and lodging away from home eight weeks out of nine. He once cleared the whole of nine tons of coal from his tender as his train to Plymouth battered head-on into gale-force winds. 'I had', he writes, 'heard of firemen "clearing the tender", but I never thought I would ever do it.'[39] Clearing the tender to the last scrap of dust was known as creating 'a bare decker'.

In the 1930s, the men stoking trains out of Euston found themselves caught up in the big-engine policy. Len Housden, a passed cleaner who had been farmed out as a railway porter during the redundancies of the 1920s, remembers:

On my return to Camden I found things had changed very little except that the Pacific Class, 4.6.2, built 1933, had been introduced.

My introduction to firing engines on the main line was in 1935. I found it both thrilling and frightening. It took a considerable time to master the skills of 'flashing' the blade, i.e. swinging a shovelful of coal through the small firehole and placing the coal around the fire-box in the manner necessary to obtain heat for the maximum steam pressure. Balancing on the foot-plate of a seventy to ninety miles per hour swaying and jumping locomotive was a feat in itself.

Long distance journeys entailed shifting anything between six and ten tons of coal from tender to firebox. The hardest job, however, was pulling the coal forward within reach of shovelling from the tender, and breaking it with a pick into the appropriate size. My hands were blistered and sore for weeks. Frequent burns and abrasions were accepted as part of the job.

Another hazard when running at speed was flying coal dust. The slaking pipe on the foot-plate was frequently used to spray water over the coal, but drivers and firemen often finished with their eyes, nose, ears and throats bunged up with coal dust, and faces as black as chimneys.[40]

In 1933, a class 8, 4.6.2 locomotive number 6202 was placed in service by the London, Midland and Scottish Railway. This engine was a scourge to firemen. It burned coal like matchwood, and towards the end of each week it was difficult, owing to boiler scaling and furred-up tubes, to keep anything like a full head of steam. On this locomotive Housden cleared the tender, except for a few bucketfuls, on the 194 miles between Liverpool and London. This was the daily reality behind the golden years of steam.

In retrospect, the work of a railway fireman was rugged, tough and inhuman, despite its physical challenge and the outside interest it created. On the Southern Railway, Bulleid's Q.I.'s, the 'Spam cans', were monstrosities, and the 'Leader' class were fireman-roasting torture chambers. The Bulleid Pacifics operating between the years 1937 and 1955 were characterized as 'air-smoothed' engines. On these the fireman laid his hands on the shovel only once on a trip. Leaving Dover, he picked up the flashing blade, worked like a demon and put it down again running through London Bridge, after which the train coasted in. Murder it was.

There was a chronic shortage of engine firemen from 1940 to 1950. During the war, long hours on duty were exacerbated by a shortage of food, which bore heavily on men who shovelled coal for a living. The engines, leaking in every pore, were hauling trains 25 per cent over the pre-war capacity load. After long hours on duty and after lodging away the fireman went on Home Guard and firewatching duties. During the Second World War there were many unsung heroes of the foot-plate, but in 1940 fireman F. R. Newnes of Birkenhead was awarded the George Medal for unloading a wagon full of munitions during an air-raid on the port.[41]

For some men, the lure of engine boilers was complete, especially if there was a railway family tradition. One of these men was Jimmy Hulme of Liverpool, who has written:

> One of my grandfathers was a foreman at Park Lane goods yard and one of my uncles was a chief foreman at Edge Hill, so I was always conscious of a family railway tradition.
>
> We lived in a terraced house about 100 yards from the mouth of the tunnelled gradient which connected Park Lane goods yard to Wapping sidings. Although not being able to see the track, we were always conscious of it; the windows used to shake with the vibrations from the goods trains labouring up the slope. Each day I went to school I crossed the road bridge which spanned this track and here I first heard the inimitable grunt and hiss of the London and North-Western Supper 'D's'.[42]

For Jimmy Hulme, the locomotive department was an automatic choice. For him to be an engine-man seemed 'so superior to all other types of railway work'. In post-war Liverpool he needed two references from prominent people before he could be considered for foot-plate work. Like many other prospective engine-drivers, he started his firing career on the Edge Hill ashpits and progressed to the shunting work, through which he familiarized himself with the intricate maze of railways near Edge Hill, and he has given us the historical background to his area:

Up to 1896, the trains were brought up to Edge Hill by stationary engine and rope working, but later, steam engines were used to haul the trains. In those days a twelve-hour working day was the accepted thing but because of the amount of smoke and steam which collected in the tunnel the men were put on an eight-hour day, a rare occurrence at the time. They were also allowed to have 'Welsh-blind' coal, which was a soft and almost smokeless fuel. This tended to swell up in a red mass in the firebox, unlike the usual Yorkshire sharp coal which ignited quickly and needed lots of secondary air from the firebox doors to disperse the dense smoke. Furthermore, they were awarded a twenty-minute meal break!

At Crown Street coal yard, where the Liverpool–Manchester Railway first started, young firemen used to explore the old engine houses, smoke shafts and tunnels hewn out of solid rock. Most of the tunnels which ran under Edge Hill were financed by Mr Joseph Williamson, a retired tobacco importer, to give work to the poor. It is thought that there are some as yet undiscovered. The old booking office of the Liverpool–Manchester Railway can still be entered to this day as it was carved out of solid rock.[43]

Railway tunnels have a certain mystery and attraction for the railway enthusiast, but for the men who needed to work in them during the years of steam they were places fraught with special problems, as Hulme discovered in his early runs through the tunnels near Edge Hill:

It was quite a frightening experience going in the tunnel for the first time with its everlasting pall of smoke which spewed out all day from the tunnel mouth. Engines always went down tender first in order to work up engine first. They were swallowed up in the smoke as soon as they entered the tunnel. Under the bowels of Liverpool we were never at any time able to catch a glimpse of the exit or even a pinprick of light. The only way the driver knew we were nearing the entrance to Waterloo dock yard was that the gradient started to level out, causing a reduction in speed. When this happened we would strain our eyes, staring through the muck, trying to see whether the signal that allowed us into the yard was off or on.[44]

Edge Hill men were masters of tunnel working. If slipping of engine wheels got very bad it was often difficult to discover which way the train was moving in the murk and gloom, and the only method of finding out, apart from putting on the brake, was to put the shovel against the tunnel wall.

Just inside the entrance of the tunnel at Park Lane goods yard, we used to couple up to the train which had been put there by hydraulic capstans. The guard would go round his train, then inform the driver as to his load; walking back out of the tunnel to his brake van he pulled a lever which was attached to a gong in the tunnel by a strong wire. On hearing the gong, the driver knew that the guard had got back to the brake van and he then 'gave the gun' to the engine, meaning that maximum steam was applied to get the train out of the tunnel.[45]

Hulme once asked a driver, 'How, in the blackness of the tunnel and with the engine blowing off steam, would the engine crew know that the guard was ready if the gong was muffled by the noise of the engine?' The driver admitted that 'A green light could not be seen, neither could the guard come forward and give the driver instructions.' He continued, 'The driver took an empty Woodbine packet from his vest pocket and attached it to the gong cable. The gong went unheard, but the furious activity of the Woodbine packet gave the driver the signal to set back.'[46] The skill of Edge Hill men working in tunnels was never better illustrated than in the story of a train worked by these men between Edge Hill and Healey Mills, and Hulme has written:

> The Healey Mills job in the link was much sought after by men, who would change their turns with others to try and work it. It necessitated working overtime; sometimes in the winter months, the men would work fourteen and sixteen hours per day on this job. They would relish this and openly boast about it. One of the old drivers told me years ago this Healey Mills job was an Edge Hill lodging turn to Farnley Junction, and he recalled the struggle they had with the return job over the 'new line' from Farnley to Heaton Lodge.
>
> They had to have a bank engine from Heckmondwike up through Gomersal tunnel, and anyone with experience with bank engines knows that they make a lot of smoke and little else. But the Edge Hill men rectified this, for close by Farnley lodging house was a tyre-disposal yard. The men booking on duty at night quite easily came across an old tyre; this they stored on the engine. When approaching the entrance to Gomersal tunnel with the return train they put the tyre in the firebox and closed the firehole doors. It doesn't want much imagining what the stench was like at the rear of the train. The bank engine men did some really stirring work in getting those trains out of that tunnel.[47]

The firing of steam boilers owed little to theory and much to practice. Firing skills were achieved on the foot-plate in traffic. Ron Smith has described for us his early attempts at mastery over the fiery furnace:

When I was sixteen I went out on temporary firing on the Southall West Junction Pilot with Ted Redrup. This was Ted's regular job. On shunting, he had no regular fireman. Ted was a nice chap and taught me a lot; he started by telling me to watch the pressure gauge and the water level in the boiler and showed me how to fire the engine. It all seemed so easy to start with but when we actually started shunting I found that I was being thrown backwards and forwards in the cab and the water level would not keep still. I was terrified, and wondered how I was going to be able to fire the engine while it was moving if I was having to hang onto the hand brake and the gauge frame to keep my balance and not let go. Ted soon saw my plight, probably because the steam pressure was dropping. Anyway, he stopped the engine for a moment and told me that if I placed my legs apart and let myself sway with the movement I would be all right.

We started shunting again and I tried to put into practice all he had told me but I think for the first hour or so most of the coal ended up on the floor after hitting the firehole doors—this not only made a mess but also jarred one's shoulder blades. By tea-time I was becoming quite proficient, and felt very happy with the job; that was until after tea when Ted told me we would have to fill the tank and clean the fire. The water column with its long cast-iron arm and its huge leather pipe was very difficult to manage and while inserting the hose into the tank I was very frightened of falling off the tank— a drop of about twelve feet to the ground. Once the hose was in the tank I had to haul down a long chain to start it filling and keep the chain held down until the tank was full. This took about ten minutes and by that time my arms were about ready to fall off. Different types of water columns that spring to mind are numerous; the one at West Ealing was drinking water while the one at Brentford docks was canal water! It was easier on the fireman if it was one controlled by a wheel valve on the ground which the driver operated, but you dare not let your mind wander on this one because if the tank overflowed it was the driver who got the soaking. In the winter it was much worse. The water columns were kept from freezing by coal-burning braziers at the foot of the column; these were known as 'frost-devils'. These did not stop the leather hose from freezing, and although the water flowed, the 'bag' had to be hammered into the tank hole with the blunt end of the coal pick.

Our meal break was rather long owing to the fact that we had to wait for trains to come in from the Midland Region—these would stop right beside our engine to take on water etc., and it gave me an opportunity to chat with firemen from other regions. I was quite surprised at some of the things I saw and learned—for instance, several of the firemen were rather old. This was because they did not want to leave their homes around London to take up driving appointments in the Midlands or Scotland; they would rather stay as firemen at their own depots until a driving vacancy occurred there. I also discovered that when they took their engines back to shed they had to drop the fire, clean the smoke-box and ashpan, etc. before they booked off. I was surprised also to learn that their drivers had their own personal hand lamps, which we didn't, and that a lot of their bigger engines had rocking firegrates, hopper ashpans and self-cleaning smoke-boxes which did in fact make life a little easier for them. They were issued with cleaning cloths whereas we only got a ball of cotton waste. Despite all these discoveries I still felt that ours were the better engines and I was a member of the better region.

Anyone who has worked with coal will know just how dirty that can be. Add a few splashes of cylinder oil for good measure and you can imagine the state of drivers and firemen. Bicycle clips round overall legs and a red spotted hanky round your neck were the best you could do to try and stop the dust. It was a dirty, dangerous and uncomfortable job. I don't want to make it sound the worse job there was from those angles; it certainly was not. I always have and always will have the greatest admiration for the coal miners, farm labourers, navvies and many others who have a damn sight more dangerous, dirty and uncomfortable jobs than foot-plate work.[48]

From his earliest days a railway fireman was caught up with railway tradition, and the most powerful connection with the past was the age and history of the steam locomotive, as Ron Smith has observed:

One of the things that fascinated me was the age of the engines. We had an engine at Southall, No. 1925, that was built about 1883 and was not scrapped until 1950. Sixty-seven years' service. We would sometimes have rare visitors such as a 'Duke' class loco. I was on coal stage duty one day when one of the last 'Dukes' came in; *Trevithick* was the name. As I moved this grand old lady up to the coal stage it seemed that generations of drivers and firemen were on the foot-plate with me, and I thought as I ran my fingers round the regulator, smooth and worn by calloused hands, 'What tales you could tell.' She had spent sixty years on the railway and I a mere two and a half. If only she could have spoken!

There were tears in my eyes when I failed my eyesight test to become a fireman. I left the railway for good in 1956.[49]

Ritson Graham, who began his railway life as a locomotive fireman at the Durran Hill engine shed, Carlisle, had a different approach to working on the main line, and he has written:

I thoroughly enjoyed the main-line journeys. Although it was a hard and long slog up to Ais Gill on the Pennines every time out, it was through some of the finest scenery in the country. I had special and personal reasons to be concerned and was deeply interested in the countryside we passed through, for I was familiar with most of it in my natural history wanderings. When it was known to my workmates that I would be sleeping in a certain barn at the foot of Cross Fell, they would give me a blast on the whistle as they passed, or if nearer at hand, as in Baron Wood, or the Eden Valley, a day-time toot or a distant wave of the hand indicated that I was recognized by the men on the foot-plate. This interest in the ever-changing line-side scene was no less during the hours of darkness when the countryside was wrapped in soft and silent mystery. The shadowy fells looming in all around us as we passed through the Pennines, the many valleys, high, wind-swept viaducts, and the plunging into countless blinding tunnels were pleasures which never palled. Winter or summer, day or night, when not engaged in feeding the insatiable furnace, I had my head out of the cab exposed to the rush of cool mountain air while noting the ever-changing scene and the details of the varied topography. To view the sun rise over the long Dent Valley, the May dawn breaking over Cross Fell, or the white moorland mist enveloping the hills are memories that last a lifetime.

The botany of the banks and the steep-sided cuttings was of absorbing interest and the miles of rail-side ditches were intently scrutinized for the effects of snow, gales and rain-started landslides.

When other people's 'weeds' were my wild flowers and their 'vermin' my small mammals, I was evidently out of step. This brought me more into my own company, to think my own thoughts and to make a fat, ever-expanding world of my own. These two factors, an attachment to the countryside and a zest for reading, were no passing phase, short-lived youthful enthusiasms, but grew stronger with practice and experience. My reading was not recreational, but a search for information, to discover all I could about the vast and wonderful world outside my very limited experience and restricted environment.[50]

Ritson Graham, 'the sparrow chaser' to men who could not appreciate his feelings for the countryside, went on to become Councillor, Mayor of Carlisle and a Freeman of the City. Included in his career were fourteen years as a trade-union lay official, President of the city's natural history society and a writer and lecturer on countryside matters. He has written: 'To have to go to bed three times in twenty-four hours to obtain six hours of sleep is not a practice to be recommended.'[51]

The foot-plate was no place for timid souls. Bucking and tossing through tired, darkened cities, pounding up the Pennines or down Grampian slopes, swallowed up in the slavering jaws of doom-black tunnels, the fireman formed an alliance with his engine unlike any other combination of man and metal. Keeping his feet, plying his shovel hour after hour, his back and legs streaming with boiling sweat, the fireman epitomized the power of machine plus man. The firebox was a red and ravenous maw which, day after day, night after night, drained his stamina and tortured his muscles. On a 200-mile run a fireman could expect to shovel up to six tons of coal and boil about 12,000 gallons of water. An express engine would consume between forty and fifty pounds of coal per mile. The coal would vary from huge slabs—'long toms'— to the finest of 'bug dust'. The largest coals were broken by a coal pick and presented to the furnace in pieces twice the size of a normal fist. Dust was shovelled in a ratio of three to one, as both large lumps and dashes of dust would reduce the white-hot furnace to a dull red glare with disastrous effects on steam pressure.

Few firemen would reckon to sit down during a four or five-hour trip on an express engine. To sit was to surrender, to accept the need for relaxation, and on an express train no diminution of concentration was possible.

Apart from the shovelling and the curtain of sweat which protected his back and legs from burning in the furnace heat, the fireman was expected to be free to observe all signal boxes on his side of the track, and to check that no emergency signal was being displayed by the signal-man. He was obliged to check at frequent intervals if the train was following in good order. Emergency signals, from whatever source, had to be communicated immediately to the driver. All this was done by sign language, for the noise in the cab of a steam locomotive made speech impossible.

For the firing of engines on the main line, conditions were rarely perfect. There was, however, a foot-plate 'Shangri-La'. It consisted of signing on duty at 9.00 a.m. (office hours) and, with a cool spring day for the journey, a nice 100-mile run on a free steaming engine driven by a pleasant mate. Foot-platemen, however, rarely kept office time. They were always more familiar with the hours between midnight and 6.00 a.m. Theirs was a job in which the battle for sleep was as real as the daily struggle in the cab. Sleep was the only balm, alcohol being a dangerous alternative. A full night's sleep was a rarity for firemen, and they often went to bed twice or thrice a day to be fit for work. Using a combination of inherited and proven techniques, plus brute strength, the railway fireman conquered his machine every hour, every day of the timetable. His like will probably never be seen again; his skills are already part of industrial archaeology.

6

Engine-Drivers

The engine-driver is no mere regulator pusher, any more
than his fireman is a mere coal heaver. For all its massive
bulk a steam locomotive is a machine as sensitive as a
racehorse . . .

L. T. C. Rolt,
Red for Danger

In the 1970s the British travelling public held two strongly contrasting
views about engine-drivers. To the railway traveller who recalled the
days of steam, the typical engine-driver was a large, beefy, weather-
beaten and heavy-booted figure excluding bluffness and geniality, a
trusted coal-stained representative of solidity and service. The newer
view, the attitude of the hard-pressed commuter on electric- and
diesel-hauled trains, presents the driver as a brash and mindless militant who, at the release of a dead-man's handle, can reduce travellers
to despair and industries to impotence. Each view contains vestigial
truths and is the result of historic development and social change.

Few people come into contact with engine-drivers. The craft remains
a mystery, despite a century of romantic publicity. There have been only
four generations of engine-men, three of these almost wholly on steam.
From the humblest of beginnings the drivers of steam engines rapidly
became the aristocrats of the line. This was based on the rigorous selection process and the respectability engine-men were to enjoy once they
were appointed. Rewards could be high, the prestige of driving royalty
being an example. But it was a cruel profession, for the smallest reduction in eyesight or other physical standards could mean demotion from
the main line to shunting on a siding, or, much worse, the humility of
messroom cleaner or lavatory attendant. One of the most fascinating
aspects of a train driver is how his eyes appear to be a decade younger
than the rest of his physical attributes. In the days of steam, the necessity to keep good eyesight was paramount, yet not until the last days
of steam power were engine-men encouraged to wear protective eye-
pieces. Drivers of steam engines were never allowed to wear spectacles
to assist in the observance of signals.

In the earliest days, drivers were free agents. In search of higher
wages, better conditions or warmer climes, a driver moved easily be-

tween companies filling driving vacancies. These vacancies could vary from opportunities presented by commercial expansion to pure strike-breaking.

Like so many others in the new industry, the first engine-man had no antecedents in his job. He was neither artisan nor journeyman, engineer nor tradesman. He had no apprenticeships or assessed examinations to offer his employer. Many of them were recruited from that hive of industrial expertise, the north-east; one writer has recorded that:

> Largely by the Stephensons' influence, men from the north-east were sought for to drive the locomotives on new railways as they came into operation all over the kingdom; even the far-off London and Greenwich sent to the north for drivers in 1838. Two drivers named Weatherburn were in charge of engines on the opening day of the Liverpool and Manchester. George Stephenson was assisted by driver Weatherburn on the foot-plate of the inaugural train on the Leicester and Swannington in 1832. . . . Years later, in 1859, Henry Weatherburn, of the South-Eastern Railway, requested and was given a place in Westminster Abbey at Robert Stephenson's funeral on the grounds that he had driven in the first locomotive, the *Harvey Combe*, used on construction of the London and Birmingham line. These men were probably brothers from Tyneside.[1]

For a worker, this was a singular honour, an early recognition that a new tradition was being born, one based upon service and responsibility.

This new responsibility did not always accord with the views of many railway officials, however. For example, Isambard Kingdom Brunel, engineer of the Great Western Railway, wished his men to be part of the engine, arguing:

> . . . I am not one to sneer at education, but I would not give 6*d*. in hiring an engine-man because of his knowing how to read or write. . . . it is impossible that a man that indulges in reading should make a good engine-driver; it requires a *species of machine*, an intelligent man, a sober man, a steady man, but I would rather not have a thinking man.[2]

In 1838, with experimental locomotives, problematic track and rudimentary signalling, it was of course difficult to expect engine-men to have thoughts very far removed from driving engines. Yet the engine-men were a new breed of artisan, a special class of worker, for the lives of passengers were the commodity in which they dealt. They needed the triple qualities of physical endurance, mathematical skill and a modicum of literary ability to perform their duties. Ignorance of printed and posted rules, regulations and amendments could not be pleaded; it was the responsibility of the engine-man to miss nothing relevant to his duties. The reading driver had come to stay, despite Brunel.

Despite the demand for such skills and responsibilities, the companies were not prepared for many years to consider the engine-man as worthy of the rights which should have accompanied those responsibilities. The Liverpool and Manchester Railway was a trailblazer in the field of draconic labour control, one of its innovations being the placing under contract of a number of its top engine-men; this decision was an important feature of the engine-men's strike of 1836. In that year a number of engine-men on the L and M stopped work in support of an increase in pay for the engine firemen employed by the company. '. . . the Treasurer asked John Hewitt, one of the oldest engine-men, whether he persisted in that [strike] notice, and Hewitt answering that he did, the Treasurer discharged him instantly.'[3] Driver Hewitt's dismissal brought out on strike most of the L and M engine-men, and Hewitt made history as the first engine-driver to be victimized for taking part in an industrial dispute. It was a reprisal which might have raised an admonitory eyebrow from the Iron Duke himself.

Four of the strikers contracted to the company were sentenced to one month's hard labour for breach of contract. The time was served at Kirkdale prison and six hours of each day were spent on the dreaded treadmill. At a meeting of the directors on 18 February 1836, a letter was read from the prisoners, who expressed sorrow for their offences and appealed to the directors for help. The directors at first refused to interfere but on the intervention of the prison chaplain they relented and the engine-men were released. A stint on the treadmill obviously concentrated the minds of the strikers on their tasks, for we learn that, in 1842, two of them were awarded £5 for good conduct. This was equivalent to at least two weeks' earnings.

The railway companies generally conceded that the engine-men were the key grade. In times of falling receipts, however, they could expect no better treatment than that afforded 'lesser grades'. An episode on the North Midland Railway in 1843 was a salutary lesson for the engine-men.

The North Midland Railway, built between Derby and Leeds at a total cost of £3 million, was by 1843 a poor investment. Dividends had reached such low levels as $3\frac{1}{2}$ per cent in 1841, $2\frac{5}{8}$ per cent in 1842 and $3\frac{1}{2}$ per cent in 1843. George Hudson, Chairman of the York and North Midland Railway, was appointed to a committee inquiring into this situation and in this capacity was able to prove that he was not only a financial manipulator but that he had also a firm practical grasp of detailed railway management.

A sub-committee of the board met at Derby on 6 December 1842 to discuss cuts in expenditure. It was agreed to discharge five drivers and five firemen from the company, and while the remaining drivers' wages stayed the same, firemen suffered a reduction to a level recommended by the committee of inquiry. Drivers' wages were 7s. per day, and firemen went from their previous rate of 4s. to 3s. 9d. per day. The men would run trains every day of the week with only one day off every other week, when they would be rested without pay. A day's work would consist of a run between Derby and Leeds and back—146 miles—without limitation of hours.

Faced with a strike, the North Midland Railway paid off its enginemen without notice and engaged fresh men, many of whom had been discharged with bad character references from other companies. The line was thrown into such disorder that the company was forced to pay a week's wages to strikers in order to keep it open.

In February 1843, the Railway Department of the Board of Trade intervened, indicating its displeasure at the inexpediency of sudden and sweeping reductions affecting the engine-men, upon whose skill and good conduct the safety of the passengers and the line depended. In a letter dated 7 February 1843, from Mr S. Laing of the Railway Department to the Secretary of the North Midland Railway, it was stated that 'making every engine-man drive 146 miles per diem for seven days in the week with the exception of only alternate Sundays is too harassing for the men and calculated to lead to accidents . . . the former system, which allows reasonable intervals of rest, should be substituted. . . .'

The reply of the company, dated 10 February 1843, argued that the action taken was forced upon the company by the refusal of the engine-men to submit to a reasonable and proper reduction. To make the engine-men masters of the line was to compromise the safety of the public by the absence of discipline and subjugation. According to the company, the engine-men had made no complaints of over-exertion and had expressed themselves perfectly satisfied with the existing arrangements. The power of the company was such that, even though the striking engine-men offered to resume work at the old rates of pay, the company refused reinstatement.[4]

The idea that discipline and subjugation were the key to the effective running of the lines was reflected in the companies' policy of fines. Drivers on the London and South-Western were, as early as 1847, fined for arriving three minutes early at a destination. In addition, they lost the trip money for the journey. Drivers could be fined for allowing engines to 'make smoke', for running short of steam, for not properly examining the engine and for not sending in daily reports at the proper time. Failure to take over an engine half an hour before departure could, on the LSWR, cost a driver half a day's pay.[5]

The North British Railway also achieved a special reputation of recalcitrance towards engine-men. The fining of engine-drivers was an early feature of company policy, and continued right up to 1914. The margins for error were very small and the fines often very severe, causing Thomas Sunter, General Secretary, ASLEF, 1855 to 1901, to write just before the turn of the century:

> If the men are to be fined, it should be done only after a thorough investigation by representatives of the companies and the men. It is a very serious matter to be fined . . . in some cases £5, plus suspension, for not being at the call of the company day and night, seven days a week, when the companies pay only for time actually worked. As they demand all time, it is only fair that they pay a full week's wages, instead of only a few shillings, for working short time.[6]

Things were even worse than Mr Sunter feared. Staff relationships on the North British were something at which to marvel, for its policy was simply that nothing must hinder the successful development of this thrusting new railway. The North British recruited its staff by offering 6d. more per day than its rival, the Edinburgh and Glasgow. When the staff was appointed the offer was withdrawn. Dismissal was summary, but staff had to give good reason and proper notice of resignation. In 1850, the driver and fireman who left their jobs without notice were arrested, taken before an Edinburgh magistrate and sentenced to three months in prison. A standard punishment for errant drivers was a spell in the workshops, where they suffered a reduction in pay. In the same year, the company decided that drivers would, on their shed day, be paid 4s. per shift, considerably less than their wages on the engine. There was resistance, the drivers agreeing to work twelve hours per day, but insisting that if the reduction took place they would resign. Before the deadline of 30 March 1850, thirty-eight men were dismissed. As the cuts were implemented, sixty-two North British men left their posts, leaving the company with two foot-platemen. As J. Thomas, historian of the North British, records:

> The striking railwaymen . . . paraded the Edinburgh streets with placards warning the public of the danger of travelling on North British trains. . . . The North British sent a blacklist of strikers to all Scottish railways and to the LNWR and GWR and other lines reciprocated by sending the North British lists of men who had been dismissed for 'forming combinations'.[7]

The men on strike were replaced by mechanics and men from the street. This was a far cry from 1849, when 200 men from the North British entertained the head of the locomotive department, Mr Thornton, to a supper at which he was presented with a case of silver-mounted mathematical instruments. On the North British, more than the Tay Bridge fell short of expectations.

Railway by-laws bore heavily on the early engine-men. Wastage of fuel could mean dismissal. Drivers who disobeyed caution or stop signals faced arrest and sentence by a magistrate. Collisions could mean imprisonment. Some idea of the harshness of the task can be seen in the treatment of driver McCulloch of the Caledonian Railway. In 1881, McCulloch had thirty-three years' service to the Caledonian, twenty-six as a driver. For overshooting the signals at Rutherglen, due to brake failure, this driver was arrested and taken handcuffed to Perth prison, where he was imprisoned for four months.

From the earliest days, drivers were subject to a ladder-type of promotion known as classification. Under this system, promotion depended upon the type of work performed, seniority and merit. Classification was a method of getting work done cheaply and keeping men in situations where betterment always beckoned. Drivers, except those at the top enjoying the benefits of the best work, argued that classification was for animals, not men, and that all drivers were responsible for the observation of rules and regulations to the same degree. In the 1850s on the London and North-Western Railway, there were five separate classes of engine-driver, ranging in wages from 8s. to 5s. 6d. per day. In the engine sheds men were known by their classification—'8s. a day men' or '7s. a day men'. In England and Wales in 1904, when the classification system was in full swing, only 931 drivers out of 21,000 were getting the maximum of 48s. per week. In this period, the average wage for drivers was just below £2 per week. In Scotland and Ireland many drivers were receiving less than 30s. per week.[8] Classification, widely regarded as humiliating and divisive, was theoretically abolished in 1931, but the system dragged on through the 1970s and will still be causing problems in the 1980s through the running of the Advanced Passenger Trains and the High-Speed Trains.

By 1858, the London and North-Western Railway had instituted a scheme whereby, under a special contract, elite engine-men performed important purchasing and book-keeping duties, which saved many hours of clerical labour in the office. By almost removing the driver from the wages grade, an illusion of association with management was achieved. Under an agreement between the company and driver Longstaff, dated 1 May 1858, we learn that the driver not only paid his fireman but also the men who cleaned his engine. Under the contract the driver agreed to any 'reasonable fine that my superintendent may inflict, pay for any damage to the engine or stock'. In the case of breakdowns, should another engine be needed to assist that of driver Longstaff, he paid for the assisting engine at 2d. per mile. Driver Longstaff bought his own stores and here is his list in 1858:

Prices to be charged for stores

Coke	24s. per ton
Coal	12s. per ton
Oil	3d. per pint
Yellow Grease	2d. per pint
Cotton Waste	2d. per pound
Firewood	6d. per cwt.
Spun Yarn	4d. per pound
Cotton Wick	1s. per pound
Tender Brake Blocks	7d. each
Tender Hoses	3s. 6d. per foot

The men upon whom such responsibilities were placed were eulogized by many writers. H. A. Simmons, for instance, wrote of the drivers he met on the Great Western Railway: 'It is simply marvellous that with such a training we have at the present day such an immense number of worthy men as engine-drivers. . . . During my railway career I never recollect receiving an unkind word or act from an engine-driver and I contend that they are marvels of manufacture.'[9]

The Scottish author R. M. Ballantyne was in no doubt about the quality of engine-drivers north of the Tweed and he wrote in his book *The Iron Horse*: 'John Marrot was an engine-driver on the Grand National Trunk Railway. This is equivalent to saying that he was a steady, sober, trustworthy man. None but men of the best character are now-a-days put in so responsible a position.' When Marrot went visiting on a particular occasion he apologized because he possessed no visiting card, but indicated that, '. . . if you'll just say that it's John Marrot the engine-driver, I daresay that'll do for a free pass.' It did. According to Ballantyne, 'Marrot, because of his superior character and abilities, was in receipt of £2 10s. weekly . . . seeing that the lives of so many persons depended on the constancy of his coolness, courage and vigilance.'[10]

In February 1888, the *Locomotive Journal* was complaining that the public at large were almost entirely unaware of the responsibilities, difficulties and hardships encountered by the engine crew as they went about their business. In that year the 30,000 strong grade of enginemen could point to the end product of their labours in the following terms.

Route mileage in Great Britain 1888	19,000
Total railway staff	350,000
Number of passenger carriages	33,000
Number of goods wagons, not including privately owned wagons	500,000
Number of passenger miles run	143 million
Total of goods, mineral and miscellaneous miles run	272 million
Number of locomotives in traffic	15,000
Railway income all sources	£70 million
Total railway expenses	£37 million
Gross profit	£33 million

At this time the London and North-Western Railway, the largest single company in Britain, had a locomotive fleet worth more than £5 million. The staff of 45,000 found themselves indebted to the company for its patronage—whole areas owed their livelihood to the presence of the 'Wessy'. In the early 1890s, another great company, the Great Western Railway, was paying drivers with ten years' service the princely sum of 7s. 6d. per day. Firemen with six years' service were getting 4s. 6d. per day.

In an article in the *Railway Magazine* of 1897, one writer records of apprenticeship that:

> The period of training is longer than the ordinary term of apprenticeship considered necessary to render a man an expert craftsman in any other particular trade which he may take up as a means of earning his livelihood, and to follow the career of an engine-driver from the time he enters the railway service until he is promoted to the position of an express passenger train driver would take more space than can be allotted to this article. In most trades the skill of the workman is equally valuable wherever he may be employed; but unfortunately this is not altogether the case with the engine-driver, whose knowledge is essentially limited to his particular line.[11]

As track layout and signalling systems become more complicated, it was essential that the men working over the lines could, in severe climatic conditions, recognize every installation on the route by shape and sound only. It was this specialized knowledge which gave drivers confidence in the worst of blizzards and fogs.

It led also to the founding of a craft union for engine-men. On 7 February 1880, William Ullyot of Sheffield enrolled as the first member of the Associated Society of Locomotive Engineers and Firemen. It was not, however, until the successful railway strike in August 1911 that the new union obtained full negotiating rights. The struggle for union recognition for engine-men was long and arduous. In the early days the very idea of a union for these men was anathema to the companies. One of the company men who expressed this hostility was Mr Daniel Gooch, Chief Mechanical Engineer of the Great Western, whose respect for engine-men would not run to recognition of the trade union for foot-platemen.

Daniel Gooch could be forgiven in the 1840s for questioning the validity and seriousness of the petitions, memorials and round robins which were circulating on his territory. A self-made young man, Gooch could see the remarkable Great Western ethic beginning to flourish, an ethic which gave every member of the staff access to management, provided housing for its key grades and insisted upon sick pay schemes. For the period, the rulers of the Great Western were model employers, light years ahead of their contemporaries in manufacturing industries, but this enlightenment did not include day to day negotiations with elected representatives of the staff. Respect for the staff was one thing—trade union recognition another. Even the engine-drivers, the doyens of the system, failed to persuade Daniel Gooch of the reasonableness of their request.

Worse still was the opposition which came from within the engine-men's own ranks. While the most craft- and class-conscious engine-men were agitating for recognition and status, a self-appointed apologist for the Great Western Railway wrote to The Times in 1862, when Mr Cobbett, MP, was trying to introduce a bill to limit the hours worked by engine-men:

> Sir, I am surprised by the motion of Mr Cobbett for the protection of engine-men that the Great Western men are classified with those who claim the protection of Parliament.
>
> I wish to advise you that so long as our esteemed Chief Superintendent is at our head we need no other protection. In twenty-two years on the Great Western I have never heard his name mentioned except with the greatest respect.[12]

Without recognition, without representation, without right of appeal, the engine-men could achieve singularity and independence of action only when they stepped onto their foot-plates, where, shackled to the clock by invisible chains, choked by fog and dashed by storm, they began to think out for themselves new philosophies and policies. The motto the engine-men eventually proclaimed to the world was 'The public safety and our own protection'.

A locomotive cab epitomized the theory of defensible space. The driver brooked no argument or interference from anyone. Without his permission, neither patriarch nor plebian passed beyond his engine-cab doors. The cab was the private place in which were plotted the tactics necessary to overcome the natural and human barriers to be faced on the daily run. Inclement weather, an inexperienced fireman, a shy-of-steam engine, a sluggish signalman and more were all sifted and sorted in the mind of the driver while he got on with the job of train driving and timekeeping.

In the days before automatic train control and colour-light signalling, the engine-driver could boast that he was master of his craft and in full control of the territory over which his wheels were pounding. In the days of steam, there were two men, but only one decision-maker in each cab. This territorial control was evident when it was stated at the Select Committee of 1891 that 'On the Mellis and Eye or Framlingham line, the railway, you may say, belongs to them, and no one else is allowed to poke his nose in.' It was difficult for management not to be irritated by knowledge of how engine-men ran the trains to suit themselves. In 1889 Sir Edward Watkin of the Manchester, Sheffield and Lincolnshire Railway divested himself of the opinion that on the Metropolitan Railway at least, 'the punctuality of the trains is admirable, but it is not the engine-driver, the guard or the signalman who is to be credited with that accomplishment, but the management.'[13] Scotland gives us another example of local fervour and territorialism. When the West Highland Line was absorbed into the London and North-Eastern Railway there remained a feeling among the staff that 'the men of that company were a race apart.'[14]

In the same period, hundreds of miles to the south, a similar territorialism could be observed. H. A. Simmons recorded an entanglement with a truculent engine-man on the Great Western Railway:

James Sandy, our branch engine-driver, was a troublesome man. He was quick, obliging and above the average of engine-drivers, so far as intelligence was concerned, but he had some dreadful failings, for he was fond of beer, fond of showing off with his engines, fond of mischief, had a dreadful habit of procrastination, was very hasty, and never saw danger . . . many a lecture I read Sandy. . . . Sandy would reform for about three days, after which he would bring me a bundle of watercress gathered from a spring a few miles up the line, at which spot, in the face of all orders, he would pull up a goods train and let it stand on the line while he gathered watercress. I did not know of this last irregularity for some time, otherwise I should have refused the cress.[15]

In the 1920s this tradition was still carried on. There was driver Bell in Scotland, a man who had previously been a gamekeeper. He always carried a gun with him, and often shot at rabbits as the train was climbing the gradient between Inveramsay and Pitcaple, sending his fireman back to retrieve the victim. It was said that when on the 12.01 a.m. goods from Kittybrewster to Elgin he would arrange his arrival at Cairnie Junction so that he was shunted for other trains. He generally used this time to replenish his larder.[16]

Throughout the years of steam, drivers would not tolerate insubordination on the foot-plate. When Victor Lockey was portering at Oxford in 1920, he witnessed a scene in which a fireman swore at a driver; the driver ordered the fireman back to the shed and refused to move the train until a fresh fireman was obtained.

What really marked off the engine-driver from his contemporaries, on the railway and off, was the length of his normal shift, the peculiarities of shift hours and the problem of the split shift. In the earliest days, excessive hours were not the exception but the rule, part of a regularly occurring, precisely calculated system of exploitation. At this time, all of the driver's time belonged to the company. In the hours these men laboured can be seen the true level of exploitation inflicted on them by the freebooting representatives of the employer, to whom 'the company' and its interests were paramount.

In those early days there existed no regulation days. The week was divided into seven units, but there were no days or nights, just periods on and off duty. Twelve-hour shifts were meant to be the rule, but could not be relied upon by the drivers. Shifts of double and treble that figure were quite blatantly insisted upon by the foremen. A day's pay was awarded when the foreman considered that the man on the engine could do no more. No shift period, limited by law, safeguarded either the engine-driver or the passengers in his care.

There was no pay for overtime. As no real working period was stipulated, overtime could begin only with the approval of the shed foreman. Sunday duty was not paid for, but engine-drivers were not prevented on free Sundays from entering the shed and making minor repairs to their engines, as well as cleaning and polishing the machines.

For many years agreed rostering arrangements were non-existent. The driver sat at home, 'on call', his nerves keyed to the tap on the door which presaged the urgent summons—'on at once'. Neither personal nor family problems could challenge this summons. Once on duty there was no telling when he would return. If he did not respond to the summons, he lost pay for that shift, with the prospect of a later fine or even suspension. There could be no 'St Monday' for him as there was in other industries, a Monday off following a Sunday spree. The first engine-drivers were largely prisoners in their own kitchens, but once at work became a marvellously flexible 'piece of equipment'. After the longest shift on duty, there existed no law which gave the driver a stipulated period of rest between his working periods. The turn of duty could be twenty continuous hours on Monday, five hours on Tuesday and fifteen on Wednesday. 'No call' on Thursday meant no wages, and the week could finish with two final turns of unlimited duration.

As early as 1842, the Board of Trade was drawing attention, through its Railway Department, to the question of the danger to the public when railway servants were kept on duty for extended hours. As late as the 1870s, the position was that many grades of railway worker had a seven-day week while others had a six-day week, competing railways providing different arrangements.[17] In 1871, the Amalgamated Society of Railway Servants was founded and its journal, the *Railway Service Gazette* soon opened its columns to the campaign for shorter hours, and many erudite correspondents graced its pages with letters which demolished the paternalistic humbug which passed for staff relationships within the industry. The ASRS argued that although wages were a matter between masters and men, working hours were a question which materially affected the travelling public, and that this was especially true of the engine-men.

In the early 1870s, the foot-platemen of the Taff Vale Railway were expected to work turns of up to twenty-six hours, and one of these advised the *Gazette* that he had been asleep at the controls of a heavy train, adding 'There are many more like me in this respect.'[18]

To argue their case against unreasonable hours, the union journal assembled a mass of evidence from men on the foot-plate. In the same era a man worked nineteen hours in a day; his train was booked out again in four or five hours, and he said he was too tired to come at that time. The company threatened him with dismissal so he was obliged to go back. Another case recorded in a letter stated:

> . . . an engine-man and fireman, having worked from 6.00 p.m. till 6.00 a.m. shunting, were . . . relieved. Just as they were going to bed, they were sent for to go on duty again at eleven o'clock of the same day. They did so, and worked eight hours, after which they were told to go on all night again without any rest, which would have made their turn of labour thirty-six hours, with only an interval of five hours. They refused to do this; and because they refused, only half-a-day's extra pay was allowed them for eight hours, so that they lost half-a-day.[19]

The continuing saga of overwork can be seen from this list of time worked by three engine-men, with their firemen, on the dates given.[20]

	On duty	Off duty	Hours	
8 December	3.00 a.m.	5.35 p.m.	14.35	
9 December	3.00 a.m.	8.55 p.m.	17.55	
10 December	3.00 a.m.	5.50 p.m.	14.50	
11 December	3.00 a.m.	12.00 midnight	21.00	
12 December	3.00 a.m.	3.50 p.m.	12.50	
13 December	3.00 a.m.	8.20 p.m.	17.20	98.30
15 December	3.00 a.m.	11.20 p.m.	20.20	
16 December	3.00 a.m.	5.40 p.m.	14.40	
17 December	3.00 a.m.	11.35 p.m.	20.35	
18 December	3.00 a.m.	12.10 a.m.	21.10	
19 December	3.00 a.m.	12.30 a.m.	21.30	
20 December	3.00 a.m.	3.30 p.m.	12.30	110.45

Total for 12 days=209 hours 15 minutes.

On the London and South-Western Railway, the men were faring little better, as can be instanced by the situation in which the 'six-wheeled goods' men of Southampton found themselves:

On the first day they work fifteen hours, and receive a day and a half's pay. On the second seventeen hours and forty minutes, and receive a day and a quarter's pay. The third day, twenty hours and thirty minutes, for a day and three quarters' wages. On the fourth day they are off duty, holding themselves in readiness for anything that may be required, and if not at home when required, are liable to be reported or fined; no payment for this. On the fifth day they work seven hours and a half in the shed for three-quarters' of a day's pay.

Second day's work: in this day's work the men have four hours at Dorchester; a half-day's pay is deducted for this. In this time the men have to attend to their engines, doing whatever may be required, and receiving no recompense. There is here a clear infraction of the promise you made to the men, that a half-hour should be allowed to get their engines ready, and a half-hour allowed to put their engines away, and that at Dorchester they should be allowed an hour and a half to do what was required to their engines.

Third day's work: work is done to the engine (for which there is a necessity, cleaning tubes, packing glands, etc.), which is evidently overlooked in paying the men a day and three-quarters' wages for being away from home twenty and a half hours.

Fourth day: is it not too much to expect the men to hold themselves in readiness in this manner?

Fifth day's work: if a principle could be laid down that the men should not work for less than a day at any one time, more satisfaction would be given. At one place the foreman does not book the men off at the correct time. With the stone train the average number of hours worked is fifteen and a quarter. The men are paid but a day and a quarter's wages for these days' work.

The following is a copy of a week's working, where the total number of hours worked were ninety-five and twenty-five minutes. Eight days' pay only was given for this week's work, so that the system is nearer the twelve than the ten hours—first day, 21 hours, 20 minutes; second day, off duty; third day, 15 hours, 20 minutes; fourth day, 13 hours; fifth day, 15 hours, 15 minutes; sixth day, 15 hours, 30 minutes, seventh day, 15 hours.

At one place the men work seventy-five hours for seven days' wages, and run 760 miles in the week. The scale of wages agreed to is not worked up to there, the driver receiving but 5s. 6d. per day, although he has been driving about seven years.[21]

It was not surprising that the men were complaining that they scarcely had the opportunity of taking food, except on the engine, and this desire for basic human treatment was heard two decades later during the Scottish strike of 1890. One of the strikers protested that this was a strike over hours and not wages by stating, 'We want more time to tell our wives that they are still our sweethearts.'[22]

By 1874, Taff Vale foot-platemen were 'enjoying' a basic week of sixty hours, but this could be achieved in three shifts of twenty consecutive hours or four consecutive shifts of fifteen hours' duration. By the end of 1874, Taff Vale engine-men had reverted to a basic week of seventy-two hours, and their appeal for remedial action was unsuccessful, the head engineer arguing that 'no other company allows shorter hours'. This was the company which inflicted fines on engine-men who left their foot-plates for a few moments to take their food in the warmth of a nearby cabin.

Drivers of the Staffordshire Railway were warned that 'if they refused overtime, they would be compelled to perform it'. Michael Reynolds, the engine-drivers' friend, wrote gloomily, '. . . eighteen or twenty hours a day on duty has been a very common occurrence, on an engine without any weather-board, and with wet sand-boxes, and in all sorts of hard weather, and we suspect in some instances with hard fare—very hard; but they have been buoyed up with the thought that their passenger days were ahead.'[23] The hope of the driver was that one day he would achieve the status of express driver, the fastest man on earth. This dream was always the top domino in the policy of the companies, who recognized the value of such a self-regulating ordinance. This dream was the basis of the legal servitude which retained such a grip on engine-men for more than a century.

In 1880, the Amalgamated Society of Railway Servants began a campaign for shorter hours. There was a new awareness that life was for living as well as for working, and that long hours precluded them from developing their mental faculties or cultivating their spiritual welfare. The new journal, the *Railway Service Gazette*, commented, 'The friendship of the past years has been replaced by mistrust and misgiving.'[24]

The mistrust and misgiving rampant in the industry seemed good for business. The year 1880 was very profitable for railway investors as the all-grades journal was quick to point out: [25]

ASPECTS OF RAILWAY WORKING, 1880

	£
Capital invested	728,000,000
Passenger traffic worth	27,200,000
Goods traffic worth	35,250,000
Passengers carried	604,000,000
Minerals carried (tons)	116,000,000
General merchandise carried (tons)	70,000,000
Miles run—all trains	241,000,000

1881 saw the beginning of the Railway Nine Hours Movement.[26] On 18 May of that year, 5,000 railway workers marched behind four brass bands to a meeting in the Exeter Hall, London, chaired by J. Passmore Edwards, MP. Except for a momentary hostility towards Sir Daniel Gooch and Sir Richard Moon, not the slightest disrespect was shown by the assembly to the railway officers. In that year of 1881, 1,180 railway workers were killed, and 6,692 injured while on duty.

In 1881 the Manchester, Sheffield and Lincolnshire Railway offered to reduce hours from ninety to seventy-two but also to reduce wages by 6d. to 1s. 6d. per day. In Sheffield, a number of drivers on this line wrote to colleagues at Gorton depot asking for support in an appeal to the company to retain hours and wages at the contemporary level. The ASRS argued that while wages were a matter between employers and employees, long hours of work caused accidents and were therefore a question which affected the travelling public.

There was plenty of evidence for their contention. There was a case in Bristol of a train being taken onto the wrong main line through overwork. Shifts of up to forty continuous hours were being worked in the Bristol area by guards and shunters. In defence of its position, the ASRS could present evidence of overwork in the previous decade which included complaints such as that of the Taff Vale policeman who wrote:

I am required to work 324 hours per month. Out of that a period of thirty-six hours is Sunday duty, for which I do not receive one single halfpenny. Through the great kindness of my employers I am allowed three days' leave of absence annually without stoppage of pay. Therefore I work six clear weeks every year for nothing.[27]

In the same period, the brakemen of the Caledonian Railway were totalling from ninety-six to 108 hours per week for earnings of 23s. On the London, Chatham and Dover Railway men of all grades were putting in the equivalent of twelve days' work in a week. Boat service men were putting in shifts of sixteen and seventeen consecutive hours when the boats were late.[28] Despite this evidence of overwork, the ASRS were still looking for co-operation, not conflict, and the union wrote to the North British Railway in 1889 regarding conditions of service:

If we are not favoured with a more satisfactory reply than that received from your Board, strained relationships between your Board and your employees may result. This committee, and the men, do not want any friction to exist, and hope that the question could be solved in a reciprocal spirit by you and ultimately be successful in promoting arrangements satisfactory to both sides, and prevent any friction on either side.

The railway companies fought hard and long against any statutory limitation on railway hours of work, but by 1890 the question had reached the stage of a Parliamentary Select Committee. The minutes of this inquiry provide one of the great social documents of the nineteenth century. By their insistence on extended hours the companies were exposed as organizations risking daily the lives of travellers and workers. Unfortunately, the elongation of turns of duty and the appalling accidents which resulted in the wake of such a policy continued long after the Select Committee had presented its report.

In that year, three accidents attributable to long hours occurred. At Westland Row Station, Dublin, on 10 July 1890, two locomotives collided. One of the drivers had been on duty for nineteen and a half continuous hours. The driver of the other locomotive had been on duty for sixteen and three-quarter hours at the moment of impact. On 12 June 1890, at Eastleigh, on the London and South-Western Railway, an engine ran into the back of a train; here the driver and fireman had been on duty for sixteen and a half hours. On the Great Northern Railway on 24 December 1890, a collision occurred in which the driver and fireman had been on duty for eighteen and a half hours.

Giving evidence to the Select Committee, Mr Henry Tennant, a director of the North-Eastern Railway, argued that in his opinion a ten-hour working day on the railway was not a possibility. He attributed this to

> ... the fluctuating character of the traffic. ... Then the weather does not admit of the work being done evenly. Then there is another reason, that the public demand train services and facilities that would place intolerable burdens upon the railway companies if the hours of the men were limited to ten hours per day.[29]

Supporting this argument, Mr Thompson, the managerial hero of the Motherwell evictions in 1890, argued that, 'The only thing which, in my opinion, would justify the limitation and fixing of hours of railway working, which also practically means the fixing of wages, would be if the state were prepared to take over the entire railway system.'[30]

In their struggle for better hours, the engine-men found a friend in Mr Charles Bradlaugh, the iconoclastic MP for Northampton, who chided the companies for their cold reception to the Parliamentary Committee when he wrote:

> Nor do I see anything unfair, when a railway company comes to Parliament for privileges and powers without which it cannot conduct its business, that Parliament shall ... annex such conditions as to hours of working in respect of signalmen, guards and engine-drivers, where inattention due to weariness has caused loss of life and grievous bodily injury to the general public.[31]

The issue was confused by the resistance of some engine-men to state interference in their affairs, the men preferring a policy of discussion between company and union. In the 1890s foot-platemen were forced to admit that during fogs and breakdowns it was impossible to finish work in ten or twelve hours; if shorter hours were insisted upon, then more lodging turns, the bane of many engine-men, would result. The accolade for loyalty went to the 300 engine-men of Stratford on the Eastern Counties Railway, who, on 26 April 1891, wrote to their superintendent protesting against any interference by the legislature in the setting of hours of work. At the same time, they appealed to their superintendent to reduce from eleven to ten per day the hours still being worked by a small number of Eastern Counties engine-men. As a sweetener, the Stratford 300 intimated that the men would work twelve hours per day during an emergency. One driver testifying before the Select Committee apparently considered seaside excursions as fitting into that category. The exchange went as follows: 'You do not think that even fourteen or fifteen hours would be held to be excessive in those cases?—Not at all. I have done it myself, plenty of times and have never felt myself exhausted.'[32] The reasons for this exercise in knee-bending and forelock-tugging by the Stratford men are not hard to find. The most advanced politically were Liberal and Conservative, not socialist, voters, and they considered state intervention an affront to individual liberty.

In the end, the Select Committee failed to make any appreciable impact on the scandal of railway hours and accidents. The slaughter of engine-men continued. As J. Thomas records, 'On 14 October 1895 an alarming accident . . . occurred at Shandon Station. The train was double-headed, with driver Thornton in charge of the leading engine and driver Thompson on the train engine. . . . Thornton had been eleven hours and Thompson fourteen hours on duty. . . .'[33] A massive derailment resulted. On 5 November 1895, driver Rathbone of Birkenhead was killed at Victoria Basin as he stepped from his own engine. He had just completed sixteen consecutive hours on duty when hit by a passing train.[34]

As we have seen, in the maintenance of control over the engine-men, the master stroke of the companies was the allocation of their 'own' engine to certain classes of drivers, and to permit these men to implement running repairs to their charges. At a stroke was formed a new amalgam of company, men and engines. Nothing like it had been seen before in British industry. Norman McKillop has written:

> The engines themselves were given a great deal more consideration than the men who worked them. My own company painted their engines a deep olive green, with the inside of the cab a deep primrose yellow, and . . . the locomotive officers, from the superintendent downwards, saw to it not only that the engines were kept spotlessly clean, but also that such embellishments as were added to almost every part of them received tacit encouragement. . . .
>
> Most of the regular trainmen had their own engines, and they regarded them as proprietorially as if they had bought them out of their own pockets. When an engine was kept in the depot for maintenance purposes—generally once a fortnight—the driver and fireman stayed with it to enjoy an orgy of gland-packing, scouring and general fettling-up which would not have disgraced some of the mechanical jobs done by the fitters of today. . . .
>
> These men had one hobby and amusement—their engines.[35]

Every bit of metal from which paint could be removed was scoured and polished, and grate blacking was utilized to keep in good outline the contour lines of the engine number which was painted on the buffer. The mundane and unromantic smoke-box door took on new dimensions, sporting brass crowns, stars and filigree work. Chimneys were decorated with brass collars. Buffers, coupling links and safety valves shone like jewels, special attention being afforded to the copper pipe fittings in the cab. A favourite location for such decoration was the engine sand-box, which allowed many a driver to show his loyalty to the Queen as well as the company. Of the fetish for cleanliness and decoration, Hamilton Ellis has written of Carlisle in the 1870s:

> Over there on the east side is one of Fletcher's engines on the North-Eastern, severe and Quakerish of outline, but painted bright green. Her driver has further embellished her with a pair of polished-brass antlered stags in her uncompromising stove-pipe chimney and there is a gaudy transfer picture of the Royal Family on her sand-box. . . . There is destined to be trouble about it later on, nevertheless, when a picture of *Venus Asleep* (or is it Goya's *Duchess Undraped?*) goes to York on the North-Eastern sand-box and attracts the scandalized attention of a very important dignitary.[36]

On the Callander and Oban Railway, at least one engine-man had the temerity to inscribe a box and compass on the fall plate of his engine which proclaimed to the world his membership of a Masonic society.[37]

The North British, as patriotic as any of its rivals, was always keen to provide an engine which would attract maximum attention, and J. Thomas has written, 'On official occasions the royal engine was so smothered in tapestry, shrubbery, flowers and painted carpentry, that an onlooker would have been hard-pressed to distinguish its permanent livery.'[38]

Among the impedimenta kept at St Margaret's was a curved board inscribed 'God Save the Queen'. A gilt crown resting on a velvet cushion surmounted the headboard and a stag's head was suspended beneath it. An elliptical arch was erected longitudinally above the boiler and the tender was draped with tassel-edged crimson velvet.

In the case of the London, Brighton and South Coast Railway, Ellis records that, '. . . the driver's name was inscribed in gilt script on the inside of the can spectacle plate, with, underneath, an indication of the mileage run.'[39] Drivers who held engines with nameplates took a dim view of the matter if their names were removed. Removal of the driver's nameplate meant that he was going around positively naked, and such men, when on the shed, kept out of sight as far as possible.

The Highland Railway was keen on the driver maintaining the engine in spanking condition and its chronicler, O. S. Nock, has written that on 25 May 1883 the following report was submitted: 'In consequence of Andrew Gray allowing No. 70 engine to get into such a disgraceful state, through want of proper attention, it is taken from him. (Signed) D. Jones. Loco Engineer.'[40] At this period, far away to the west of England, Great Western drivers were scrounging champagne bottle corks from the dining cars to fit the big ends of their engines. The South Midlands were not to be outdone in this fetish for cleanliness and smart work.[41] At Bletchley, engines were glossy and gleaming, their brass plates shining like gold. On the Hull and Barnsley Railway, around 1898–1900, engine-men were honoured with locomotives which were black picked out in ultramarine and vermilion lines. Engine lettering was gold with red shading. By 1913 engines were painted invisible green, a greenish black, like oil spilled on a road, with yellow and vermilion lining.

The Hull and Barnsley Railway was taken over by the London and North-Eastern Railway, and the latter company continued the practice of allocating engines to men on passenger duties. The passenger engines were apple green, lined with black and white; buffer beam and connecting rods were in red. These comparisons were meat and drink to North-Eastern men who kept them spotlessly clean inside and out, until the amalgamation of 1923.

In the 1920s on the Great Western, the record of every large engine was exhibited, together with its driver's name and its coal consumption over the previous three months. According to Wilf Turner, who was a foot-plateman at Bristol, the larger Great Western engines burned about forty-three pounds per mile in normal conditions.[42] Any increase in coal consumption beyond the norm was the subject of much chatter among the engine-men. Great Western men were, in the 1920s, allocated such engines as the four-cylinder King Edward VII, and took pride in their possession, doing lots of work themselves to keep the machines spotless. There is nothing today to compare with the freely given, unpaid labour of British engine-men in those days of company pride.

The main-line companies had no monopoly on the fetish for beautiful steam engines. Many of the early photographs of the Lynton and Barnstaple Railway

... show the polish worked into a fish-scale pattern, while the brasswork—chimney, cap, dome and safety-valve covers, etc.—was invariably glittering. The basic colour was a deep green, often referred to as dark emerald or holly green. . . . The frames, cylinders and other gear below the tank sides and running plate were painted in a reddish-brown shade, while the buffer beams and headlamps were vermilion. . . .[43]

The L and B was small, but it was beautifully marked, the crest of the company appearing several times on the lower panels of the reddish-brown and white carriages.

When Anthony Sperdutti began his firing career on the Great Western at the end of the First World War he found that the drivers at Millbay were all in love with their work; their engines were their castles. According to Sperdutti:

The drivers in those days had to buy their own overalls, so they would try to cadge jackets and waistcoats from guards and shunters. Most drivers were tidy but some were scruffy. The flat cap was normal headgear. Many of these men liked a smoke and a drink, but others, church-going men, would report bad language or cleaners smoking on the shed. Smoking on the engine was strictly forbidden. Many of these old drivers thought more of their engines than they did of their homes. They would go down the shed on Sunday and work for nothing on their own engine, taking up brakes and packing steam glands. If not at work, they would be hanging about behind the door awaiting the caller-up. If working on an engine in the public gaze, these old gentlemen not only forbade smoking in the cab, but insisted that the firemen should at all times stand up in the cab. The drivers at Millbay had to be called 'mister', the title by which they addressed the foreman. Many of the older men had great difficulty in reading and writing. Yet they were proud men and could get a train home on time against fearful odds, whether naturally or mechanically created. This allegiance did not receive its just reward. In the rationalization panic of the 1930s many Great Western men were forced to retire at sixty years of age, at the very moment when the top-paid work was within their grasp.[44]

According to Sperdutti, several of his acquaintances had to sell mortgaged homes and, after forty years on the company, apply for public assistance. 'I have seen grown men crying with the unfairness of it all,' he wrote.[45] Anthony Sperdutti, working in the heyday of the Great Western Railway, nevertheless recognized a particular company spirit but believed that it was destroyed, along with many other railway traditions, by the nationalization of the industry.

The history of railways in Britain contains many stories of industrial heroism based on job loyalty, but only two examples need to be chronicled here as evidence of loyalty by engine-men to the companies they served and the passengers they protected. The times and the circumstances could hardly be more strangely contrasted yet both examples portray the best aspects of human beings under stress.

In 1927, Britain endured one of the most severe winters then recorded. In Hampshire, the usually lush and woody Meon Valley somersaulted into climatic change. Snow-drifts over twenty feet occurred and the Meon Valley line of the London and South-Western Railway was closed to traffic. In the worst snowstorms in living memory the engine-men of the Meon Valley ploughed into the snow-drifts to clear the line. The men on the first snowploughs were exposed to the full fury of the snow-storms. With throttles opened full out, and with the engine crews being thrown from side to side on the foot-plate, the engines smashed undauntedly into the enormous drifts. In the open air the men were drenched with falling snow; in the tunnels they faced constant danger from the huge icicles dripping from the roofs. As the engines could not be turned, they were driven head on into the mighty drifts, until foot by foot the engines were snowed under. Standing in waist-high snow, the engine-men of the South-Western cleared the snow from the engine ashpans and oiling points, and with engines minus sidesteps, headlamps and identity discs the tracks were cleared bit by bit. On 29 December 1927, blinded and frozen by the forces of hurricane nature, the men and engines of the Meon Valley line smashed their way into Winchester. The lines were open again.[46]

In direct contrast to this episode was the desperate courage displayed in the doom-laden darkness of Primrose Hill Tunnel on the morning of 20 May 1937. On this day, driver Joe Ball and fireman Cormack Higgins, of Edge Hill shed, Liverpool, hooked up at Euston to the 10.40 a.m. express from London to Liverpool. They were unaware that in the engine smoke-box a deflector plate had not been securely fastened in position and within a few minutes of departure from Euston this plate would fall across the engine blast pipe, causing a most appalling accident.

As the train entered the tunnel, the blast pipe was partially blocked by the faulty deflector plate falling across the orifice. Instantly the engine cab became engulfed in roaring flames. In the darkness of the tunnel, jumping from the moving cab would have meant certain death, but such an abrogation of responsibility never entered the heads of the engine crew. For three and a half burned and scalded miles, Ball and Higgins stayed at their posts, bringing the train to a stop at Willesden Station, the first place where help could be guaranteed. First aid and medical attention were quickly available but the severe injuries proved fatal to both men. At the inquests the coroners paid high tribute to the heroism of Ball and Higgins whose calm fortitude and devotion to duty were worthy of the highest traditions of the railway service.

In the railway city of Carlisle, Ritson Graham, whose previous loyalty had been to the army, was looking, not for a new loyalty, but for a job with regular wages. He had no stars in his eyes about the prospects of a life of shift work, feeding a fiery furnace day after day, often with lodgings away in strange towns as an extra drawback. He was, however, prepared for the challenge, and he has recorded:

We had no romantic notions about engine-driving; it was not a boyhood dream of any driver that I ever met, but most of them could not have followed any other occupation more efficiently or to their greater satisfaction. It was an extremely rare event for a foot-plateman in the line of promotion from cleaner to driver voluntarily to leave his employment. It was a job for life and security of employment was one of its greatest assets.

Apart from my life-long pleasure in country pursuits and in selective reading, I shall always regard as maturing years those spent as a fireman at the Durran Hill depot in Carlisle. This, though we may not have realized it at the time, was one of the best run engine sheds in the country, a model of efficiency where both men and machines were respected and where decency and order prevailed.

Cleanliness and a high standard of respectability was maintained and, best of all, it was mutual. As a random example of this, there was a modest notice in the engine shed which read, 'Please do not drop matches on the shed floor.' Most engine sheds I have visited have been littered, not with match sticks, but with brake blocks, discarded engine springs and brick-arch material by the barrow-load. The significance of this, however, is not merely the message it conveyed but the lamentable fact that men brought up at these other depots could only sneer disdainfully at such a request. It was a symbol of an atmosphere, and an indication of an environment. The old Midland Railway maintained high standards, that at least was not denied, and high standards, or low ones for that matter, rub off on those who constantly come into contact with them.

On the 'road', our name for the line, we lived up to our training, the example of our seniors which had become established as the tradition of the company. The engine-drivers did drive. They handled and nursed their engines according to the ever-changing gradients, which they knew intimately. The load, length and type of train and the condition of the weather were also factors to which they gave constant attention, not to mention the obvious ones of signals, indicators and warning notices, etc.[47]

Ritson Graham observed several examples of this tenacious dedication to job and line:

During the long winter nights the inactive driver was literally frozen stiff, for a swiftly travelling locomotive, with a small cab, is the coldest place on earth on a frosty night. It was not the practice of the old school of drivers to take a turn with the shovel though the tradition was beginning to be broken by the younger men and was a regular practice on the 'Lanky' (London and North-Western Railway).

We on the Midland did not wish it otherwise. 'He does his job and I do mine,' was the mutual understanding. We were, by necessity, fairly silent on the foot-plate but the mute relationship was rarely an unfriendly one. We communicated by signs to indicate the position of signals or possible hazards.

While this attentive application to the job was general on the Midland it would be wrong to assume that it was unknown elsewhere. On being transferred to the 'Wessy' as a passed fireman and spare driver, I met some excellent foot-platemen, men who had little to encourage them other than the pride in their work and in their rough-and-ready set up, no one to appreciate their worth. Self-respect is a forerunner to fellow-respect, and this is easier where the environment is conducive to both.

My fellow workers, most of them my seniors, possessed a strong fraternal spirit. They lived for their work and it was the main topic of their conversation. In attempting to understand the character of these men, it must be borne in mind that they were performing a duty of great responsibility without any strict supervision whatever. They were on their own from signing on to signing off. In fact, so removed and remote was the 'boss' influence, that it was strictly forbidden for an official, even when travelling on the foot-plate, to interfere with any of the foot-platemen's work. They could report and comment after the trip, but offer no remarks or instructions on the job.

This conscientiousness, pride of craft and sense of responsibility, was the hallmark of the steam driver's performance of his duty. The attachment of the men to their work and to their engines had to be seen to be believed. At its best it was stronger than was desirable, where the men concerned often possessed more regard for the success of the journey, the timekeeping, etc. and above all for the care of their engines, than for anything else.

In the passenger links the drivers were allocated their own locomotives, and plates carrying their names were hung on the sides of the cabs. While I did not agree with this over-personalized attitude, I did however admire these men and no doubt this recognition of their many sterling qualities urged me to join with others in working for their richly deserved rights, deserved both as honest, devoted and skilled workers, and as first-class citizens.

It was a personal relationship, the men were working for their own satisfaction, living up to their self-imposed high standards. Such men, and there were many, literally begged, stole and even bought extra oil to keep their engines in perfect running order. They 'examined' all round and oiled everything within reach at every stop en route, be it a signal at danger or when shunted into a siding, day or night.[48]

This obsession with perfect running order was a significant factor in the Ais Gill disaster on the night of 1 September 1913. On a wild night in the Pennines the 1.35 a.m. express from Glasgow to London was rammed in the rear by the 1.49 a.m. Edinburgh to London. Fire fed by escaping gas caused the deaths of fourteen passengers and serious injury to thirty-eight others. Driver Caudle, the driver of the 1.49 a.m. train, had actually left the foot-plate to oil the left-hand driving wheel axle box. The force of the gale held up his movements around the engine framing, and by the time he reached the foot-plate again he found the engine short of steam and the fireman desperately trying to get some water into the boiler. In the crisis the train passed all the signals at Mallerstang and ran into the rear of the earlier train, which had stopped through shortage of steam and had not been protected in the rear.[49]

The economic slump following the First World War made railway work very attractive to many youngsters. Frank Mason, who joined the railways at this time, wrote to me many years later of the lure which railway service possessed:

We lived in a railway street; the sidings, with a slag-heap mound, were at our back gate. Those black shunting engines with the inter- minable back and forth movement instilled no romantic admiration in me. If I stared through my bedroom window when rain flooded the pane and the wind rattled the frame, the supposed objects of my ad- miration could be seen crouching wretchedly, dripping, cold, but vigi- lant for hand signals that never came, or fixed signals that tarried. My drowsy last minutes were spent under the counterpane on many nights, to deaden the crash of buffers—the 'ouch' of drawbars pro- testing.

Dad was a driver at the shed. On previous occasions I had heard there might be a chance, but Dad seemed reluctant—on the rare occasions I saw him—to help me to get on the railway. This Satur- day, however, Mum had won her way and Dad had 'asked for me'. Why did Mum do this? in later years I wondered, for not only had she led a deprived life of uncertainty and anxiety, but all our neighbours were foot-platemen and many tales of hardship could be told.

As a fourteen-year-old I used to enjoy a visit, with a mate, to feed their hens. His father, a driver, had constructed his hen-pen by the line-side of a coal storage siding, and three of the sidings held unusual contents; about fifty 'MM' engines. The Ministry of Munitions engines were relics of the First World War; they had been transported from Flanders and then stood 'in grease', waiting allocation to Britain's railways. A large proportion eventually went to the LNER, though some were retained on the LMS.

Naturally we boys trespassed on them when no shunters etc. were about. I received an unfavourable impression of locomotives by this experience. They were clumsy, ugly brutes, massively built and, of course, covered in dirty grease. I had some idea of the controls but could hardly imagine normal men being strong enough to operate them; certainly the reversing wheel frustrated the strength of both of us. I had carried from that experience therefore an antipathy to such a world of massive, dirty drill.

But *now* I was a railwayman. Now on boarding a foot-plate a warm glow hit one. There was the sensation of wisps of rising steam, the smell of hot oil, the coal-strewn lap-plate and the unconquerable urge to open the firehole door and marvel at the size and heat of the fire. So my indoctrination commenced into the cult and personality of the 'iron horses' with which I was to be associated for forty years.

A storeboy had no right to be on a foot-plate, and if the foreman or shed master approached one had to slide down the opposite handrail pronto! But if I was caught I could justify myself by one of two reasons: that I was taking oil bottles to be filled for the driver; or, that I was getting coal for the boss's fire. The latter had to be proved by the evidence of a coal bucket. The reason was quite valid, for we knew on which engines to look for good Yorkshire coal and the office fire-grates were particularly partial to 'a bit o' good Yorkshire'. So we robbed Peter—the engine—to pay Paul—the boss.

Often I got into trouble over engine oil. We issued it from the stores to engines according to their type and the mileage of the trip they had to perform. The driver or fireman brought the oilcans and watched, with keen eye, that I measured the right quantity. The cylinder oil was very tricky—it was so thick and slow to emerge from the tap of the large tanks. The ration of cylinder oil for a shunting engine was only one pint and about a quarter of the thick stuff would remain in the measure after pouring. As the driver watched the operation, with anxiety or anger, according to his disposition, my storesman adjudicated, with biased regard to his stock book record. Many were the quips or threats from the drivers: 'You're not in the chemists now!' or, 'Just wait till you get firing for me!'

I had learned a lot in the nine months of my employment, and my second boss badly wanted me to become apprentice, but with national unemployment at 1½ million, fully qualified chemists were two-a-penny, and, when employed, only raised two-thirds of the 90s. that a driver could boast weekly. Apprentices only earned 'buttons' for several years. I had landed a job at 24s. a week, with an eight-hour day and time in the evenings to enjoy myself with my fellows—that is what I thought!

Jim Walker was also fascinated by the sight, sound and smells of the railway. When he left school in 1932, Jim could not wait to get down to the engine shed at Stoke to apply for a job. He was told he was too small, but later, at eighteen years of age, he made a start as an engine cleaner. His references were impeccable, one from his old headmaster, another from a Justice of the Peace whom his mother knew 'through the chapel', and a third from a clergyman. Backed by the educational system, the judiciary and the church, Jim was a certain starter as soon as he gained the requisite inches. Promotion, however, was to be slow and painful, necessitating many transfers and many lodgings. Once they reached the position of driver, the men held on as long as they could. At Saltley shed, Birmingham, Jim Walker found that:

> It was not until 1926 that drivers on the Midland were required to retire at sixty-five years of age. There was plenty of evidence to the statement that the drivers were so old that they were taken to the shed in bathchairs and lifted onto the engine.
>
> These men received a pension of 7s. per week between the ages of sixty-five and seventy, after which the allowance was reduced to 4s. 6d. More than movie actresses found it necessary to lie about their age in those days.[50]

Retirement was a terrifying prospect for some. I heard of one driver who had always said that when he was ordered to retire he would commit suicide; when the time actually came he did just that.

Midland tradition died hard, as Mr M. F. Higson found when working at Lancaster engine shed in the 1950s.[51] Lancaster was an ex-London and North-Western shed which had gone into the London, Midland and Scottish Railway in 1923. The amalgamation of Midland and North-Western traditions was never really effected, as Mr Higson discovered when he met the archetypal ex-Midland man:

> He was all that typified the old Midland Railway to me. A great hulk of a man, smartly turned out in a white shirt and black tie with that wretched little wyvern . . . set high in the front of his cap, this so and so made no bones about his dislike for young hand firemen . . . Every remark was a command, snapped and snarled with great contempt. His whole attitude was one of sheer disgust.[52]

The ex-LNWR men would not surrender to such treatment. At Lancaster in the 1950s several drivers still wore the Lancashire and Yorkshire symbol in their hats just to show that the 'wretched wyvern' was not the only survivor of the glorious days of the individual companies. The hierarchy of grades inaugurated by the companies was matched by the staff, which created statuses and jealousies based upon territory, ritual and taboo. These distinctions were more marked in the foot-plate world than anywhere else in the industry. The men of the city and town sheds, who usually worked long-distance trains, had a friendly contempt for their colleagues who operated out 'in the sticks'. The men born on the millstone grit were always more abrasive than their counterparts in the chalk and clay areas. On granite, or fen or coastal area, however, engine-drivers always considered themselves separate within themselves as well as distinct from other railway workers, and this differentiation was illustrated by the attitude of passenger to freight sheds. In the hey-day of steam, the rivalry between Camden and Willesden sheds had to be experienced to be believed.

In foot-plate terms, Camden shed, star of the old London and North-Western Railway, was a name to conjure with. A mile north of Euston Station, it was a small dark shed, jammed between the bustle of the main line to the north and the quiet green of Primrose Hill. It worked practically nothing but express trains between London, Carlisle, Man-chester and Crewe. Its drivers and firemen were the self-anointed car-dinals of the main line. At Camden there were few shed days on which to relax from the rigours of main-line work as almost every day there was a main-line locomotive to be manned. Come rain, fog, snow, or boiling summer heat, those six tons of coal were the daily challenge.

The great rival to Camden was the ex-North-Western freight shed at Willesden Junction, a shed as conglomerate as Camden was select. Triangled between two main roads and the festering dark waters of the Grand Union Canal, Willesden was a splendid mixture of main-line freight, local passenger work, including the *Tring Flyer*, and a vast amount of local freight trip work. Willesden men were masters in the art of making overtime, constantly setting at nought the attempts of dia-gram makers, controllers and foremen to produce an effective and effi-cient programme. Willesden men went to work not for eight hours per day, but for 'six or ten'. They wanted either a short day, giving some much-needed leisure, or a long day with overtime payments. From the two roundhouses and the long shed of Willesden, under the continuous gentle perspiration of the squat cooling towers of the adjacent power station, the men of Willesden ranged from Lillie Bridge to Liverpool, from Camden Town to Crewe and from Kensington to Carlisle. It was a marvellous mixture of machines, men and patois.

When Camden shed was short of staff, the vacancies were filled by men from Willesden. The supermen of Camden were always furious when a Willesden driver, employed the day previously on knocking a few wagons about Chelsea Basin, would suddenly appear at the controls of a stream-liner bound for Manchester or Carlisle. Few Camden men ever saw or wished to see the interior of the Willesden sheds, and any Willesden engine appearing on Camden shed was an irritant to dispose of as quickly as possible.

On the ex-Midland lines, Camden and Willesden had for counterparts the passenger shed at Kentish Town and the freight shed at Cricklewood. The passenger men of 'The Town' characterized their freight colleagues on the Edgware Road as 'the enemy' or 'Huns'. These two depots were separated geographically by Finchley Road tunnel, and once through it, hostile territory was encountered, many young firemen at Cricklewood being given dire warnings of what lay beyond the dark and grime of that famous 'hole'.

Like Camden, Kentish Town was the doyen of the system, dealing in a high proportion of long-distance express work, casual vacancies being covered by specially trained Cricklewood engine-men. To the chagrin of the glossy-capped, shiny-booted passenger men of Kentish Town, the foot-plates of their passenger engines were often manned by Cricklewood men whose uniform seemed to consist of an old brown raincoat topped by a civilian cloth cap.

Such intense shed loyalty also operated in the north of England. At Carlisle, when the city boasted sheds belonging to the LNWR, the Midland, the North British, the Caledonian and the Maryport and Carlisle, it was said that engine crews would cross the street rather than recognize the men of another company and, such was the jigsaw type of fragmentation of the foot-plate crews, that men of one company would rarely encourage romantic attachments between their own children and the offspring of men working engines for a rival company.

Drivers' nicknames gave a new dimension to a shed, for once a man was labelled, he would rarely be referred to again by his proper name. New starters had to find for themselves the man behind the name, for little or no help was forthcoming in translation. Between the wars, Cricklewood had a driver who applied for the job of public hangman.[53] He was called 'The Noose'. Another was 'Coal Cellar Charlie', whose wife insisted that he deposited coal dust in her basement, not on her linoleum. There was 'Shadrach' Sharp, a driver who claimed to have married the prettier of two sisters. The girl Shadrach married was said to make horses rear up, leaving little to be said in favour of the other belle. 'Blind Charlie' Chance was so short-sighted that he felt his way round the shed by fingertip control, often ending up in the inspection pit. This joke highlighted the difference between the high standard of eyesight demanded of main-line men and the lower level required by men restricted to the shed limits because of defective vision. Poor old Charlie would pull his own teeth by tying string round the offending molar, the other end being attached to the handle of a bucket of water which was lowered quickly to the ground.

Polmadie, the Caledonian shed at Glasgow had a varied store of characters. Among these was 'Gentleman Jim', an expert on the work of Thomas Carlyle, much of which was read and explained to engine cleaners more interested in Glasgow Rangers than *Sartor Resartus*. 'Dandy' was another; here was a man who liked his dram and who discussed painting, writing and the art of good living with his colleagues. 'Dandy' could stagger home in full Masonic regalia at 2.00 a.m., and a few hours later, the fuzziness gone, he was sober, overalled and capped, on his way to work.[54]

The types of accidents which had always befallen engine-men continued to plague them throughout the 1950s and on up to the present day. Technological advance was unable to put a stop to the maiming and killing of man by machine. Engine-men were burned by blowbacks from the firebox and scalded by unexpected rushes of steam; they fell out of engine cabs or from smoke-box framing. They tripped over heaps of clinker, or on fire irons left in dangerous places. They fell off tenders, they were injured lifting up the leather hosepipes on the water cranes. The turntable in the shed strained their backs, and sometimes flung them over the driving mechanism into the pit. These facts baldly stated give little indication of the weeks of pain and worry sustained by men working in an industry where every accident had to be contested at Common Law if any compensation was to be granted. For many years, accidents to railway staff were attributed to acts of God or personal negligence. Compensation was difficult to obtain. The table below shows the increasing ability of the engine-men's union to obtain compensation not only for men killed or injured on duty but also while travelling to work.[55]

ACCIDENTS TO ENGINE-MEN
AND COMPENSATION AWARDED 1956–76

Name	Accident	Sum awarded at Common Law
1956		
Fireman Jones Wellingborough	Leg amputated in collision	£1,429
Fireman Hulme Old Oak Common	Eyesight lost when whistle chain broke	£1,400
1966		
Fireman Watson Blyth	Killed by passing train	£6,812
Driver Martin Motherwell	Killed while riding cycle to work	£4,725

Name	Accident	Sum awarded at Common Law
Driver Brown Carlisle	Killed in motor cycle accident	£4,878
1976 Secondman Bruce Ayr	Injured in collision 1971. Not working in 1976.	£12,000
Driver Madge Paddington	Seat collapsed on a shunting diesel. Incapacitation with spinal trouble, 5 years 8 months	£15,000
Driver Fletcher Blackburn	Two years incapacitated after accident	£23,000

Engine-drivers always had a great respect for properly constituted authority; indeed it was the basis for their own power on the foot-plate. They would as a group of men, however, oppose authority which they considered unfair, unfeeling, ill-informed and abusive. In defence of such principles they fought hard for the eight-hour day, differential payments based upon responsibility, and for public ownership of the railways. We have already seen the strength of the opposition which the engine-men faced in the struggle for their rights. Nevertheless, by presenting a united front these men were able to make significant gains. Two organized strikes, which were thirty-seven years apart, will illustrate how such progress was made.

For engine-men, 1887 was the year of 'The Midland Strike'. Conditions on this company were not any worse in general than on any other company at this time, but in 1886, the Midland began a minor reign of terror against its engine-men. Fines were imposed for such crimes as coal falling off the tender and for refusing to pass signals at danger. In 1887, the Midland abolished the guaranteed week and precipitated the strike.

On the Midland, one third of the engine-men belonged to ASLEF; some were members of the ASRS, but the majority were unorganized. On 5 August 1887, the Midland timetable became a fictional document. The Midland men did not consult anyone—they just did not report for work, their attitude being 'smash us if you like'.

The foot-plate union took three days to size up the situation. It then called out all its members on the Midland Railway. ASLEF decided it would not furnish strike pay, but it would also not allow its members to work while others were on strike for basic conditions of service.

The Midland Railway won that fight by importing unorganized foot-platemen from other areas. The strike cost the foot-plate union £3,000, none of it in strike monies. Under its own rules, the union paid 'out of work pay' of £1,685 to 402 members. At a cost of £261 each, fifty-six members were assisted to emigrate. Two members of the Executive Committee were among those dismissed and six delegates who were discharged were allowed £100 each under the union rules. The 1887 strike was still a burning issue for engine-men in 1924 and was referred to in the Circular of 29 January of that year as 'The Fiasco'.[56]

The engine-men were not going to make the same mistake in that year of 1924. A fundamental test of democracy is the right of people to oppose blind obedience to authority and this concept, even if it was imperfectly understood, was the reason for the foot-plate strike of 1924. Since 1921, the companies had shown a reduction in their wages bill of £55 million; between 1921 and 1922 net receipts had increased by £5,654,078, yet in November 1923 they were applying to the National Wages Board for an annual reduction of their wages bill by £4 million.[57] In December 1923, the National Wages Board agreed to a reduction of £½ million. On 24 January 1924, 70,000 members of ASLEF, seriously affected by the cuts, shut down the railway system, defying an Act of Parliament and abrogating a document signed by all the major railway unions. The striking foot-platemen received letters of support from the Red International of Labour Unions and from the Russian Railway Union, but were condemned by the weekly newspaper of the independent Labour Party, the *New Leader*. The incoming minority Labour Government of Ramsay MacDonald was politely informed by John Bromley of ASLEF, 'If the success of the Labour Party and of a Labour Government can only be built on such serious losses in wages and conditions, then I am sure that the workers will not welcome a Labour Government under such conditions.' Bromley's men were certainly under attack, a significant minority of them, the main-line drivers, standing to lose up to one fifth of contemporary earnings based on mileage. Despite the criticisms and the press campaign against the union, the mileage strike of 1924 was a triumph for the engine-men, a justification of the view that they were a special group of men.

Their troubles were by no means over, however. At the opening of the 1950s, the engine-men could look back on thirty years of redundancies, transfers and dismissals. They had endured reductions in salary, 2½ per cent in 1929, restored in 1931, and a further 2½ per cent in 1931, not restored until 1937. Now in 1955 they were plagued on three fronts. First, there was the prevarication over wages and pensions. Second was the announcement in 1955 of the £1,500 million plan for the modernization of the railway industry, a development which could only lead to the decimation of the foot-plate union. Third, morale was very low, due to outworn equipment and lack of spares. Engines which were creaking in every joint were expected to maintain speeds with loads which taxed to the utmost the ingenuity and physical strength of the men. W. Murphy, the editor of the *Manchester Evening News*, who went along on a night express run from Manchester to London recorded in the May 1952 edition of the *Locomotive Journal*:

Four hours on the foot-plate of a long-distance express leave a fairly deep impression on mind and body. Disillusion is the strongest of them. *Solomon Islands*, the huge black three cylinder 4–6–0 on which my journey from Manchester to London was made, lost no time in putting a stranger in his place. Her opening gambit was a succession of awful shuddering noises accompanied by terrific jolts and jars as she strained at the load. . . . so loud were the complaints of her driving wheels that even the mighty puffs from her chimney were lost in the din.

Night had closed in by the time we left Stoke . . . for the driver three hours of unremitting concentration began. The night was moonless, and he could not see the track. Nothing could be seen through the forward glass spectacles but the succession of tiny red and green lights, each and every one of which the driver knew by name. It is by this and his recognition of bridges, viaducts, embankments and cuttings that he can know what lies immediately ahead. . . . Too soon for me we emerged from Kilsby tunnel and really began to pile it on. Gradually our speed rose until I was practically stunned by the noise. Tucked in a corner on the fireman's side I hung on and felt sick. I saw the driver blow the whistle but I couldn't hear it. . . . Passing through Wolverton in a tempest of sound and motion a most horrible convulsion fairly stopped my heart. 'This is it,' I thought, 'we're running on the ballast.' The fireman must have seen from my expression that I thought we were about to run through the Pearly Gates, for he yelled in my ear 'wet rails'. This terrifying performance had been due only to temporary loss of grip and consequent racing of the engine. I've sampled most forms of transport including Service aircraft and Bren-gun carriers across open country, but for sheer terrifying pandemonium give me the engine of a night express.

Between 1953 and 1955, long negotiations between railway unions and the Transport Commission produced the following scales of payment for engine-men: [58]

Grade	per week	
	s.	d.
Adult Engine Cleaner 2nd Year	135	0

Grade	per week
	s. d.
Fireman and Assistant Motorman	
3rd Year	164 0 (Max.)
Driver and Motorman	
1st Year	175 0
2nd Year	185 0
3rd Year	195 0 (Max.)

(A London rate of 3*s*. higher than the provincial rate to be applied to Engine Cleaners employed in London)

Hardly was the ink dry on this decision (Railway Staff National Tribunal, April 1955) than the foot-platemen put in a logical claim for their differential payment to be secured. Their comparisons were as follows:

WAGES AND SALARIES 1955[59]

Grade	Weekly wage in shillings
Station-master	254
Signalman	193
Male Supervisor—Inspector	254
Head Shunter	160
Senior Porter—Passenger	146
Senior Porter—Goods	143
Foreman—Yard	174

WAGES AND SALARIES—MINING INDUSTRY 1955[60]

Grade	Weekly wage in shillings
Craftsman—Underground	212
Craftsman—Surface	192
Signalman	164
Deputies: Grade 1 North East	340
Shotfirers	320

For engine-men, 1955 was 'the year of differentials', the year of the longest strike within the history of railway trade unionism and the year when the relationships between the craft union and the industrial union reached the lowest ebb since the mileage strike of 1924.

The Transport Commission countered this demand for differentials with a proposal to bring back a new system of classification and a possible increase in mileage payments, arguing that a differential payment could be conceded neither wholly nor in part.

On 28 May 1955, the foot-platemen began their seventeen-day marathon strike. It was a strike that was very costly for the country and for the railway unions. The National Union of Railwaymen, which retained a nucleus of engine-men within its ranks, argued that agreements were made to be honoured and advised its members to work normally. This decision, correct in procedural terms, led to open and unashamed blacklegging all over the country, and left the stain of inter-union hostility long after the strike was settled. The engine-men were undoubtedly of the opinion that differential payments were the key to the whole future welfare and status of their craft and society. Despite this feeling, the Executive Committee of the union advised its members on the London Transport Executive not to infringe on the dispute in existence on the main line.[61]

On 14 June 1955, the Government set up an inquiry under Lord Justice Morris and his rapidly produced report awarded the following rates of pay:

Grade	Per week in shillings
Drivers, Motormen	
1st Year	176
2nd Year	187
3rd Year	198
Firemen	
3rd Year (Maximum)	164

For wage increases of 1–3s. per week the engine-men successfully pursued their principle of relativity. The Government, which for two weeks had refused to negotiate while the strike was in progress, was forced to grant an impartial inquiry. The Transport Commission, which had argued that the railway negotiating machinery was sacrosanct, was obliged to surrender this principle and the engine-men, 'bloody but unbowed', were able to claim a victory over government, Transport Commission and the national press. One result of the engine-men's success was that small increases of pay were awarded later to some signalmen and foremen whose work theoretically controlled the activities of engine-men. For the engine-men a circle was completed. The fear of the Stratford engine-men in 1891 that the state might interfere in the relationships between the companies and the men was reversed, the engine-men insisting that the state should now examine, judge and publish its interpretation of the rights of engine-men.

The years 1954–6 were notable for a serious decline in the financial affairs of the railway section of the Transport Commission and the long strike of 1955 did little to improve traffic receipts, the decline in revenue over three years being as follows: [62]

BRITISH TRANSPORT COMMISSION NET
TRAFFIC RECEIPTS—RAILWAYS

Year	Receipts
1954	+£16,569,000
1955	+£2,149,000
1956	−£16,292,000

In the 1960s the modernization of the industry bit deeply into the numbers of engine-men as single manning of engines and trains replaced the driver and fireman. Staff upheaval, promotion, transfer and redundancy were major problems for the engine-men, who again had to negotiate against a background of technical and social change in an atmosphere of much public hostility to the industry. A new redundancy system was devised. Rather than release the younger engine-men the new policy allowed men at the top of the promotion ladder to leave the industry on the basis of resettlement grants, the maximum payment being in the area of £1,200 after forty years' service. Most of these long-serving engine-men were taken on by big departmental stores as doorkeepers, messengers or lift attendants. Others became attendants in gentlemen's toilets. Within six months many engine-men plummeted from a situation in which they could be called up to drive the Royal Train to one where they dusted toilet pans for anyone who cared to visit. Loyalty had not paid off for these men; for the younger men the message seemed clear—'Get what you can now—the future offers little.'

The last human drama of the age of steam was the reluctance of engine-men to accept as fireman young men who came to Britain from the ex-colonial countries. For many men, brought up to believe that an engine cab was the last bastion of the aristocracy of labour (and of white supremacy), coloured men at the controls of a high-speed locomotive meant that the job of engine-man had reached an all-time low. Tempers ran very high in some areas, especially London, and withdrawals of labour were threatened. The railway trade unions took a highly principled stand on the question of the internationalism of labour, but in some areas they could not carry the rank and file with them. The issue was a running sore until the mid-sixties, when the engine-men's leaders, official and unofficial, accepted that indigenous labour had to some extent advised the railway industry what it could do with its low pay and poor conditions; railway work no longer carried the status it once had, and the men were leaving their jobs, leaving them open to immigrant labour.

For engine-men, 1955 had been a power peak—the organization, united and determined, forced the Government to negotiate while the men were on strike; this was a notable first in British industrial relations. For the railway management, however, 1955 was the year of the Modernization Plan for British Railways. Within half a decade the proposals for modernization had raised a spectre of a union decimated by depot closures, voluntary redundancies, and the single manning of engine cabs. From a peak of 90,000 in 1955, ASLEF entered the 1970s with a membership slashed to around 30,000. But the smaller it became, the more militant was its posture—the men of the Southern Region being especially truculent in the 1960s and 1970s.[63] Almost any subject was grist to the mill of those who considered themselves unjustly treated. Redundant men transferred hundreds of miles to retain a livelihood and facing the prospects of the high rents of south-eastern England were not unwilling to lead or take part in militant actions, if only to show their dissatisfaction with official union policy. At this period, a section of men on the South-Eastern Division of the Southern Region were contemplating a breakaway union catering only for electric trainmen. Their argument was that of classical economy—high wages would derive from labour shortage. By these terms engine-men on the southeast routes would gain the maximum return for their labour.

The South-Eastern Division men opened up their campaign in 1962 in support of a one-day strike by Underground workers against cuts in the national railway network. They followed this in 1963 with a work to rule over the implementation of the forty-two hour week, agreed but not implemented because of staff shortages. The engine-men were trapped—they could not get wage increases when labour was plentiful, and now they could get neither wage increases when labour was scarce nor hours of work lessened for the same reason. Because they were tied to nationally agreed rates, they could not argue for district settlements. Resignation was an alternative taken by many; militancy was the road taken by those who wished to retain their job and claim a just reward.

In 1965 the Southern Region cut Sunday services on the south-east routes, making considerable inroads into the engine-men's pay packets. A work to rule followed which produced such chaos that trains were queuing for entry to Charing Cross and Cannon Street stations for a distance of five miles. The local union organizer asked the men to go back, promising 'pounds plural' as the outcome of the stoppage. The General Secretary of the union however, addressing a meeting of the engine-men at New Cross, would have none of it, arguing that 'if you go out into the wilderness don't expect me to come and get you'. The

General Secretary had held his union together and was later able to present the men with a short mileage payment scheme. The Minister of Labour, Mr Ray Gunter, an ex-railwayman, was unable to impose any authority on the situation, much to public annoyance. At Charing Cross and Cannon Street, drivers had to be accompanied to their cabs by policemen, so high was the possibility of physical assault. During this work to rule, the seventeen-mile journey between Dartford and Charing Cross could take up to three and a half hours. Two words have enshrined this strike in railway lore. An enraged lady passenger hurled the epithet 'Bastard' at a Victoria motorman. His reply? 'Mother'.

The 1970s saw no let-up in the problem. In 1970, when management wished to introduce the 'Frowd' radar line-side speed recorder, the motormen, by threatening to work to rule, prevented its installation. In 1971, Southern Region proposed to axe eighty trains per day during the summer. Apart from the inconvenience to 100,000 commuters, the motormen were to have around £3 eased weekly from their pay packets. A threat of working to rule saw the withdrawal of the proposed cuts. 1973 and 1974 saw a running battle between management and men on the question of engine-cab speedometers. The speedometers, which cost approximately £1,000 each, were fitted but blanked off and were ineffective. Southern management insisted that train drivers caught overspeeding would be disciplined. The motormen countered with, 'Put two men in each cab as a safeguard, or make the speedometers effective.' Drivers who refused to take out the trains were sent home, providing a grisly two days for commuters before the issue was closed—the motormen having their way. At the time of writing the 'Frowd' line-side radar speed recorder was still not fitted in the London area.

The militancy of the Southern men showed the official and unofficial aspects of railway trade unionism in high contrast. The Southern men also demonstrated the power of work to rule and the officials of the union were always able to use this as a trump card in negotiations.

The passing of steam on the railway marked a point of no return in a driver's relationship with both his engine and his employer. Mr N. M. Lera, of Harley Street, London, who attended the last rites of steam at Tebay engine shed in 1968, has written:

> After completing its last duty of the day, banking on Shap, the engine, a British Railways Class 4 (known as a Chinese Four), returned to shed and was greeted by a sentimental crowd of enthusiasts mourning the demise of yet another outpost of steam.
>
> The engine stopped in the shed yard, and while the fireman attended to the routine tasks of coaling and watering, the driver

climbed from his foot-plate, wiped his hands on a piece of cotton waste and addressed the crowd: 'Well,' he announced, 'that's the last of them cast-iron bastards!'[64]

G. Bishop, a firebox repairman from Eastleigh on the Southern Region, was aware of what this meant, and has written:

Gone is the driver who would get to the depot before his signing-on time, so as to be sure that his engine was in good condition for whatever journey it had to do. He would have with him his bag with his food and rule books in; these bags were sometimes as big as small suitcases. His shining copper tea can would be hanging on the side of it, his cap badge and boots were also well shone. Gone is the fireman who would clean his fire and break the coal into suitable size so as to make his firing easier for the journey. Also with him went the cleaner who would put that little extra in cleaning the engines. Gone also are the fitters and boilersmiths who would not let any engine leave the shed until all repairs had been completed. Last, but no less important, were the boiler workers whose job was to keep the boilers clean. All these were true railwaymen, gone, and they will never be seen or heard of again.[65]

The decline of the steam locomotive meant much more than the passing of a picturesque and romantic form of transport. It was the breaking-up of a close-knit community of men, whose skill, initiative, sense of responsibility and devotion to duty can never be replaced by the button-pushing diesels and the electric-powered machines of today. The steam men were not, however, hostile to the change. They all saw the advantages of the cleaner, less laborious and more comfortable type of power. Introduced judiciously, and accompanied by better conditions and pay for fewer men, this could be a step in the right direction, and undoubtedly, from the engine-man's view, it has proved to be so.

In his smart uniform, with a monster diesel or electric train under his fingertip control, the modern railwayman is still the monarch of his working area. He owes this glorified position to those bearded and fustian-jacketed men who originally mastered the revolutionary power of iron wheel on iron rail, who fought bitter battles for their rights, but who still had the compassion to refuse to shunt a wagon in which a bird was nesting.

The Double Homers

Lodging away from home by train crews first came to my knowledge in 1942 when, in a schoolyard at Carlisle, I heard the son of a railway guard relating how his father had been obliged that week to wait five hours for a bed in a railway hostel. As an errand boy in the city I often cycled past the huge brick building on Gallows Hill which housed lodging trainmen from London and the north-west of England. Scottish crews lodged on the northern side of the city at Kingmoor hostel. The lodging men, coal-stained, grey-faced and red-eyed, with their brass-bound lodging tins and unfamiliar dialects, were a feature of our main railway centres for many years. Lodging men were a hardy breed, a unique combination of natural restlessness contrasted with an inimitable acceptance of rule and ritual behaviour.

The history of railway workers lodging away from home had three phases: first, the imposition of lodging by the private companies; secondly, the growth of disaffection with the system; and lastly, the unofficial strikes against lodging which resulted from years of unheeded protest through normal lines of communication.

The lodging trainmen of Britain had little in common with earlier itinerant workers, such as the medieval guild journeymen, the travelling masons, or the tramping artisans of Victorian England, all of whose histories have contributed to the social fabric of Britain. All of these groups had ports of call in other towns where they met at hostelries with such names as the Mason's Arms, the Carpenter's Arms and the Bricklayer's Arms. In these hostelries, a travelling craftsman met a committee of his colleagues, was given refreshment, money and information about jobs. In a strange town he was among friends. The lodging trainman and his engine were, even when lodging only thirty miles from home, always termed 'foreign'.

From the earliest days, the larger railway companies found it useful to have engine-men and guards 'on tap' in places both near and distant from the home depot. Such men, with wide route knowledge, could be moved across the system like pieces on a chessboard, and the cost of such activity was minimal.

Despite the drawbacks of lodging away, almost every depot had its 'lodging king', a man of whom it was said that he would hang up like an overcoat, his lodging basket on the table, ready to dart to the shed on the heels of the caller-up who had advised him that he was required to lodge on a 'special' train.

For many years, lodging away affected only engine-men and guards, but was extended later to sleeping-car attendants, ticket collectors and dining-car attendants. For the companies, men away from home overnight were 'resting', but the train crews had other names for the system, such as 'double tripping', 'lodging out' or 'booking off'. The Great Western men originated the term 'double homing', and this is the term we will use.

The earliest double homers stayed in private houses, quickly nominated 'diggings' or 'lodges'. The origins of private lodging are lost in history, but we know that foremen at engine sheds kept lists of private addresses where men could stay at very short notice. Such foremen were authorized to loan small amounts of money to men asked to lodge when signing on at the home depot. Pocket watches were available to drivers under the same arrangement. Engine-men who lodged could build up their own list of available premises, a procedure at odds with the stringent control over the movements of staff normally insisted upon by the railway companies. From the haphazard start, lodging away grew into a strictly regulated system which was to endure throughout the age of steam and into the age of diesel and electric traction. Begun by the railway companies of old, it ended only when British Rail decided it was no longer economically feasible.

In the 1830s, the Newcastle and Carlisle Railway banned lodging allowances, arguing that wages were adequate to 'cover that charge'. Ten years later the London and Brighton Railway was paying 'away from home' allowances of 2s. per night to engine-men and guards. As P. W. Kingsford records:

> In the 1860s on the Great Western, engine-men were paid 2s. 6d. for lodgings, but subsequently, because of the danger that they might profit from it, it was reduced to 1s. 6d. In the early 1870s the pay of brakesmen on the London and North-Western included any such allowances, but a little later the regulations provided for them to have 1s. per night if no company's lodging house was provided.[1]

If the lodging continued beyond two days, the allowance increased to 1s. 3d. per day and 2s. per night.

Before trade-union activity influenced the working of lodge trains, there was no limit to the detention a man could endure. Nor was he paid extra for long detention in strange towns. A man often lodged only thirty or forty miles from his own backyard only to be advised on reporting to his foreign depot that he was not working home, but to another depot. Carlisle men lodged at Dumfries, Bletchley men at Newport Pagnell, Crewe men at Salop, Patricroft men at Wigan and St Helens. In the 1920s, Wigan men lodged at Sutton Oak, which was only seven miles from home, and at Widnes, only eleven miles out. A man could be away a week, short of money, tobacco, and enduring the misery of clothing long past the scent of attar of roses. These men lodged at home and lived away.[2]

The lodging men had to create for themselves a special web of personal and social relationships. Passenger men on the Great Western Railway always used premises different from those of the freight crews. At Hereford, passenger men were guests of Mrs Davis, while the humbler freight crews lodged with Mrs Sadler.

The Great Western engine-men had a fearsome loyalty to their craft and extended this to behaviour on lodging duties. O. S. Nock wrote of Mr G. Grant, a divisional superintendent at Plymouth in the 1860s, who recalled

> . . . the case of the old 4.00 a.m. daily goods [train] from Swindon to Weymouth, which called and did shunting at nearly every station en route. This train was regularly worked on alternate days by two brothers, and they were often sixteen, seventeen or even eighteen hours on the trip of ninety miles. What 'lodging' at Weymouth then entailed Grant does not reveal, but he does record that however late their overnight arrival it was a point of honour with both the brothers never to be a minute late in starting away on the return trip at 4.00 a.m. from Weymouth.[3]

This is a prime example of loyalty to the company and job, where the needs of the service took precedence over the need for rest by track-numbed limbs.

Many of the private lodges were small houses built near to the engine shed or marshalling yard and bedroom windows were often kept shut to keep out noise. Some landladies were the widows of railway workers. In the days before social security, taking in lodging trainmen was in some cases their only source of income. Often landladies earned 'pin money' by letting bedrooms to double homers. Other proprietors were fellow railway workers buying their homes on mortgage.

According to Mr Wilf Turner, a double homer from Bristol, 'The life of a double-home landlady was sad and unrewarding.'[4] The double homers usually cooked for themselves, but many landladies would cook a few potatoes in order to earn a few coppers. In the main, the double homers did not have the run of the house—the kitchen and the bedroom were the limits.

The houses had to be left open all night. The position of the key was known to the double homers, and in the more popular houses men were coming and going at all hours of the night. Most kitchens contained a blackboard which informed the new arrivals who had preceded them and at what time the beds would be vacant. If the house was full, then the men simply tramped to another address. The kitchens of these houses, piled with the equipment of engine-men and guards, resembled an engine-shed messroom more than the pride and joy of a housewife. Sunday brought little easement, but the kitchen, like Dr Barnardo's Home, was always open to the boots of trainmen.[5]

The pressure on space was tremendous. Very quickly a tradition arose where the engine-men shared a bed while the guard slept alone, reinforcing the separateness of engine and brake van. As few of these homes had hot water laid on, the engine-men would wash off their grime in a bucket on the engine; many would rinse socks in the same way. In the dead hours, the driver would rustle up some wood and the fireman would smuggle out a knob of coal to freshen up an ailing kitchen fire—this coal became known as 'the pocket piece'.

To be caught carrying firewood was a minor offence but stealing coal could bring down the wrath of the railway gods. In a cold house beds would be examined for dampness by placing a watch between the sheets. If on retrieval the watch face was damp the men would shift out to another lodge. Many beds in those days had straw mattresses, so the precaution was necessary.

The inside toilet was almost unknown; the chamber pot was on regular duty, so there was no place for false modesty on cold nights. On such nights it was regarded as a bonus that the beds were often still warm from the last occupant. The third occupant of such a bed was rarely in the mood to demand room service at 4.00 a.m.

In his regular lodge a man left part of his identity in the bedroom, yet he could go for years without passing more than the time of night with the others who shared the accommodation. There were always men who could not stomach sleeping in houses which bulged with weary, snoring humanity; these men would sleep in the engine-men's messroom at the shed, or sort out a coach in the carriage sidings which looked stabled for repairs. Some drivers would not allow firemen to smoke in the bedrooms, not because of fire risk but because tobacco could harm the drivers' eyes.

Although friendships were struck, the relationships were usually businesslike, the men paying immediately on arrival. As little entertainment was available in the houses it was not unknown for the men to take their sleep and pleasure simultaneously by bedding down in a local cinema. Sometimes there was little alternative, for the landladies in seaside towns, glad enough of the custom in the dull months, would, 'in the season', relegate the men to attic or basement. One lady at Nuneaton covered the legs of bedroom and kitchen furniture with old stockings as a defence against heavy-booted lodgers. At Blackpool men were lulled to sleep by North Sea breakers and the dull roar of the Golden Mile; sand found its way into some of these bedrooms. At Stratford in east London it was the roar of engine valves and soot on the bedclothes. Guard Mosley of Wigan had a brother who found the lodge at Birkenhead riddled with cockroaches. By contrast, the private home at Westhouses, Derbyshire, always had a warm fire going and a bottle of beer ready, day or night. Masborough, near Rotherham, was probably the showpiece of lodging houses on the Midland section. The hostess, Zita, always provided a warm Yorkshire welcome; 'her' men had hot food on arrival and while they were resting she set about cooking another meal. The fireman always had the bed behind the door, and the winter cold was tempered by a hot brick wrapped in a towel placed in the fireman's bed. Zita had a parrot which picked up some railway slang and would screech as the men arrived, 'Kentish Town men—double trip, are you lodging?'[6]

Lodging in Scotland, as with most places, had its ups and downs. When William Watt of Carlisle arrived at Ardrossan with a train in the early hours, he and his fireman slept in the engine-men's messroom until the landlady drew her bolts at 8.00 a.m. In the late 1940s private lodging was still operative in Scotland and Mr William McLagan has left us a pen picture of how he lodged in a private house in Stranraer on the west coast:

> I stayed with a railway family who had a comfortable cottage near the engine shed. The bedroom was occupied every day by a driver and fireman from Corkerhill depot, Glasgow. When they left, the room was made over to another youngster and myself. The rooms were lit by ornate glass-funnelled paraffin lamps which gave off a soft light and a pleasant aroma. Food was good and plentiful, because all kinds of game, including pheasants, were killed on the track and ended up in our stewpot.[7]

A great amount of lodging work was on night freight trains, and although landladies would cook for a small extra charge, they would not arise between midnight and 8.00 a.m. The double homers preferred to cook their own meals, and this was the reason for the large black and brass bound tin known as a lodging basket. Into each man's lodging basket would go pre-heated puddings, pies, sugar, jam, tinned milk, cake and biscuits, bacon and eggs. The Edge Hill men carried a cloth-covered basin of 'scouse'—a type of Irish Stew—and the west of England men relied upon a pasty known by its shape and texture as a brake-block—history is silent on its taste. Cardiff men, known as 'railbenders' when lodging, carried pre-cooked meals in enamelled basins. In the depressed 1930s, the lodging-men, with their black brass-bound tins, were well known to the street urchin of all the main railway centres. All double homers had the experience of young children approaching them at the depot exits asking, 'Anything left in your basket, mister?'

The lower half of a lodging basket was a symphony of railway memorabilia—*Rule Book*, appendices, train notices, boiler gauge glasses, woollen 'trimmings' for big and small ends and a pack of cards with which to do the devil's work when the train was pounded in a running loop. In these loops was enjoyed the great lodging meal of bacon and eggs sizzled on the firing shovel. Fresh tea, made with water boiled in the firebox via a tea can perched on the shovel blade, washed down the potatoes which had been cooking slowly on the engine manifold.

Lodging away made an early appearance on the companies which were to consolidate as the Southern Railway, but it never became a feature of train working. Firemen on this railway were not allowed to lodge until they reached twenty-one years of age. In 1938, Bricklayer's Arms men lodged at a 'hell hole' in Snargate Street, Dover. Ramsgate men were concurrently lodging on one turn in the Old Kent Road. In the mid-1930s, while lodging at Ramsgate, driver Green and fireman Blake of Bricklayer's Arms attempted a spot of fishing from a boat; a heavy sea pushed their craft around the coast to Deal, where they were retrieved. Reporting for duty at Ramsgate they were told that their families had been informed that they had been 'lost at sea'.

Many of the private lodging houses left much to be desired. When Wally Chalmers was a fireman on the Cornish Riviera, he stayed in a private house at Brockley Road, Plymouth. He recalls that the landlady, who shall be nameless, was a poor woman, whose pickings, at 5s. per man per visit, did not permit much in the way of material comforts.[8] The winter months brought arctic conditions to the bedrooms; the blankets, of the cheapest and coarsest material, were supplemented by the men's own overcoats. At times the rugs on the floor were put on the bed to gain some warmth. The undying memory of Brockley Road, however, is that of the slippers; trainmen in the house were expected to remove boots and to use slippers worn by countless men over the decades.

At Fishguard, Ma Thomas had been taking lodgers since the harbour was a fishpond, and she would cheerfully put to bed any engine-man who had foolishly 'gone on the oil'—the Great Western term for alcoholic excess. At Fishguard rabbits could be bought cheaply and many London engine-men brought a dozen home to sell about the shed to eager customers.

The GWR—God's Wonderful Railway—had one completely satisfied double homer. When guard George Smith of London lodged at Carmarthen he stayed at a public house—the Red Cow Hotel—where ex-shunter Dai Rees and his wife treated him like one of the family. At the hostelry, Smith kept an old 350 cc Ariel motor cycle with which he explored the Gower coast. Mrs Smith would at times travel on the train which the double homer was working and spend the period of the lodge turn as a guest. For Smith, double homing meant getting paid for enjoying himself.

The GWR was not always able to satisfy the basic needs of the men which it sent on lodging turns. Bill Parker, who spent his entire life in the service of the 'Royal Road', as the GWR called itself, has written:

> At Paddington we had eighteen guards who lodged regularly at Plymouth, Truro, Penzance and in south Wales. The average pay per double home was about 6d. extra per shift. Some of the places at which we were expected to stay were indescribable. At times, refusing to sleep in filthy beds, we would snatch a few hours' sleep in the station waiting-room before working our trains home. On other occasions, men would refuse the proffered accommodation and would sleep in the driver's cabin at the engine shed. Others would find a resting place on the cushions of a carriage stabled in the sidings adjacent to the station.
>
> During the busy summer season, Western men on lodging trips often had to give up their bedrooms to the summer visitors and make do with a camp bed in the basement or attic. On one occasion we were expected to lodge in a railway carriage which had been sent to Torre for that purpose. On entering the coach we found it reeking of old boots and blocked toilets. We refused to lodge there and as we did not wish to let the company down we slept in deck chairs on the beach. This way we did not break faith with our employer or our public.
>
> In the worst days of lodging, men on short rest between Plymouth and Truro were expected to 'book off' and 'book on' again at the away station. Payment was not continuous so a man could perform a day's work spread over sixteen hours, yet be paid only for the hours actually in traffic, which could be as low as nine hours. There was, however, little difficulty in filling vacancies in lodging links.[9]

In the 1950s, train crews from Plymouth and Penzance were lodging at the trim little home of Mrs Hines in Wells House Road, Acton. Mrs Hines was the widow of an express-train driver; on his death Mrs Hines was left with a weekly income of 18s. With two children to keep and a weekly rent of 21s. Mrs Hines went into the double-homing business. She had one room only available for lodgers. She took only engine-men and guards and had twenty of them in her home every four weeks. The engine-men shared one bed; the guard, following tradition, slept alone. There was no bath and only an outside toilet. The price for use of the bedroom was 2s. 6d. per man per trip. The men brought their own alarm clock and cooked their own food, usually the great lodging repast of bacon and eggs.[10] It was questionable how much sleep the men had, for the house backed onto the Broad Street–Richmond line, where a procession of freight trains laboured morning, noon and night to 'catch a path' or be squeezed in between two tightly scheduled passenger trains.

Entertainment and leisure were constant problems for men lodging in private homes. If engine-men arrived at Wells House Road in the afternoon, they would rarely stay in the house, preferring to go to local cinemas and public houses. Mrs Hines recalls the Great Western men who stayed with her as being quite elderly, a demonstration of how long it took the men to reach the best-paid work. In the days before social security, the double homers were a lifeline to those too proud to ask for state assistance. At the home of Mrs Hines, the fees were paid immediately the men entered. This was the usual practice at the private homes. When the men left their own homes for a lodging turn, the ritual was no less regular; ex-railway guard Sid Mosley has written: 'We were a London and North-Western family. My father and I were lodging guards, two brothers were lodging engine-men. The whole of the kitchen table was needed to pack the lodging baskets.'[11]

Some of the men were adventurous enough to savour the sights of strange towns and cities. A youngster lodging in London could enjoy delights not readily available in Carlisle, Carnforth or Crewe. Petticoat Lane was a favourite haunt of men double homing in London, and London men lodging in Newcastle-upon-Tyne could always find contrasts when visiting fishing or holiday centres in the homeland of railways.

Private lodging existed into the 1950s, but as early as 1890 the larger companies were building hostels for the double homers. The hostels displayed many styles and designs, but the common element was proximity to engine sheds or marshalling yards. Many of the new hostels were in the charge of matrons, an aspect of the theory that males away from home need the controlling influence of a female. In the earliest days the matrons played a macabre game of musical beds, and many complaints were made by men about the shortage of accommodation.

By 1891 the London and North-Western Railway had hostels for trainmen in most large towns and cities on its routes, and its manager, Mr George Findlay, commented:

We have comfortable lodging houses built by the company for the men, where we have provided lavatory accommodation, baths and things of that kind. And a man, the moment he is taken off a train, is put to bed and gets the amount of rest necessary, he is called up when it is his turn. In many of these lodging houses we have fifty or sixty beds where men get relief of that kind.[12]

In the mid-1920s, engine-men from the Chalk Farm Depot were lodging at Carlisle and men from Crewe were lodging at Perth. The Camden men 'took their turn'; that is, they could not escape the lodging turns as part of natural promotion. At Crewe, the Perth work was eventually done by volunteers, and there was never a shortage of engine-men willing to earn 'the big penny' on work which needed muscle power and dedication.

When the train crew arrived at the hostel, tradition took over. The driver entered first, followed by the fireman, who marked the train-crew board, indicating what men had arrived, what meals would be needed at which times, and what time the men wished to be called. In the 1950s, the arrivals were presented with a piece of hard yellow soap and a hessian towel. The soap would not lather and the towel, once wetted, simply refused to dry anything.

Mr Davis, a driver at Crewe, has vivid memories of the dining-rooms of company hostels. He has written of brown and green paintwork, of cast-iron saucepans, black-as-night frying pans impregnated with the juices of a thousand onion-topped steaks and of fat-bellied teapots whose interiors were as brown as their chipped exteriors.[13]

For the instruction of the travelling men the Gideon Society provided a Bible in most bedrooms. The volume was very useful in levelling up listing wardrobes, or wedging wobbly windows, but rarely was it put to its proper purpose. However misused, the Bibles were never mutilated.

Washed and fed, the men would either go out or remain in the recreation room, which usually sported a small billiard table, cards, dominoes and perhaps a dart board. A radio with earphones was a real luxury. The yellow and black covers of the *Railway Gazette* were an inevitable part of the accoutrements of these recreation rooms, but the pages of this famous magazine were turned about as often as those of the Gideon Bibles. Men who were being thumped and bumped for 200 and more miles were not interested in reading how smooth a ride the passengers were receiving as a result of the sophisticated equipment advertised in the famous railway journal.

An early hostel on the London and North-Western was built over the engine shed at Camden and caused an engine-man to complain that he had no bed to sleep in after fourteen hours on duty. The *Railway Service Gazette* commented:

He had to wait for men to get out of bed and they had done the same. For seven years this had been reported and nothing had been done.

In summer, some men had been overcome, presumably by the stench, had been taken ill and had to return home. The beds were smoking hot with sweat. If they waited for the matron to make the bed they would lose the bed to someone else, unless they stood by the door while she made it.[14]

The later Chalk Farm hostel, built in 1929, was fronted in Romanesque style, a veritable fortress of archways and embrasures. The hostel was only a few feet from where the fussy North London electrics burnished the rails of Primrose Hill Station. A few yards to the west was the clangour of Camden goods yard, and across the roar of the west coast main line could be heard the constant rumble of the coal hopper on Camden shed. The Crewe men who lodged at Chalk Farm were held in such esteem that they were always given the beds they requested, well away from the noise and smoke of Camden.

At Willesden Junction, the LNWR had a lodge in Stephenson Street which catered for ninety-eight lodgers at a time. It boasted central heating throughout its brown-linoleumed interior, and a speciality of the house was that all chamber pots were emptied by the domestic staff. According to Mr Davis of Crewe, who lodged there as driver and fireman, Willesden 'was noted for its stone stairs and iron railings, through which the wind whistled viciously. The bedrooms were rather like wooden horse stalls, divided by wooden partitions about seven feet high; many men who used this lodge compared Willesden with a prison— reminiscent of Wormwood Scrubs. A man coming in suffering from a cold or too much "liniment" could wake up every person on the floor.'[15]

Mr A. E. Grigg of Bletchley also lodged at Willesden; he has written:

The Willesden lodge, situated in the dingy streets near the loco shed, gave the appearance of a strongly built Victorian abode for down-and-outs. Solid brown-painted woodwork, cream-painted walls that had turned sourly yellow over the years, a spiral stone staircase that echoed the sound when heavy-booted inmates laboured their way to bed. The bedrooms, or sleeping cubicles, a more apt phrase, were just a number of wooden stables with small iron bedsteads, with reasonably clean linen provided you were the first to sleep in the box-like apartment. Furniture would have been an extravagance, even if there was space to fit it in, but a practical pot under the bed often gave evidence that the last incumbent had not long departed. There was consolation in knowing that if one fell out of bed the heavy density of bedroom fluff would make a soft landing. The gloomy surroundings and the numerous smells had the advantage of making a return to work a pleasure.

Meals were provided by a staff recruited with no particular quali-
fication for cooking or enticement to a happy stay. Many of the wary
inmates cooked their own meals. They probably decided on this
course when on their first visit they saw Old Nell, one of the staff in
this Dickensian abode. With stockings hanging down around her
ankles, matted shoulder-length hair and a face that showed youth
had been left far behind and washing was not one of her favourite
pastimes, Old Nell reminded you that it was not the Savoy Hotel.[16]

Steaming north from London, the next lodging place was Mr Grigg's
home town, Bletchley in Buckinghamshire. According to Mr Jim Cox, the
sleeping quarters were under the shed water tank and in the lodge the
cockroaches were as big as mice.[17]

At Rugby, the lodge was connected to the engine shed by a short
staircase; trainmen lodging there were invited by the foreman to 'climb
the golden stairs'—local slang for lodging. Rugby lodge was built of
Crewe-fired bricks, set in black mortar. In the fifty years it was opera-
tional, such was its quality that no major repairs were carried out on
the premises. The lodge was exclusive to engine-men, guards being
accommodated in a building in the goods yard.

Mr Grigg has also described Rugby lodge from the point of view of
the train crews of Bletchley:

Rugby lodge was used by Bletchley men, but staying there was a
dubious privilege. It was a part of the frontage buildings of the loco
shed and its interior followed the same pattern as Willesden and
Leicester. Food was brought and cooked by the inmates so a common
sight when walking into the dining-room was a number of men cooking on the large coal-fired range with its multi-purpose railway line
fender. As the men reached over to attend to their frying pans, one
foot would conveniently rest on the sturdy fender. A plate containing
an egg was balanced on the fender while other items were frying.
Frying time ended, large lumps of coal were crashed against this
unbreakable object to bring them down to suitable size for rapid
burning.[18]

At Crewe, even the local pick-up trains were lodging turns. The 'pick-
ups' were jobs which shunted at all sidings and stations, delivering coal,
cattle and goods. Crewe men had to lodge at Salop, thirty-two miles out,
Heaton Norris, thirty miles out, and Mold Junction, twenty-five miles
out. At Crewe, if a man was in the 'Extra' or 'Spare' link and wanted to
be at home on a particular day, he had to put his name down for a
'single trip'. This gambit was not always successful, and the applicant
was warned, 'Don't come this too often.'

In the inter-war period the London, Midland and Scottish lodge at Upperby hostel, Carlisle, was alongside the coaling plant; the windows facing the coal chute were never opened because of the flying dust. This lodge was replaced early in the Second World War, on a high piece of ground called Gallows Hill.

According to Jimmy Hulme of Liverpool there was plenty of good-natured banter between the 'cream' from Camden and the 'serfs' from Liverpool. This banter, however, could turn to nastiness if a non-Camden engine-man dared to sit at or place a utensil on the Camden table. This was like swearing in church. When Jim Walker was a fireman, he often wondered why tables were left vacant when they were obviously needed. Mr Walker once witnessed a scene where a Patricroft (Manchester) man threatened to punch the nose of a Camden fireman who had placed a lodging tin on the 'Manchester' table.[19] Pride and exhaustion formed the basis of such behaviour—pride in a long journey successfully completed matched by an exhaustion which screamed from every limb and numbed the consciousness. Like many other men, Jim Walker often saw Camden firemen coming into Upperby lodge and falling asleep at a table during their meal. Jimmy Hulme, when lodging at Upperby from Liverpool, was a 100 mile per day man. This, according to Camden engine-men, was boys' stuff. The trip from London to Carlisle was the true test of masculinity. Camden men asked for and obtained the best accommodation on the quietest side of the building.

The north-west of England was the heartland of lodging away, the Midlands and London following in that order. On the west coast route, Crewe, Stafford and Mold Junction hostels were all handsome in gabled stone. By contrast, Preston was a brick monstrosity where the wooden partitioned cubicles lay over the engine shed—a nightmare that the fire officers of today would not tolerate. This building also had a bad reputation for infestation by cockroaches.

Manchester had large hostels at Newton Heath, Belle Vue and Trafford Park, Birmingham boasted Aston, Bescot and Saltley. While none of these buildings were beloved by the double homers, the conditions had improved greatly since the time a brakesman felt compelled to write to his union journal:

> . . . The building in which the brakesmen have to sleep was formerly called the Queen's Hotel, but has for many years been used for office purposes, with the exception of five bedrooms and a mess room, which the men have to mount sixty-three steps to reach, loaded with the following articles (there being no place to leave them behind): coupling stick, oil can, grease knife, hand-lamp, a set of flags, a tin of fog signals, a large basket containing sufficient food for two days,

a large time book and appendix thereto, a *Rule Book*, and a train book. The furniture in the mess room consists of three chairs, two stools, and two forms, besides an old broken-down sofa. . . . The bedrooms, I am informed, are situated on the same floor, two of them containing three beds, the other three two each, which is only sufficient accommodation for twelve men, and there are, I believe, fifteen at the present time. As the men come in and go out at various times, some of the rooms are occupied from Monday morning until Saturday night, and several of the men have to make their own beds as a regular thing. Some of the chamber utensils are left standing two or three days together, the matron having no opportunity of doing the necessary work. Moreover, the bedroom windows are continually closed, so that no fresh air can be admitted.[20]

The Midland Railway had a passion for lodging and their premises could be found in all major railway centres. According to Jim Walker, this company had a nasty habit of placing their lodges in either the most insalubrious districts or within the shed perimeter. If the lodge was within the shed limits the company posted notices: 'Men asleep— please keep engines quiet.' On the Midland section, men struggling for sleep counted not sheep but engines.

This company had its defenders, however; F. S. Williams wrote:

There is also a fine three-storied building erected especially for drivers' lodgings in the event of the men being unable to get back to their homes the same night. This building is fitted up with a large cooking stove, with a room with fires and steam pipes for drying wet clothes, and with a lavatory. There are about twenty-two bedrooms, all comfortably arranged, so that each man has a separate chamber, a clean and comfortable bed. The corridors and landings are all heated by hot water pipes, and hot and cold water can also be obtained in abundance. Downstairs is a small room supplied with newspapers and periodicals for the use of the men.[21]

On Edgware Road in north-west London stood the huge red-brick hostel of Cricklewood, shielded from road noise by a large hoarding. When I visited it in 1973, the building was an empty hulk, a museum to the men who pummelled freight from the sodden, unkind Midlands to the markets of a voracious capital. At Cricklewood all the cubicles were half tiled and each contained a Gideon Bible. Cricklewood had a fantastic cast-iron 'pull out' clothes drier and that rarest of items, a 'night lavatory', the significance of which still eludes me.

Going north, the next Midland hostel was Wellingborough, another massive brick structure built within football-field distance of the crash and slam of the Wellingborough ashpits. Whatever double homers got up to in Wellingborough the ancient role and status of Midland Railway engine-men was maintained. Drivers and firemen sat at different tables. The driver could and did order his stoker to bed. These bigots would proudly inform young firemen that in earlier times promotion for firemen was dependent upon drivers' reports, regular attendance at work, the condition of the engine and the smartness and punctuality of the fireman.

Beyond Wellingborough lay the lace and hosiery city of Leicester, and Mr Grigg has once again left us an impression of the hostel there:

As trainmen walked in the door Victorian practical decor would meet the eye. To complete the scene, Old Bill, the one and only steward, would shuffle towards the newcomers and give a grunt to signify they were unwelcome. As he rose unwillingly from his chair, the oversized head on a bloated old body and unsteady legs could quite easily cause a hungry body suddenly to lose its appetite. Bill's cupboard of saleable food was limited to tins of sardines, beans, perhaps Irish stew and packets of biscuits; only on request and with great reluctance would he open up for business.

In the dull solitary confinement of the cubicle bedroom where creature comforts were of little importance, spiritual comfort was always at hand. The Holy Bible, clean, undamaged and conspicuous by the absence of other articles, was there if guidance was required.

In the greyness of the morning, if Old Bill was on duty, the tea, sugar and milk when tipped toward the tea cup was closely watched by Bill's watery eyes. If the upturned tin remained too long in that position Bill could no longer stand the sight of precious milk draining away. His hand would shoot out at surprising speed with the remark, 'Go steady, I got to get sixteen men out of that.'[22]

Between Leicester and Sheffield was the lodge at Long Eaton, near Trent. This building, which soaked up like a great sponge train crews from as far afield as London and Sheffield, was an island situated where traffic ebbed and flowed between the Toton marshalling yards and the main line. When I was there in the late 1950s, time had stood still for two decades, and the staff seemed caught in their own time warp. The huge fire, characteristic of the heyday of lodging, was a great compensation on freezing nights, for the cubicles were so cold that many of us preferred to snatch our sleep by its eternal flames. Each bedroom had its own Gideon Bible, and in the dining-room men sat on wooden forms and dined off scrupulously clean butcher-block tables. Those of us too young to have taken part in the pre-1939 lodging situation were regaled by the hostel steward with the great folklore of lodging in the days of steam. A great deal of the information in this book was mentally recorded in Long Eaton hostel.

The Midland lodge at Sheffield was known as The Nunnery, after a coal mine of the same name which operated beneath the building. The Nunnery, despite its insalubrious surroundings, was known to the engine-men as a home away from home, where men liked their 'own' beds and where this was usually accommodated. The Nunnery had sixteen bedrooms, warmed by a Jumbo stove. It was decorated in 'dingy green' railway paint and it sported the inevitable railway brown linoleum. Spitoons were an interesting embellishment, but somehow The Nunnery lost out on Gideon Bibles.

The bedrooms, usually single, but sometimes with two single beds, were equipped with a wardrobe, bedside lockers and a mirror for each man. For many years Mrs Maillard was the lady in charge of The Nunnery and it was due to her efforts that it enjoyed such an enviable reputation among trainmen. The door was never closed, but on arrival all men were greeted by the notice 'Please remove shoes before going upstairs to bed in order not to disturb the sleeping trainmen.' The Nunnery completed seventy years of soot-blackened service to the Midland train crews.

Holbeck, the Midland lodge at Leeds, was in the tradition of the large house. Built of brick with stone facings, begrimed with the smoke of half a century, it stood within the perimeter wall of the locomotive depot. Thirty yards away was the ashpit with its squeaking ash elevator and grumbling coal hopper. Day and night the snick of the coal pick, the clash and clatter of rake, shovel, and fire iron, contested the right of a man to sleep.

The Holbeck engine-men did their best to muffle the traditional sounds of a busy engine shed, but steam meant noise and their task was an unenviable one. For men lodging at Leeds, the atmosphere of the lodge was a great compensation. In the 1950s, Holbeck lodge was a historical relic, a monument of Victorian industrial archaeology, yet its faded walls rang to a rich assortment of dialects which ranged from Glaswegian and Bristolian to chirpy north London accents.

The train crews were always assured of a warm welcome from the hosts, Mr Wilf Thornhill and his wife. The food was good and there was always plenty. Leeds lodge was an important clearing house where, between trains, engine-men from far-flung areas discussed the issues which affected them.

Sometimes the lodge job allowed a few hours out in the evening. In Leeds, the Yates Wine Lodges were popular with the men, as well as the Friendly Inn at Holbeck. Theatres were rarely visited, for unless spare clothing was kept in the lodge, the obligatory blue cotton shirt, crumpled trousers and boots of the foot-platemen were out of place at all except the lowest class of music hall.

In the 1930s, Leeds abounded in seedy dives. According to Jim Walker:

> The 41 Club provided pleasure-seeking trainmen with a 'speakeasy' atmosphere, and very daringly supplied drinks after hours. Before 1939, many public houses had lounges where women of doubtful virtue were only too willing to accept drinks from affluent railway-men. And affluent they were. Men on lodging turns could earn up to £10 per week when the usual earnings in the country were about £2 10s. It was no wonder that the best lodging turns were jealously guarded by the depots at which the turns were allocated.[23]

Very different from the grime of Leeds and Sheffield was the Midland lodge at Hellifield, a converted house which nestled in pastoral splendour at the end of the scenic descent which had begun at Ais Gill summit. The matron at Hellifield was responsible for the excellent meat pies enjoyed by men from as far afield as Carlisle and Heaton Mersey.

The Midland lodge at Saltley, Birmingham, was situated at the railway end of a sad and dispirited street. It was dominated by the local gas-works, the fumes from which permeated every hole and corner of the building. There was no escaping the smell. When a man rose from bed his nose and throat were impregnated with the smell and taste of municipal gas. In the 1950s, Saltley was a hybrid lodge, catering for double-home men but also taking in large numbers of permanent residents, mostly young firemen and guards who had been transferred into the area to offset the huge staff shortages. Saltley had an institutional air, with long dingy passages leading into tired-looking rooms. The behaviour of the youngsters played havoc with the sleep of men on double-home working. In my time, many of the double homers refused to eat the meals provided, preferring to bring their own food or using a local fish and chip shop.

In the 1960s the position had altered little. When Noel Cox was firing into Birmingham from Scunthorpe 'the place was a pigsty'. Rarely was hot water available and the washbowls were plugged with news-papers as they had been in the 1950s. The fish and chip shop was still the main source of sustenance for double homers. In the 1970s, how-ever, Scunthorpe men lodged in splendour in the Market Hotel, Birmingham, a far cry from the days of straw beds and breakfasts cooked on the firing shovel.

On the Western Region, between 1945 and 1952, a small proportion of railway lodging was in de-wheeled carriages. Before Laira engine shed provided huts for lodging men, engine-men from Old Oak Common slept under these conditions when lodging at Plymouth. Mr Wally Chalmers remembers that when lodging with such trains as the 'Cornish Riviera'

> . . . the lodge at Laira was a converted passenger coach near both shunting yard and loco shed. One compartment of the coach was the bedroom; the washplace was the toilet compartment, but there was no water supply. Cold water was available from a tap out in the yard and this was brought by bucket. Heating the compartment was the task of a small cylinder containing an electrode; it would not burn a man's hand no matter how long it was held. The bed was so narrow that any turning over would deposit the double homer on the floor of the compartment.[24]

The alternative to the coach was the private house—not much of a choice for the crack engine-men of the Western Region.

The Southern Railway introduced another form of railway lodging, an activity known as 'tidal lodging'. To maintain a pool of men in the Southampton area who had route knowledge to London, the Southern built a hostel at Eastleigh. This building was between the engine disposal pits and adjacent to the coal stage from which a Niagara of coal, dust and noise poured incessantly. Above the bedrooms gurgled the tank which supplied the shed with water.

Before the turn of the nineteenth century lodging away both privately and in company hostels was in full spate on the Eastern Counties Railway. One of the earliest company-built hostels was at Stratford in east London. This hostel was built over the main offices in the centre of one of the largest railway establishments in the world. Trains ran within a few feet of the bedrooms. A number of conflicting views of the Stratford hostel have been handed down to us, the managerial attitude being quite different from that of the men who used the building and its facilities. At the 1891 Parliamentary Select Committee on Hours of Labour on the Railway, the General Manager of the Great Eastern, Mr Birt, said of Stratford Lodge: '. . . we have excellent accommodation in the shape of dormitories for the men; we have spent £2,000 in its constructions, and are spending another £1,000 in additions to it.' Asked if one of the motives in building dormitories was to keep men out of public houses, Mr Birt gave his answer firmly in the positive. It was also, he remarked, the intention of his company, '. . . to construct dormitories at all our principal stations'.[25]

The men of the Great Eastern were faced at this time with the alternatives of long hours on duty or the prospect of lodging away. Guard Ellis of Stratford was asked, 'Would you prefer to work a longer day if you knew you would finish at home, or would you prefer to lodge?' He replied, 'To lodge away is what every railwayman hates; I am very much opposed to it.'[26]

Although the Eastern Counties Railway was proud of its Stratford dormitory, there was another view of the situation, and it was expressed by a socialist engine-man who wrote:

> One hostel in east London was situated over the offices in the middle of the locomotive yard, where engines were moving around twenty-four hours every day. The sleeping accommodation was in a dormitory without windows, the ventilation coming from louvres in the roof. These let in large quantities of soot, and it was common to wake up in the morning to find a thin layer of soot on the bed.[27]

Stratford had a fan in the roof to keep the air moving, and this helped to bring in the soot from the shed. Later, a part of the roof was converted to glass, which turned the dormitory into a sun trap during the summer months. The rattle of passing trains, the shunting operations in the yard and the all too often sudden emission of steam from a tortured safety valve must have made Stratford a very unpopular place to stay. It gives credence to the legend that for many years men lodging at Stratford were not reluctant to have a few pints at Dipples, just outside the station, in the hope of dulling their senses into sleep. Stratford had 300 engines and every one was a menace to the man trying to sleep. It is no wonder that in the earliest days engine-men talked of 'wooden engines and iron men'. In the days of the Eastern Counties Railway guards and foot-platemen used separate buildings; the engine crew went to the hostel and the guards to a large and gloomy building which stood in the centre of the original goods yard at Temple Mills near Stratford.

Halfway across north London from Stratford, the King's Cross depot also had its problems in lodging away. Mr Bob Lunniss, who was a driver at King's Cross, has written:

> Prior to 1939, lodging on the Eastern Counties main line was provided in old company hostels, many over seventy years old. In many cases, a trainman on leaving home would not know whether or not he would be expected to lodge when he reached his destination.
>
> When he signed off at the foreign depot, the man could be given the address of a householder who accepted lodgers and he would go there. If the householder took him in, the man would wait there until called for duty. On many occasions a man would be refused accommodation or would be told he could lodge there if prepared to wait until another man vacated the bed.[28]

Of the hostels used by the east coast men, Farnley in Yorkshire seemed to be the most disliked. This Leeds hostel was in the centre of an angle of rails which was heavily used for the turning of engines. It was, according to various correspondents, a forbidding workhouse type of building. It had a stone floor with two large tables in the centre, and a fixed form running round the walls. There was a heating boiler in one corner and a gas stove in the other. The sleeping quarters were on the first floor, and the cubicles were large enough to take only a single bed. The cubicle partitions reached neither to the floor nor to the ceiling, so a snorer, the bane of lodging men, made sleep very difficult. Farnley had four washbowls and its saving grace was that it possessed a big old-fashioned bath into which limbs racked by 200 miles of bump and clatter could sink for merciful relief.

In the eastern counties the men of March in Cambridgeshire could well be termed 'lodging kings'. In 1940, 'when 750 men were employed on foot-plate duties, two-thirds of the men were employed on main-line duties which involved lodging away. The work often consisted of fifty-two week rosters, fifty of which were lodging away.'[29] The spread was enormous, and March men faced the following long detentions:

Location	Hours detained
Norwich	18
Doncaster	18
Cambridge	12
Yarmouth	15–16
Grimsby	16
Longwith	23
Retford	20
Sudbury	16
Dereham	12

On Sundays, March men would work special trains and they were lodged at places only a few miles away from home. The excursion men lodged at Peterborough, fourteen miles away, King's Lynn, twenty-three miles away, and at Cambridge, thirty-three miles away; all these places could be reached within the hour from March. Before 1921, engine-men lodging at March made individual arrangements or stayed at the Railway Mission Hall where they slept on ex-army beds and were fed at the Temperance Hotel in the station yard. After 1921, the company took over a private house for its lodging men. There is on record a case of a driver and fireman from Doncaster who were lodged at March for fifty-one hours. When March men got home from lodging away they were expected to fill up their working day by helping out with shed duties. One foreman at March would forestall any column dodging by locking the door to the messroom, ensuring that men ate and relaxed at his discretion. March men lodging at Annesley slept in ex-army huts and were looked after by a caretaker.

When March men lodged away they often carried 'pocket pieces' of coal with which to maintain the fire in the houses used as lodges. Coal was very much more expensive in the eastern counties than it was in South Yorkshire. Few of the private lodges provided bathing facilities and the train crews rarely looked for such luxuries, the cost of which would have to be borne from their meagre lodging expenses. Cases of men sleeping on the floor in private dwellings were not unknown when sixteen to eighteen men were billeted in three-bedroomed houses.

The price for lodging away for these men was for many years $1\frac{1}{2}d.$ per hour, so overspending of the allowance was not very hard. As one railwayman observed, 'I hated being a $1\frac{1}{2}d.$ an hour man.'

Some of the men lodged away for twenty years as firemen, and on being made drivers were marked up immediately on lodging away turns. There is little doubt that the men of March hated lodging away and when the real struggle for abolition began the Cambridgeshire men were among the staunchest and most vociferous campaigners.

In 1927, when the LNER was contemplating non-stop running between London and Edinburgh, it was clear that the great barrier to success would be the physical exhaustion of the engine-men. Before 1928, no engine crew had worked a non-stop train for anything approaching the proposed 392·7-mile journey. Mr Nigel Gresley, the Chief Mechanical Engineer of the LNER, solved this problem by designing locomotives which eliminated the need for the train to stop en route for engine-men to be relieved. This was achieved by constructing a passage through the tender of the locomotive. When the engine was coupled and gangwayed to the train, a spare crew sitting in the train was able to pass from a coach to the engine.

The first five of the Gresley Pacifics to be provided with corridor tenders were Nos. 4472, *Flying Scotsman*, 4476, *Royal Lancer*, 2573, *Harvester*, 2577, *Night Hawk* and 2580, *Shotover*. The eight-wheeled tenders were 25 ft 10 in long, carrying nine tons of coal and 5,000 gallons of water. Fully loaded, the tender weighed sixty-two tons eight cwt. The 5 ft high, 18 in wide corridor was lit naturally by a round port-hole front and rear. Nigel Gresley was a big man, as were many of his main-line crews, so he made the corridor just large enough for his own frame to pass through, reckoning that where he could go, so could his beefy engine-men.

The double-crewing on this London–Edinburgh run had, on leaving London, a crew from King's Cross depot on the engine; sitting in a reserved compartment in the train was a crew from Edinburgh Haymarket. Approaching Tollerton in Yorkshire, the Scottish crew would come through the tender and relieve the London men, who would then ride as passengers to Edinburgh, where they lodged in private houses.

In the summer of 1927, a relief Scots train from London to Newcastle, by running the 268 miles non-stop, created a new record, previously held by the Great Western for the run between Plymouth and Paddington. Encouraged by this, the LNER in 1928 booked the *Flying Scotsman* to run non-stop between London and Edinburgh. On 1 May of that year, the *Flying Scotsman* left London on the down inaugural run. Simultaneously, the other half of the new service left Edinburgh for London. At King's Cross the engine and train were inspected by Sir Charles Batho, Lord Mayor of London, and Sir R. L. Wedgewood, the General Manager of the LNER. The train was 700 feet long and weighed 500 tons. The trip from London to Tollerton was under the control of driver A. Pibworth and fireman W. Goddard of King's Cross shed.

At the same time the up *Flying Scotsman* was being recognized in Edinburgh by a visit from Bailie Hay and his daughter, who presented driver T. Henderson and fireman R. McKenzie with black and white rosettes (the city's colours), and silver badges in the shape of the city's arms. Henderson and McKenzie were relieved at the half-way stage by driver J. Day and fireman F. Gray of King's Cross.

All along the line from Edinburgh to London there gathered groups of people keen to watch the passage of these record-breaking trains. On arrival in London, Mr Whitelaw, Chairman of the LNER, presented the train crews with beautiful pocket books suitably inscribed to mark the occasion. This was easily the longest non-stop journey in the world, and the men working these trains became a new elite among the enginemen. They were stationed at King's Cross, Gateshead and Edinburgh Haymarket; here are their names: [30]

King's Cross engine-men

Driver B. Glasgow	Fireman A. Austin
Driver H. Miles	Fireman W. J. Bridle

Gateshead engine-men

Driver H. Pennington	Fireman J. Ridley
Driver J. Gascoigne	Fireman J. J. Williams
Driver J. W. Halford	Fireman J. F. Cairn
Driver J. G. Smith	Fireman J. Bambra
Driver J. G. Eltingham	Fireman J. Slinger

Scottish engine-men

Driver T. Roper	Fireman J. Todd
Driver R. Sheddon	Fireman L. Taylor
Driver T. Smith	Fireman J. Redpath

Lodging away was not an issue here; these were the top-paid, prestige trains on which a favoured few were privileged to work. Until 1946 the Edinburgh men lodged privately in London; after this date they used the ex-Midland lodge at Kentish Town, the front door of which was only a few yards away from the busy branch line between Kentish Town and Barking. There was nothing like the thud and smash of wagons shunting at nearby Holloway yard to ease a man into sleep.

In Scotland, double homing had, as might be expected, its own flavour and texture. At that end of the British Isles the Highland Railway found it necessary, in the Naughty Nineties, to provide temporary accommodation for foot-platemen. The penalty for misuse of the premises was severe, as this letter demonstrates: [31]

26 March 1894
Dormitory at Blair Atholl
This dormitory has been fitted up for the benefit of engine-men and firemen who may be stationed at Blair Atholl as spare men, and will also be for the use of engine-men and firemen arriving at Blair Atholl, and having time to rest themselves, but not having sufficient time at their disposal to look for lodging elsewhere.

It must be distinctly understood that the dormitory will be used solely as a bedroom for the benefit of those requiring it, and as such must be kept clean as circumstances will permit. It will be under the charge of the loco fireman and will be locked up when not in use.

Should any damage be done to any portion thereof by any of the occupants during his stay he will be held responsible for the cost of repairs.

(Signed)   D. Jones
Loco Engineer

Lodging away for Scottish trainmen was determined by traffic requirements; social considerations never entered the matter. The men of Polmadie in Glasgow, working between Carlisle, Perth and Dundee, were sometimes away from their depot for a week at a time. Hamilton train crews on the London, Midland and Scottish lodged at Hurlford, thirty-five miles from their home depot, and men from the North British shed at Eastfield lodged in private homes at Bathgate, thirty-five miles away. These were 'private home lodges', and the trainmen often had the problem of being unable to enter the house until they felt the landlady would unbolt the door. Men had been known to sleep in the shed messrooms, and even in the guard's van of stabled freight trains.

Dundee had no lodge, so men lodging out sought and found a variety of places to sleep and eat. Two of these buildings were in Dock Street. They were termed 'model lodging houses' and both had the same type of institutional air about them. In these lodges two types of industrial workers rubbed shoulders and swopped tales—the steady, hardworking railroaders and the seafaring men whose permanent abode was the 'model'. These men probably slept more soundly than the men lodging at Eastfield, for the hostel there was inside the engine shed. It was very different at Mallaig, near Fort William. Here the hostel was at the end of the No. 2 platform; it could take up to forty men at once. If the fishing industry was booming, Mallaig lodge was a busy place.

At Fort William, the engine shed and hostel were built inside the old fort. It could accommodate about twenty men, and in common with many other Scottish lodges its affairs were in the hands of a matron. In Aviemore stands Spey Lodge. Surrounded by a cluster of sturdy railway cottages and backed by some of the most spectacular scenery in the Highlands, Spey Lodge, once the lodging house for Scottish train crews, is one of the few places left where visitors can use the facilities originally provided for trainmen lodging away from home. Different again was Stranraer, where accommodation progressed from an old hut fitted with camp beds used by painters to third-class sleeping cars, the millennium being reached when a new single-storied lodge was built in the little windswept town on the coast. Controlled by a matron, this trim building could accommodate fifty men. Affectionately known as the 'Clayhole' by the lodging men, the thick local dialect contrasted wildly with the Cockney slang of the London sleeping-car attendants who lodged at Stranraer off the Irish Mail from Euston before the service was suspended and the line closed. Stranraer specialized in fish and chips—even for breakfast—but it was one of the friendliest places we knew. After one of the huge meals the lodging men would usually enjoy a stroll on the quayside and then repair to the Smugglers' Bar.

In Oban, the trainmen lodged in Alma Crescent, utilizing the bottom flat of the house, a rare treat for the men of Glasgow, Stirling and Grangemouth who lodged there. Inverness was probably the doyen of the Scottish lodges, possessing sixty bedrooms; among its regular users were men from Perth and a number of sleeping-car attendants from Euston. The building, on Longmoor Road, is now the headquarters of the Scottish Gas Board.

Lodging in Perth also provides a chequered history; the early lodging men slept in guards' vans and even in engine-men's messrooms—'the bothies'. A pinnacle was reached when train crews were allowed to use a building which Dewar's Distillery had provided for its male employees. The place had one drawback—Dewar's woke their employees for duty with a loud bell, so trainmen arriving in the early hours would wait up and go to bed only after the morning tocsin had cleared the premises. Despite the delightful aromas from the distillery, many Glasgow men lodging at Perth nipped back home and spent their rest period in their own homes, returning to Perth to work their own train home. This illicit practice was probably unknown to the railway authorities; if they did know, they turned a blind eye. It was a rare official who would consider tangling with a Polmadie engine-man who wished to sleep in his own bed.

The hostel in the Aitkenhead district of Glasgow was a sixty-six-roomed structure called Larkfield. Its lyrical name mocked its soot-stained exterior and the surrounding complex of factories and working-class tenements. The people of this area, railway and non-railway, contrasted sharply with the dismal environment. Larkfield eventually closed up as a lodge in order to be converted into a social works department. It was my experiences among the men of the Glasgow engine sheds and the hostel at Larkfield which encouraged me to write this history of lodging turns.

Lodging in Glasgow had many compensations. There was football at Ibrox Park or Celtic Park, or listening to the speakers at Glasgow Green. An English voice either at football matches or in a street debate always created great interest, although a foreigner had to keep his comments short and guarded. Glasgow had many street orators in the late 1940s, anarchist speakers always drawing interested crowds.

The one thing the Scottish hostels had in common with those throughout Britain in the late 1940s was the amount of movable engine equipment the lodging men carted through the streets and on buses. The engine-men's lockers in the lodges contained firing shovels, boiler gauge glasses and coal-slaking pipes. Only by toting this equipment to and from their engines could the men guarantee that their return trip would run to time.

Before Larkfield was opened in 1929, dining- and sleeping-car men from London travelled back from Glasgow to Motherwell to use the single-storied wooden building adjacent to the engine shed. The lodge was still being used in the late 1940s and during this period visiting trainmen would find the washroom occupied by two local football teams, getting the Lanarkshire mud from their bodies and gear. Englishmen were advised not to ask questions or raise objections. They didn't.

Engine-men lodging at Motherwell trod very warily when walking or working in the shed. In the late 1940s, when tools and tackle were in short supply, it was often necessary for foot-platemen to cannibalize dead engines for pieces of equipment. The men at Motherwell did not take kindly to such liberties. It was at Motherwell in 1948 during the tool shortage that I found a group of engine cleaners sitting in the cabin of a dead locomotive cleaning a vast selection of knives and other sharp implements. One cleaner had a revolver which he spun expertly on his trigger finger while I beat a rapid retreat.

Until the advent of the high-speed internal combustion engine, the main-line lodging men were the fastest men in the world across ground. Such a status could turn the head of any man. But the price for such status was heavy, for unless his health or eyesight failed, a man would lodge until the last day of his main-line career. Such lodging men were often referred to as 'hobos of the line'.

The lodging men were tied more tightly to their job than their colleagues on local work. They often worked over the tracks of more than one company. They were issued with more appendices, more working timetables and more weekly notices than non-lodging crews. With constantly changing speed restrictions, closing hours of signal boxes and the shutting off of water supplies, they could afford to miss nothing of importance in the mass of continuously amended printed material with which they were issued. They signed for every document issued and were held responsible for all errors.

The senior men did the bulk of the lodging work. For engine-men at depots such as Camden, Crewe, Carlisle, Polmadie, King's Cross, Gateshead, Doncaster, Old Oak Common, Cardiff and Bristol, the lodging house was the inevitable climax to a firing or driving career. A fireman would achieve the glory of long-distance work when he was about twenty-five years of age and could reckon on ten years of high-paid mileage turns; at the end of each run the lodging house awaited. At the age of forty-five, after ten years of shed, shunting, and local driving, the main line and the lodging house again became his dogpatch. It was his duty; he simply had to go. The *Royal Scot*, the *Flying Scotsman*, the *Cornish Riviera Express* would be his responsibility; the money was good, and the lodging houses, usually unattractive and utilitarian were part of the job.

The lodging train crews were divided into two groups of unequal size and occupation. In the first, and smaller, group were the express drivers and their firemen, the aristocrats of the line. In the large second group were the men who worked all the other types of trains, from express fish, fruit and meat trains down to the humble colliers and the empty wagon trains returning to the collieries.

Much of the lodging work was on freight trains which ran outside the heavy passenger timetable. A lot of this work was done between the hours of 7.00 p.m. and 3.00 a.m., that is, neither day nor night work, but a distinctive railway split-shift system. The regular railway shift system of days, nights and afternoons was not the world of the lodging man; he lived half-way between night and day. Weekend lodging turns and bank and public weekend holiday lodging away were other great social disenfranchisers.

The men lodging on freight trains waited for dead men's shoes, but it was far from being a period of inactive waiting. These slow trains were the basis on which the express driver of the future built his intimate knowledge of the lines he regularly worked over. Facing a trip of 200–300 miles in rough conditions, the express driver was able to call on experiences gained by years of lodging away on freight trains. Blinded by fog or snow his ears told him what his eyes could not as they listened to the changing sound of the ground beneath his wheels; this would give him an unfailing guide to places and distances. Without this knowledge his ability and technique would be flawed.

Should his health and eyesight continue to satisfy the railway doctor, a driver would retire full of years, miles and memories; if unable to meet the required rigorous standards, the driver 'came off' the foot-plate. He might be lucky and retain a place as the driver of a shunting engine in a railway backwater, but if the damage to physique or eyesight was severe, the options were messroom attendant, shed sweeping or lavatory attendant. In order to prepare for this possibility, the drivers of freight trains—the express men of the future—simply set about earning as much overtime as possible. While running between closely diagrammed passenger trains, the freight men often 'discovered' mechanical failures which slowed down their trains, disrupting the passenger service and leaving the signalman no alternative except to shunt the freight train into line-side loops—exactly what the engine-men wanted. In the sidings the men earned overtime; in the lodging houses they earned nothing. While in the loop, the lodging repast of bacon and eggs, fried on the shovel and washed down by fresh tea, was enjoyed by the engine-men; this black art was followed by several hands of cards while waiting for the signalman's decision. In the winter of 1955, when I was the fireman on a freight train between Somers Town, London, and Saltley, Birmingham, the driver and myself took advantage of a dense fog to drag out a rostered six-hour run to seventeen hours. This record lasted twenty-four hours. The crew of the same train on the next night took nineteen hours to complete the shift. Next payday we laughed all the way to the bank. Many engine-men bought their own homes and secured their own financial futures by such inimitable forms of social control.

Few men reached the top-flight passenger lodging jobs before their middle forties; often it was much later, and at a time when his family was 'getting off his hands'. His wife, who had managed the home and children for long periods without his presence, now faced a further two decades of shift work, lodging away and a particular type of loneliness.

There is little doubt that a sizeable minority of these top-flight drivers were shareholders in the old companies; these men advised the young starter, 'Look after the company, boy, and the company will look after you.' These were the men who would retrieve discarded oily cleaning rags from the shed or yard floor and dutifully return these to the stores. Others of this ilk would save drops of oil from cans left on the engines, and once they had achieved a good supply would triumphantly produce the oil from its storage place and oil up an engine without going to the store. Others were more concerned with their own financial security. One man I knew, a main-line lodging man, regularly sold his issue of overalls and came to work in ordinary clothes. Some of these men enjoyed rents from inherited property, although in the 1960s and 70s the emphasis seems to have shifted to the purchase and rental of caravans as security against eyesight failure or early retirement from main-line duties.

The engine sheds which bore the heaviest burden of lodging were usually those to which company housing estates were attached. Examples of such sheds were Carlisle, Crewe, March and Peterborough. In London, lodging men lived on company estates at Willesden, Acton and Cricklewood. Until the late 1930s, railway companies insisted that if men did not actually live on company estates they had to move into the 'calling up' area. This meant that a man had to move himself and his family within reasonable walking distance of the shed. Whatever its location within the city or town, the railway estate always developed a separate identity, and this separateness fostered a specific community spirit. For families of lodging men this community spirit had a special significance.

To set a man off at night to face hundreds of miles of fog, snow and darkness and to wonder if he would ever return was the unspoken dread endured by thousands of women throughout their lifetimes. Sometimes these men did not return alive. On 30 September 1945, driver Swaby and fireman Jones of Crewe, coming to lodge in London, made a serious error when they ran through a crossover road at Bourne End at more than twice the laid-down speed. These two, along with thirty-eight passengers, were killed on the spot, and five more people died later; in addition, sixty-four people were seriously injured. No satisfactory answer to this lapse of concentration was ever provided.

Lodging men were involved in the worst disaster ever to involve passenger trains in this country—the Harrow and Wealdstone disaster of 8 October 1952. In patchy fog, the overnight Perth–Euston express, which had passed two signals in the danger position, crashed into the back of a local train from Tring to Euston. Within moments, the down 8.00 a.m. Euston–Liverpool express smashed into the wreckage, the collision costing the lives of 112 people. Both Crewe foot-platemen on the Perth express were killed, along with the Edge Hill driver in charge of the down express. The fireman of the down express was flung from his cab, but survived the impact.

The knock at the door or the measured tones of a radio announcer bringing a railwayman's wife news of an accident were ever-present fears. Railway accidents make dramatic national news, but the effect on railway estate dwellers was always personal and poignant. These were the dangers which faced the lodging men and their families throughout the man's career.

The wives of the lodging trainmen were often the daughters of an earlier generation whose working lives had been dominated by the railway lodging house. In early married life the wife of a lodging man would be the partner of a coal-streaked fireman, whose lodging away would be done on freight trains. His hours of duty, sleeping and leisure would dominate her plans for shopping, cleaning and visiting. If he was a 'spare' fireman, she would rarely know from hour to hour what shift he would be working or where he would be required to lodge. As most of the lodging work was done during the night hours, there would be few weeks when she could sleep without disturbance, for between midnight and 6.00 a.m. were the hours when lodging men were most active.

These women were not impressed with thrilling runs, length of piston stroke or the benefits of super-heated boilers. They accepted the fact that they were fourth on a list which ran, in order of priority, engine, train, lodge, home. They were resigned too to the fact that lodging away was to be, except for one decade, something to be suffered for thirty years. Hers was to be a special type of loneliness. Unlike the wives of seafaring men, who could attune to long separations broken by long shore leaves, the wife of the lodging man was tied to railway shift hours as firmly as her husband.

The great task of the wife of the lodging man was to protect her husband against noisy callers and flippant disturbers of his rest. A casual caller at the home of a lodging man would often find the door knocker screwed down or its clamour numbed by a strategically placed cloth. Frivolous visitors were discouraged, as were barking and screeching pets; stray animals were rarities on railway estates. Public utility men servicing the estates used the back door of the premises, always aware of the excitement engendered by a front-door visitor. Errand boys, delivering to the railway estates, abandoned their traditional whistling after admonitions to keep quiet in the vicinity of daytime sleepers.

Wives also had to learn the art of coping alone with domestic crises. Come pregnancy, toothache or matriculation, she was well aware that at the critical moment her husband would probably be fast asleep in a town or city she could probably find on a map only with difficulty. It was a rare occasion when lodging men were excused their duties, exceptions being made if there was infectious disease in the house or if the latter stages of pregnancy were difficult. For the engine-man, duty called and he was obliged to go. It was the task of the lodging man's wife to ensure that when her man left the house, his mind was as calm as his body was rested.

She had to prepare meals and 'put up' lodging baskets at times which bore no relation to normal hours. She had to call her husband for work and ensure that he was prepared at all times to answer the urgent summons 'On at once, be prepared to lodge.' Many of her evenings would be spent alone at her fireside, until the clock reminded her that it was time to call the trainman for his supper before he left on a night run. Never knowing exactly what time her husband would arrive indoors, she could never stray far from the domestic hearth.

Shift work and lodging away made the lodging father a very shadowy figure in the early years of his children's lives. In the home, the railway children quickly learned the behaviour expected of them. Noisy games were prohibited and doors were never slammed. Even when he was in bed the house was dominated by the father, because his rest was essential to the financial security of the family.

Few lodging men would deny that they saw little of the formative years of their children's development. A man lodging away twice or thrice a week, at weekends, at holiday times, for a whole lifetime, paid a heavy penalty for stability of work and wages. He lost something irreplaceable —the sight and sounds of children growing up.

In his absence it was natural that the family would revolve around the mother, to whom the children would usually turn for advice and encouragement. In a lodging home, the woman ran the ship. It was usually the woman who took the children on outings, excursions and visits to the dentist or the hospital. Entertainment involving all the family was minimal. Not for these families the regular evening get-together to mull over the doings of the day. At the time when most families were settling in for the night, the lodging man was reaching for his cap and basket. The children in bed, the woman had to settle down to an evening alone or, at best, a visit from the wife of another shift worker with whom she could discuss a common problem. Such women would likely be her daytime companions as well. It was at such times that the solidarity of the railway estate was asserted.

In the larger families there would often be more than one double homer, for, as the sons grew up, the older men would be 'asking down the shed' about employment prospects for the coming generation. The ritual which enmeshed the parents was upheld by the offspring. William Watt, who was an engine-driver at Carlisle and lodged away for almost half a century, has written: 'My father was an engine-driver, as were his five sons. Within our family we completed 300 years of foot-plate work. We all lodged away, taking our own food. My mother baked twenty-four loaves every week, and sixteen of them went into lodging baskets.'[32] In the days when lodging away was mandatory and largely unquestioned, five wage packets would produce a high standard of living, but the problems of feeding and sleeping five men, who would rarely be on the same shift, must have been enormous.

In days of economic depression, the family of a lodging man enjoyed a very favourable economic and social position. The basic wage of a top-flight engine-driver in the 1920s and 30s was £4 10s. per week, about 33⅓ per cent higher than a top-flight tradesman; this was often supplemented by Sunday work, extra pay for night duty, overtime and, at the highest level, mileage payments. Many trainmen had allotments on company ground, and this produce was often augmented from the kitchen garden of a company house. Free and concessionary travel provided opportunities denied to millions. Given these conditions, a woman could not be expected to rise in anger against the principle of lodging away. Like her husband, she was in the business of serving the railway company and travelling public.

We can only guess at the number of lonely, worrying nights endured by these women. What is certain, and what many railway historians have failed to reveal, is that behind the traditional view of the sober and dependable engine-drivers, firemen and guards was the household stability provided by these unsung heroines of the iron road. It was not without reason that these women were known as 'railway widows', or the unpaid servants of the railway company.

From the 1890s to the 1950s two other types of double homing existed throughout the system—the 'long' and 'short' rests. Short rests were put on for day excursions, such as race meetings or combined railroad excursions to places of interest and beauty. For short rests the train crews would sign on early in the morning and work the excursion to its destination; here they would stable the coaches and place the engine in the local depot. The men were left to their own devices until the evening, when they worked the train back to its starting point. In the rest period the men could take a stroll through the town and then find somewhere to sleep, usually in a coach in the carriage sidings. Often these men took their rest on the sand, or slept on deckchairs. The shift could spread over twelve or sixteen hours. The compensation in later years was that payment was continuous.

The long rest came in during the mid-1950s, and was the method used to operate the low-priced 'Starlight Specials' between London and Glasgow. London men lodged in Leeds. The same coaches which worked

the outward trains formed the train back to London; the lodging engine-
men waited for their own coaches. Payment on the long rest period was
continuous, but never enough to compensate for eighteen or nineteen
hours in sweat-soaked clothing.

The Second World War created a new situation as yards and depots
were denuded of key staff. There were vacancies galore at places which
had not taken on new staff for two decades. The question was: where
could men drafted in 'on loan' be housed? The answer was: in
stationary railway coaches, dewheeled and refitted as living quarters.
One of the first experiments with coaches was on the London, Midland
and Scottish Railway at Little Brickhill, near Bletchley. Mr A. E. Grigg,
who was a fireman at Bletchley, remembers that as lodging facilities in
the town were non-existent, the carefree youngsters sent for foot-plate
duties found themselves 'in the coaches'.

As many as sixty men could be sharing such coaches. The Welsh, Irish
and Scottish contingents segregated themselves, using the English lads
as both connectors and cementers. Many of the youngsters did their
celebrating at odd hours, and very often the shift foreman at Bletchley
would appear at the coaches, stick in hand, and root out for work some
of the more reluctant youngsters.

There was frivolity and indiscipline in the coaches, which were a
magnet to a certain section of the local girls; many of these had an unofficial view of the coaches, not always in daylight. A group of youngsters from Nuneaton found guilty of robbing the Bletchley Co-operative
Society of rainwear were eventually found lodgings less palatable than
the coaches at Little Brickhill. If there was mischief in the town, the
police of Bletchley made early inquiries at the railway coaches. On a
warm summer evening passengers on the Cambridge–Oxford line could
often see naked young men taking advantage of the engine water
columns of Bletchley.

In the early 1940s London engine sheds were gravely short of firemen; the Government's answer was to send in air crew men from the
Royal Air Force. These men had done their statutory number of raids
over Germany, and rather than lounge about their billets, they volunteered for firing duties on the railway. Pilots, navigators and air gunners
on loan to Willesden wore blue dungarees with RAF wings displayed.
The Willesden men took the RAF men into their homes and developed
a sound comradeship, but would not permit them to work on main-line
trains. The RAF men were allocated duties on the ashpits, the blunt end
of railway work.

As 'D Day' approached, the flyers returned to their squadrons, leaving a huge gap in the railway workforce. This was filled by the transfer
of many youngsters from the provinces to London. An appeal to the

Willesden men to take these lads into their homes was largely unsuccessful; two men on different shifts in one home was a recipe for domestic mayhem. The answer was again railway coaches, dewheeled and placed near to the place of work. Mr Eric Doody, who was a trade-union representative at Willesden, wrote to me of those days:

> The first of these were two old coaches placed adjacent to the fitting shop. No food was provided, only a bed in the coach. Sleep was very difficult for the youngsters. The lads were fed from a small caravan canteen which dispensed tea and sandwiches only. Most of the youngsters were totally disillusioned with railway work and only the Essential Works Order kept them in the industry. I have seen a loco foreman enter the coaches, pull a lad out of bed and order him straight to an engine.

By 1945, London was suffering a chronic shortage of key railway staff, especially firemen, guards and signalmen. The railways, in conjunction with the unions, opened three hostels for such men: the Craven Hotel, the Hampden Club and Old Oak Common. Each hostel had a distinct flavour.

The Craven Hotel, in Craven Street, the Strand, was a former Southern Railway hotel. The Craven brought the north of England into London's West End. Fireman, overalled and often wearing clogs, contrasted strangely in dress and speech with the bowler-hatted commuters at Charing Cross Station. The Craven was resplendent in crimson carpets and mirrored pillars in the dining-room. The diners were a rare assortment, however, engine-men, guards and signalmen with a humour and language quite unknown to the local inhabitants and shopkeepers. In the early 1950s the hostel was a magnet for the buskers. On Saturday nights performers of all kinds would appear in Craven Street, entertaining the hotel residents and staff until the law moved them on. A visit to the Craven usually paid the busker very well, the coins being collected in a grimy hat sent into the dining-room. Across the street Lyons Corner House diners often drifted from their tables to listen to the entertainment. A dozen or so of the boys belting out 'Maggie May' or 'Liverpool Lou' was another sight and sound often enjoyed by visitors to the Strand or Trafalgar Square on a Saturday night. More decorously, every weekend would see a group of Cravenites inviting the off-duty nurses of Charing Cross Hospital to a free evening at the Lyceum Ballroom in the Strand.

In 1951, the Southern Region of British Railways repossessed the hotel and transferred the staff to the Hampden Club, Polygon Road, St Pancras. The Hampden Club was situated in the hinterland between the stations of King's Cross and Euston.

Putting 200 mainly young and footloose railway workers into the Somers Town district of St Pancras might have been a disaster, but Somers Town, basically a railway area, took the lads as they came, spicy north London language mixing easily with dialects as diverse as Diss and Doncaster.

One year after the opening of the hostel there occurred an outstanding example of workers from other areas attempting to establish an identity on foreign ground. The very affluent social committee of the Hampden Club booked the Fountain Ballroom of the Cora Hotel in Holborn for an Annual Dinner. Every ticket to this function was free and each resident was allowed to bring one guest—female. The committee made a tour of nearby hospitals, distributing free tickets for a function which included a first-class orchestra. This illustrated the famed generosity of railway workers and the effect of the dinner was to incorporate the railway hostel into the community.

On paper its 200 lodgers were among the most cosseted men in London. Most of them had separate rooms, many of which were unofficially redecorated by the men and fitted with radiograms and tanks of exotic fish. The Hampden Club had cheap meals, good beds and a billiard room with three full-sized tables. At weekends the games room was the scene of card games of staggering length and massive pots. From the Hampden Club every day went the drivers, firemen and guards of the *Royal Scot* and the *Flying Scotsman*, and signalmen working the most vital signal boxes in the capital. Shunters and dining-car personnel completed the list of grades which every day kept the rail service of London alive.

The dining-rooms of the Hampden Club were studies in territorialism. The larger dining-room was for non-overalled staff, the smaller for men eating before going on shift; no matter, the men divided up not by grade but by geographical area. Liverpudlians laid claim to certain tables and kept closer together than two ferrets in a sack. Welsh and Scottish let expanses of floor divide them and the Irish contingent was, as ever, divided between the major ideologies of republicanism and loyalism.

In 1949, the Western Region built a new hostel at Old Oak Common. This hostel had its origin in a pair of coaches adapted, in 1942, to house a small number of men employed as labourers at the engine shed. By 1946, with sixty men living in coaches, a permanent building was needed and the company provided it. In 1949, amidst a plethora of potted plants and speeches by Very Important People, a complement of 280 men was afforded new quarters. A twenty-three year stay is still the record. Most of the residents of the Old Oak Common hostel were young Welshmen, many in the city for the very first time, causing spells of anxiety for the parents left behind in the valleys. The youngsters enjoyed individual rooms, with unlimited hot water, electric heating and drying facilities, billiards and early television. The crowning glory of Old Oak Common, however, was the 500 seat lecture theatre.

Before the mass motoring of the 1960s there were few jobs for which a man could be paid while watching the early sun chasing the Mersey mist from the latticework of Runcorn Bridge, or see the glow of London reflected in the sky on the descent from Tring in the Chiltern Hills to platform level in Euston Station. A young fireman, sleep nagging at his eyeballs, could still thrill to the descent from The Peak into Derby Station. The glare of Motherwell's Glasgow and the lonely hills and sky on the run from Ais Gill were always a supreme contrast to the bustle of Carlisle Station. Plymouth Hoe, Tiger Bay, the Cider Counties, high spots of Western lodging, were, however, insufficiently attractive to the Western engine-men who kicked against lodging away in the early 1950s.

Resistance to lodging away began long before the anti-lodging strikes of 1949 and 1953. At the Select Committee of 1891, a Great Eastern man, reflecting that the Stratford lodge was full up every day with 'countrymen', argued during an exchange, '. . . If I was working a train which would bring me to my home . . . I should be willing to do fourteen hours with that in view.'[33] A reduction in hours, said the witness, would increase lodging turns on the Great Eastern and this the men of Stratford did not wish.

Before the railway trade unions were able to influence the question of lodging, men were often kept for long hours in the lodge with very little financial recompense. The following is an extract from a set of rules governing lodging before the First World War:

> 2s. 6d. will be allowed each man per lodge. If the lodge is more than twelve hours, 6d. per hour will be paid each man for each hour or part of an hour over the twelve hours, providing that he has been on duty ten hours or over before going to lodge.
>
> When men are booked to lodge eighteen hours or over, but prefer, subject to permission, to travel home and back in their own time, 2s. 6d. will be allowed to each man.[34]

Unions did campaign against lodging but, at least in the early days, were unable to make appreciable differences in the practice. By 1918, a section of the double homers were campaigning against lodging away in private homes but the issue petered out against the larger packet of improvements gained by railway workers as a result of the national railway strike of 1919. The gains, when they came, were very small. The

ASLEF *Conditions of Service Book* contains the following agreement from the twenties:

> After being booked off, a man should be worked back to his home station, but, if in unforeseen circumstances it is necessary to book a man off again, the allowance shall be at the rate of 2*d*. per hour from the time of signing off duty for the second rest to signing off duty at the home station. Where the company provides lodging, a reduction of 1*s*. per night or day will be made.

The situation was bound to erupt at some point, however. The strain lodging away placed on the men could not be ignored indefinitely. Call these places lodges, call them barracks, call them hostels or just thieves of engine-men's time, the buildings and the behaviour of the men who used them and their interaction with other railway grades were all brought to public prominence in the severe anti-lodging strikes which occurred on the railway system between 1949 and 1955.

By 1940, lodging away had become a major issue among engine-men on the eastern lines, from London to Edinburgh. In the middle of the Second World War, the engine-men of Scunthorpe and Grantham simply refused to lodge away and insisted on changing foot-plates at roughly half-way stages. This was a dangerous tactic in wartime, but the engine-men got away with it, thus building up a store of confidence for when the storm broke later.

The situation seethed, rather than simmered, throughout the war years. Food was in very short supply in the lodges and men were reluctant to lodge in London or wherever bombs were dropping.

Even in the late 1940s, the top-flight engine-men at King's Cross were lodging at Newcastle-upon-Tyne in circumstances which were completely unacceptable. Engine-man Blazey of the King's Cross depot has recorded in a letter to me:

> At Newcastle, we lodged at Dollie's on the Westmoreland Road. As she had no hot water on tap, we washed off the dust in a bucket at the station boiler house. At Dollie's even shaving water had to be boiled. The stairs were devoid of linoleum and the beds were minus sheets, although these were later supplied to drivers only. The proprietress of this establishment and her daughter were no lovers of hot water, and the London men were often joined at breakfast by the youngest child, clad only in a dirty, urine-stained nightgown.

In 1946, a desire on the part of railway management to introduce more lodging turns was rejected by the loco and traffic grades of the National Union of Railwaymen, despite the managerial plea that more lodging meant higher productivity in the industry. The winter of 1947 tested the railways almost beyond endurance. Engine stock was depleted by war and spare parts and tools were in nightmarish short supply; all this was compounded by chronic staff shortages and long hours of duty. To ask for more lodging by trainmen was the match to the petrol.

The Railway Executive, the organization established by the Labour Government of 1945 to act as the agent of the nation and discharge the financial obligations of the industry, decided in 1948 that more lodging turns were necessary in the struggle to boost both the railways and the economy. ASLEF and the NUR were then asked to consider extra lodging turns with the undertaking that men would not be expected to lodge less than seventy-five miles out from home station or less than 150 miles in the case of passenger trains. The Railway Executive agreed to provide clean hostels with clean beds, wholesome meals and with reasonable facilities for entertainment. They were to be supervised twenty-four hours a day. The minimum lodging expenses for each man would be 6s. per trip—minus his food. Further, the Railway Executive agreed to a minimum of nine hours' rest between turns, and a maximum of sixteen hours in a railway hostel. The attitude of the Executive was that more and faster trains were the key to successful operation and that an increase in lodging turns would be a great help.

Early in 1949, the Railway Executive offered three lodging turns at Gateshead and Heaton depots. On 17 May a driver and fireman turned up to work the Gateshead train out, but refused to lodge. They were warned, but not disciplined. On Friday, 20 May, a number of foot-platemen at York met and agreed not to work lodging turns to Gateshead; their resolution was that they would refuse to work Sunday duties until all proposals on lodging turns were withdrawn.

On Sunday, 23 May, more than sixty expresses failed to run in the Eastern Region. In Yorkshire, sixty local trains were cancelled. The entire electric train service on the Tyne was stopped. On 24 May the Railway Executive told ASLEF and the NUR leaders to get a grip on their members. The NUR reply was to advise its affected members not to work the extra lodging turns and to warn the Executive that should any action be taken against any member of the union the entire resources of the union would be used to protect that member.

The Daily Express asked for a common-sense approach to the problem, and The Times argued that railway work had advantages as well as disadvantages. The Yorkshire Post, after a quiet approach, suddenly discovered that a small group with foreign allegiances were behind the stoppages. It attacked Mr Jim Figgins, General Secretary of the NUR, for wanting the railways run not for the nation, but for himself. The attitude of Mr Figgins to the wage freeze policies of the Government was common knowledge, but the anti-communist crusade now directed its energies to discrediting the man with the least amount of real influence on the situation.

The Railway Executive negotiating team was led by Mr William Allen, a former General Secretary of ASLEF, appointed a member of the Railway Executive after nationalization in 1948. Mr Allen cut little ice with his former comrades and less with the representatives of the NUR. The NUR had a number of foot-platemen and guards involved, but the great weight of people employed in the hostels as supervisors, cooks, cleaners and stewards were members of the NUR. An extension of lodging may have meant promotion for some of these grades, but the union found the proposals unsatisfactory. After much debate, Mr Allen announced that a number of new lodging turns would be introduced with the timetable of 23 May 1949.

At this time, Britain was experiencing a bout of hysterical anti-communism. The Chinese communists had entered Shanghai, and in Berlin riots and arrests at the main railway station highlighted the divisions over the post-war status of the city. In London, the John Lewis Partnership was threatening to dismiss all the communists on its staff and Sir Hartley Shawcross, KC, was exposing the communist threat behind labour unrest in Britain. Into this atmosphere the National Union of Railwaymen injected a demand for a 10s. weekly increase for its half-million members. The railways countered with a plea for increased productivity, including an increase in lodging turns for train crews. On Sunday, 23 May 1949, on the eve of the proposed new lodging turns, 3,000 foot-platemen in the Eastern Region did not report for work. All that the men wanted was to return home at the end of each shift. From depots as far apart as King's Cross and Dundee, the engine-men defied both employer and trade union. Did the men have a case?

At York, Mr Blazey had experiences of lodging which he could well have done without. The lodge at York was a small hotel and restaurant open to the public. In the dining-room the men were served meals in a curtained alcove; on occasion, the bedroom used by Mr Blazey would be let to a paying guest and the fireman could not get to bed until the guest had vacated. At this hotel, according to Mr Blazey, a coin-operated toilet was the last straw. The men were sleeping on the top floor 'so to get to a free toilet, the men had to get up, dress, and pass through lounge, restaurant and kitchen to answer nature's calls'. In the mid-1950s, the proprietor of a York hotel refused to accommodate senior firemen from King's Cross because the men had originated from the West Indies. The reply of the King's Cross men was simply, 'You take all of us or none of us.'

The view that the stoppages were communist-inspired held no fears for the men of Darlington and Tweedmouth, both sheds swinging behind the policy of no more lodging turns. In the meantime, ASLEF, committed to honouring agreements, was not averse to properly controlled lodging turns. The *Yorkshire Post* returned to the fray in its editorial of 23 May, calling the actions irresponsible, and arguing that, as public servants, the first duty of the railwaymen was to give efficient service, otherwise 'changes worse than lodging are possible'. On 28 May, King's Cross and Middlesbrough engine-men joined the stoppage, despite a statement from Mr Baty, the General Secretary, that 'the strike is unjustified and we do not condone it in any way'. On 29 May, men of Mr Baty's union in Carlisle formed up behind the campaign, although in fairness it was the Eastern shed only which acted.

As part of its campaign, the *Yorkshire Post* sent a reporter scudding to London where an examination of a hostel at Kentish Town revealed both an institutional air and an atmosphere of friendliness. Reporting from 'where highwaymen once had roamed' the *Post* advised the engine-men that whatever grievance they had it could not be the hostel at Kentish Town. This simply avoided the question, which was really the desire of the men not to become once more wanderers in the industrial environment. Now they had a cause, new leaders and a powerful body of men in support.

At the ASLEF Annual Conference in 1949, the General Secretary expressed his concern for the division in the union and urged the honouring of agreements. He was supported by the Kentish Town delegate who argued that, 'The Kentish Town men who lodge are there because they agree that express work and lodging cannot be separated.'

Despite the public statements by the union that the Eastern men were not concerned with lodging throughout the country but only with an extension of lodging in their own region, *The Times*, referring to the NUR, claimed on 16 June 1949 that 'The combination of braggadoccio and vanity and obtuseness to the public interest of this union has caused great inconvenience to the travelling public and to the railwaymen themselves.' The NUR—involved, but least able to control the situation —expressed at its conference on 28 June the view that, 'Having fully considered all the facts, conference expresses its profound disgust at the scurrilous and totally misleading statements in the press directed against our General Secretary and our organization.' The Labour Government of Clement Attlee was transfixed, unable to say a word in defence of one the founders of the Labour Party—the National Union of Railwaymen.

Relationships between the two unions involved sank to a new low. Mr Baty, in agreeing that lodging was the curse of the foot-plate grade, nevertheless accused the bigger union 'of lack of practical approach; the meddlesome bombast which they have displayed in connection with lodging has been such as to beggar description', and he urged his members in the *Locomotive Journal* of June 1949, 'not to become the sport and plaything of the conglomerate of Euston Road'.

The Railway Executive now had to think big, and it did. A meeting was called of all representatives of the striking engine depots—something unprecedented in railway history—and it broke the deadlock. The Sunday strikes had cost the industry dear in lost revenue, but it had saved more than £150,000 in wages. The unofficial strike committee, by raffles and collections, had raised £259 plus a few shillings, and with this sum the Eastern men challenged a Labour Government and a state corporation. As a result of this unofficial action, the National Agreement of 1919 was revised in favour of the engine-men, and the engine-men held off proposals which would have reduced them to men who lodged at home and lived away. The engine-men had given notice that there was more to trade unionism than official negotiations; the voice of the Vigilants had once more been heard.

In the mid-fifties the days of crank and clank were clearly numbered, owing to the Modernization Plan which was announced in 1955. Yet in 1954, a rash of anti-lodging strikes spotted the Western Region. The axes of the new campaign were Old Oak Common and Banbury, with clear support from Cardiff and Newton Abbot. Again, secret committees were established and an all-line committee co-ordinated the activity. The proposal from the Western Region had been an extension of lodging away on freight trains and places such as Banbury and Newton Abbot were especially hostile to the new proposals. On 28 May 1954, 1,323 engine-men on the Western Region stayed away from work as a protest against an extension of lodging away. The *Daily Express* bemoaned the possibility of the worst railway trouble since 1926. At their Annual Assembly, ASLEF men decided by forty votes to two to insist on a total abolition of lodging turns. The unofficial stoppages showed the extent of their feelings.

The unofficial stoppages ceased after an eleven-hour meeting of the strike committee in Bristol on 28 May 1954. The Government had decided that a strike situation was preferable to capitulation, and that if necessary, troops would be utilized to clear the traffic. The engine-men knew that this was more than they could surmount.

In the late 1970s, King's Cross men were lodging in modest splendour at the County Hotel, York, and at the West Parade Hotel, Newcastle-upon-Tyne, the latter known to trainmen as 'Handa's Palace'. The non-lodging men working out of 'Cubitt's Pile' were relieved en route, took a break, then worked back to the home depot. Newcastle men were lodging at Ilford in a modern railway hostel and Frodingham men were lodging in comfort at the Market Hotel, central Birmingham.

Mr Reg Burnett has kindly provided us with a model non-lodging turn at King's Cross. This diagram will serve as a model for non-lodging turns throughout the industry today.

King's Cross	Turn 12	Sats. Ex.	
On Duty		21.30	
King's Cross Depot	Dep. L.E.	22.10	
King's Cross	Dep.	22.30	(1572)
Doncaster	Arr.	01.22	
	Relieved	01.27	
Relieve 01.51	Doncaster	02.00	(1A35)
King's Cross	Arr.	05.13	
Immobilize		7 hrs. 47 mins.	

This turn of duty, encompassing some 300 miles of train working, is worth eighteen hours' pay. These turns, of course, are spread over a trainman's roster. Such duties are not performed every day, not even every week; what they do show is that much of the main-line train work can be performed without lodging away.

In the 1980s the high-speed and Advanced Passenger Trains being offered by British Rail may raise again the economic value of railway hostelling. The engine-men's union is still officially opposed to lodging out, but a stream-lined and well-paid system might appeal to the younger engine-men.

The main question to be asked about lodging away is simply, why was it tolerated for so long? For the lodging men it could be argued that in the days of steam the main-line engine-man occupied an honoured place in our society. From wielding an oily rag around the wheels and boiler of a railway engine they had become stars in the railway firmament. Few other jobs could provide such a dizzy ascent.

8

Language on the Railway

In the 1960s, a large body of academic thought argued that working-class children failed at school because they were linguistically deprived. This argument, now largely refuted, said that the thinking processes of working-class children were inferior to those of middle-class children; the former were said to use language which was context-bound, emotional, and often illogical. By comparison, the speech patterns of middle-class children were unemotional and reasoned. In this chapter we hope to prove that working-class children are inferior neither in conceptualization nor in the use of complex language patterns. We will argue that the use of humour, wit, satire, metaphor, simile and allusion shows that working-class speech is richer in every way to that of the middle class.

Since the Industrial Revolution and the widespread development of language the rulers of society have, in order to retain their power, inflicted a style and pattern of language on those set below them in society. This ruling language is characterized by its demands for report writing, form filling and the handling of complicated documents. Language became the guardian of privilege and the method by which one class fastened its ideology on another.

In Victorian England, the working class went by a variety of titles, such as the 'lower orders', the lesser breeds', the 'dangerous and propertyless class'. Other epithets of abuse were the 'servant class' and the 'great unwashed'. They were viewed from society's upper echelons as an uncouth, illiterate and bestial mass, fit only for economic subjugation and defined by such legislation as the Master and Servant Acts.

The reaction to this was twofold. It consisted on the one hand of written challenges to the ruling ideology via trade-union and socialist literature and on the other in the foundation of a richly potent industrial slang. In both cases the working class appropriated language in defence of its own interests. In the first instance, a highly skilled and erudite section of the working class, led by the engineers, became conscious of the need for linguistic skills as a method of approaching employers, as a means of separating the skilled from the unskilled workers and as crucial to the emancipation of the working class. Chartism, trade unionism, socialism, Institutes of Technical Education and the Workers' Educational Association stemmed from the desire to uplift the disinherited sections of society. Advanced trade unionists always saw the conquest of literacy as basic to the development of the mechanical arts, artistic skills and potentialities of their members.

Slang is a general term for all non-standard English except dialect. In the nineteenth century, three specific aspects became identifiable: the working class had its lingo, the middle class its jargon and the upper class its argot. In 1921, the German linguist Edward Sapir wrote: 'Peculiar modes of pronunciation, characteristic turns of phrase, slangy turns of speech . . . are so many symbols of the manifold way in which society arranges itself and are of crucial importance to the understanding of the development of individual and social attitudes.' Every trade and profession possesses a unique linguistic form. Its context is singular, inimitable, closely woven, where language by arcane forms guards the secrets of the group from hostility and surveillance. Language must grow from a web of personal and working relationships. It cannot exist apart from cultural aspirations or from the socially inherited assemblages of beliefs, practices and taboos which create the texture of life.

Responsible, heavy and dangerous work demands close companionship and a condensed, vivid terminology. Such language examines and comments upon complex questions in ways which make nonsense of most theories of linguistic deprivation. New phrases planed and honed on the whetstone of diurnal reality displace profanity and introduce colourful, bittersweet and brimstone comment which illustrates the baroque linguistic power of the lower echelons of society. The American writer Carl Sandburg has told us, 'Slang is language which takes off its coat, spits on its hands and goes to work.'

Slang is created and burnished in the workplace—at the point of productivity. It combines immediate reaction with aptness of description and comment. Slang is a transformational technique, neutering the hostile and relabelling the horrific aspects of daily life. If Chomsky is right in arguing that much scholarship has leagued itself against the aspirations of the people, a linguistic backlash will be one important form of social protest; the language of the technocrat will be rejected by those further from the source of power and replaced by a blacker, spicier language. The process works as shown:

Stimulus	Internal Behaviour	Response	Characterization
A new and possibly threatening situation.	Consideration of human and social effect of machine.	Re-objectivization. Relabelling and neutralization of hostile phenomenon.	Relabelling based upon ridicule. Contrastive features. Absurdity used for fusion of concepts. Metaphor, simile, satire, humour.

I do not claim slang as a separate language, but its great variety of forms entitles it to be described as the language of kinship groups. This type of language has to be learned, and when its secrets are mastered the individual slots into the group. Even before school the working-class child will hear the language of the workplace. This language will be full of references to other industries, other places, and will often be as subtle as it is variant. Slang stems from real situations; it is often created by speakers quite unaware of their ability to produce new and vivid language forms and shows a natural joy in language-making by its originators. This is the language of the group's own world, by which they analyse and reinterpret their view of social reality.

The railway industry is an excellent example of industrial language-making. On the railways, there was a language of the orderer and a language of the ordered. Railway managerial language always demonstrated a clear knowledge of the power of language, spoken or written —a society of 'them' and 'us'. On the railway, even in the 1970s, one side institutes the concepts, makes the rules, writes the textbooks and largely decides the punishments. The word 'must' was, and is, the most potent word in railway instruction manuals, especially in the 'Railway Bible'—the *Rule Book*.

The railway was the first paper-dominated industry. Here everything was written down and posted up; important documents were signed for individually, the railway worker being held responsible for all posted literature which affected his working arrangements. Rule books, appendices, special train notices, even the minutiae of railway literature screamed out the language of the orderer, the group which, by language skills, occupied the seats of authority.

The early railways demanded a high standard of literacy on appointment, and it was this demand for a literate staff which gives the railways a special place in our industrial history. Unlike the cotton and weaving industry, or the coal mines, railways could not advance without a continuous increase in language skills. The history of industrial relations on the railways is the story of how the staff turned a managerial demand for literacy into a means of their own social and political betterment. For the ambitious railway worker, particularly engine-drivers and signalmen, the increased technical ability leading to promotion was dependent upon language skills; for the trade unionist, language acquisition and mastery was viewed as a weapon in their struggle for better working conditions.

The changing form of language in industrial relations on the railway can be seen in three distinct stages. In the earliest times, the potential railway worker abased himself before his prospective employer. An applicant 'begged to apply' for work and was 'your obedient servant' at the end of his application. The second stage was the period of request, when railway workers, overworked and underpaid, approached their masters with round robins and memorials in support of their claims for higher wages and shorter hours. Today we have clear-cut demands for shared power. The railway trade-union journals, the seed-beds of ideas, argue for national policies for their industry and for full recognition for trade unionism as a positive force for planning within the industry. This has been a linguistic and ideological revolution.

The coming of the railway likewise created linguistic ramifications within the external social order. In the late 1820s, the Duke of Wellington feared the dissemination of popular literature by railway because he knew it would lead to a new consciousness of social inequality. By the 1830s this was a reality and there was a rapid increase in working-class literacy as trade-union literature and cheap journals such as the *Penny Magazine* found their way into many homes. This literature provided the foundation for a great increase in social class consciousness and political organization.

Railway talk is a magnificent example of working-class speech. Though largely unknown to the professional students of language, it possesses a unique richness and demonstrates a delightful inventiveness in the creation of language. In the wider sense, railway talk is a strategy for coming to terms with a muddled world of rapid decay and technological advance. Such speed cannot be measured by the usual sociological methods. There are ritualistic, even superstitious elements involved, but the basic idea is to manipulate society and machinery in order to protect the individual or group from the negative aspects of authority and technological change. New techniques, new machines must be relabelled, and hence neutered.

Railway workers have a general view of the world which is largely defensive. The outside world, with little real knowledge of railway operating procedures, tends to be critical of dirty, late-running trains, unco-operative staff and continual financial crises. Such criticism only forces a social group into industrial bunkers. This is especially true of the railway where, many years ago, began that territorialism which we now call the railway bailiwick.

On the engine, in the signal box, in the guards' room, out in the marshalling yard can be heard the language of the bailiwick. On a bailiwick a new language is taught and learned; the gift of speech, often crushed at school, is invigorated and pushed to a central position. On the bailiwick, the indecipherable instruction, the unworkable rule, is diminished by the hallowed activities and phrases of custom and tradition. The language of the bailiwick is not a dog of low descent, but a working organic language which crackles with wit and social criticism. Such a language stems from a knowledge of a specific task within a specific territory. It has nothing in common with railway jargon—where cows on the line become 'bovine interference with services' or a human being is translated as a 'unit of labour'.

On the bailiwick, language is not confined to railway terminology. It has internal and external sources of refreshment. Such talk recreates, enlivens and enriches our language by reaching out into other industries and other activities for source materials which are then reshaped to match the local situations. There is profanity on the railway, a diverse, intimate, complex profanity, but there is also a rich store of vigorous and colourful phrases which have entered the common stock of the English vernacular tradition—such as 'full steam ahead' and 'there's light at the end of the tunnel'.

Apart from slang, there are other communication systems operating on the bailiwick. There is technical language, written as instructions to people occupying specific places at particular times. Visual language is used when the human voice is unable to transcend space. Examples are semaphore signals, hand signalling and flag waving. Aural communication is when bells, gongs and whistles originate and control behaviour between people who cannot see one another. Many of these bailiwicks rejoiced in names which illustrated the flora and fauna of their regions. Signal boxes revelled in such names as Thrustle Nest Junction, Sutton Oak, Etruria and Bo-peep Junction. Smoky, dust-laden engine sheds were designated Belle Vue, Botanic Gardens and Dairycoates. Dusty, draughty marshalling yards had names like Daisyfield, Freshfield and Mayfield, conjuring up visions of pastoral serenity.

Language can be hammer or anvil, and although for many years the railway worker was the anvil, his particular use of language became, if not a hammer, a shield, behind which the group was cemented, and the area defended so that all things hostile and strange could be rejected. Language on the railway turned the commonplace into the rare. The following is an example of railway talk which could have been heard almost anywhere on the railways of Britain in the days of steam:

> We were humping the bricks with a short of puff Black Five. It was as thick as a bag. At Stone Crossing both squirters packed in, but we got inside without blocking the fast. A set of Huns with a tender first crab hooked up but we still made a rounder.

Translation
Humping the bricks: Working a brick train.
Short of puff: An engine steaming poorly.
Black Five: A Class 5 Mixed Traffic Engine LMS.
Thick as a bag: Very foggy.

Squirters: Water injector mechanism, taking water from tender to boiler.
Getting inside: Entering a loop line or siding.
Blocking the fast: Blocking the main line.
Set of Huns: Engine-men from another depot.
Tender first crab: 'Crab' was a freight engine; tender first meant that the
engine was wrong way round for train working.
Making a rounder: A twelve-hour shift—half-way round the clock.

Another example is the skill with which railway workers gave new
titles to the companies that employed them:

Staff nickname	*Railway company*
The Clog and Knocker	Grand Central.
Let me sleep Lord, my shepherd Elleva Mess	London, Midland and Scottish.
Go when ready Greatest way round God's wonderful railway	Great Western.
Late, never early	London and North-Eastern.
Muddle, goes nowhere	Midland, and Great Northern.
Slow and dirty	Somerset and Dorset.
Languish and yawn	Lancashire and Yorkshire.

The great variety of signals on the railway system gave rise to a
special nomenclature. Semaphore signals were named sticks, pegs and
boards—the distant signal being designated the 'back board', or the
'back 'un'. The yell from fireman to driver 'back 'un off' meant that the
distant signal was at clear. 'A brown 'un' meant that the distant signal
was at yellow, as did a 'ginger 'un'. The cry 'two labour gain' meant a
double yellow aspect at a colour light signal. 'One labour gain' meant
one yellow aspect at a colour light signal. A 'blue 'un' meant a green
aspect. 'Forever amber' was awarded to signals which seemed permanently set at yellow. The terms 'Christmas Tree', 'Feathers' and 'Fairy-
land' related to signal gantries, direction lights and a colour light mal-
functioning, in that order.

Railway workers often created words of their own. 'Womming' was
a word for rail turning by plate-layers. 'Wimbling' was the use of an
auger; i.e. to wimble—to drill. 'Weasling' referred to porters with time
to spare from platform duties who raced off to earn tips by carrying
passengers' luggage.

There was always a railway measurement based on the length of the
four-wheeled rail wagon ranging from 'bring it up a wagon length' or
'half a wagon length away'. The power of this is exemplified by the story
of the shunter who apprised a non-railway friend, 'I saw you in church

last week, you were sitting two wagon lengths in front of me.' There was always a shunter who went by the nickname of 'The Mystic'; this was the unorganized man who could never find a shunting pole and was to be found wandering around muttering, 'Where's me stick?' The classic shunter's story must be how a particular inspector obtained the cognomen 'Thrombosis'. 'We call him Thrombosis,' said the shunter, 'because he is a bloody clot wandering round the system liable to stop everything at any moment without warning.'

Railway language seems a closed area to historians of the age of steam. Who has recorded the engine-driver's breakfast—'two Woodbines and an aspirin'—or the contents of the fireman's head, which, when devoid of the daily racing information, showed 'twenty inches of vacuum'? Who has heard of the 'fifty face man', whose word could not be trusted?

The foot-plate was a rich tapestry of nicknames and uncomplimentary titles such as:

Abadan: This was a driver who hoarded engine oil in hideaways around the shed.

The Desert Drivers: These were engine-men who had a permanent fear of running short of water in the tank or sand in the boxes.

The Whispering Baritone: Every shed had a loudmouth, a barrack-room lawyer; this was his title.

His Master's Voice: Generally an ex-foot-plateman turned foreman's assistant. A crawler, a sycophant.

Little Sir Echo: See above, for interchangeable term.

The Bugler: Before the steam whistle was invented drivers had bugles which they used to give warning of their approach. The Bugler was an excessive whistler.

Captain Hornblower: Another excessive whistler—especially during the night hours.

Foremen were not immune from nicknames and were never overjoyed by such linguistic handles as 'The Scarf'—a title bestowed because a foreman was always around the necks of his men—or 'The Balloon', the designation of the foreman who was always pleading, 'Don't let me down boys.'

Much railway slang reflected the high peak of British Imperial power. Without the railway the conquest of India and much of Africa would have been impossible. The terms 'coolie' and 'banjo player' clearly echo overseas expansion as does 'Chinese labour', the work of unpaid porters at London railway stations in the 1930s. The famous 'thin red line' was transposed from its military setting to the red mark on the pressure dial which signalled a full head of steam. Likewise, 'showing the white feather' was removed from the heat of battle to describe the lazy wisp of steam at boiler safety valves. On the railway the minutiae of tasks spawned a language of the baroque, a coupled relationship based on work and its experiences plus a joyful use of language.

It is interesting finally to look briefly at American railroad slang. In *The Railroader* (1940) Fred Cottrell introduced us to the idioms of the American railway worker. He pointed out that railway men were to some extent looked down upon by white-collared workers who could only be jealous of the monthly bank statements of key workers on American railroads. By comparison, the key grades of railway workers in Britain had high status unreflected in their take-home pay. Cottrell found that the speech patterns of the 'self-made' railway officer were quite different from the lingo he had absorbed and used 'on the road'.

American railroad slang is a social group language which postulates a sardonic view of the men's tasks and supervisors. Like British railway slang it is couched in linguistic and semantic forms which are the despair of non-speakers of the language. I give here a few similarities and contrasts between the two language systems.

	British term	American term
Driver:	Engine-man	Engineer, throttle puller
Fireman:	Banjo player, coolie	Bakehead
Guard:	Brush, tail lamp	Big Ox
Conductor:	Submarine commander	Captain
Foreman:	Whiplash firecracker	Ringmaster
Control office:	Nerve centre	Beehive
Guard's van:	Flea box	Louse Cage
Signal light:	Bullseye	Eye
Fully-loaded train:	Rafter	Jigger

GLOSSARY

Austin Seven: Midland Railway Class 7 Goods Engine.
Bang road: Opposite direction to normal traffic flow.
Banjo: Firing shovel. Repeating signal—black band on white disc.
Banjo player: Fireman on steam engine.
Barracks: Railway hostel.
Basic English: Amendment to *Rule Book*.
Beginner's luck: Derailed on first shift as a driver.
Bescot tarsprayer: LNWR Super 'D' Goods Engine.
Bible: The railway *Rule Book*.
Big Penny: Overtime, bonuses, premium payments.

Birth Controllers: LMS 'Garrats'.
Black Five: LMS Class 5 Mixed Traffic Engine.
Black light: An empty bulb socket.
Black oil: An unlit semaphore signal.
Black Princes: Engine cleaners.
Blinkers: Smoke deflectors on engine smoke-boxes.
Blister: Managerial request for information.
Blunderbuss: Train incorrectly signalled.
Bogie man: Carriage repairman.
Boomerang: A return ticket.
Bostons: Lincoln engine-men.
Bread Bins: Great Central Pacifics.
Bug dust: Small coal.
Bugler: Driver whistling excessively.
Bunny: Driver conducting another on an unfamiliar stretch of track.
Butterfly: Communication cord reset valve.
Canteen cowboys: Men awaiting work.
Captain Hornblower: See Bugler.
Captive audience: Men on training courses.
Chinese Fours: British Rail Standard Class 4 Engines.
Chinese labour: Part-time, unpaid porters of 1930s.
Coolie: Railway fireman.
Cripple: Wagon for repair.
Dead heat: All fire out of the engine.
Desert drivers: Engine-men always worrying about water and sand.
Flashing blade: A firing shovel.
Foreign Legion: Engine cleaners on loan to other depots.
Frost Devils: Coal braziers for melting ice at water columns.
Glassback: A reluctant fireman—lazyitis.
Gnat's blood: Tea.
Green fire: Unburned coal—Emeralds.
Hairspring tight: Mean—greedy.
Half dirties: Men employed partly on steam and partly on electric traction.
Head shrinker: Railway doctor.
Iron Lung: A Franco-Crosti Class 9 Goods Engine; the chimney was
    outside the fireman's window preventing him from putting his head out
    to breathe. Supposed to burn its own smoke, the Franco-Crosti sent
    most of it into the engine-men's lungs.
Jazzer: NER K 3.
Jocko-Jinty: Shunting engine.
Juice: Electricity.
Jungle juice: Beer.
Knobbing up: Changing the points.
Lanky Bomber: LNWR Freight Train.
Latch lifter: First drink of the evening.
Launching pad: Turntable.
Leccy: An electric train.

Little 'un: Calling an arm-shunting signal.
Lizzies: LMS Class 7 Passenger.
Lonesome Pine: Man with unpopular opinion—isolation.
Long toms: Yorkshire coal.
Mickey Mouse: Colour lit signal with position lights.
Mindbenders: Tutor drivers—instructors.
Miner's Friend: LMS 'Royal Scots'.
Navvies' wedding cake: Bread and margarine.
On the blood: Full steam presure.
Razor gang: The railway auditors.
Shrimps: Tamping machines for track relaying.
Side winder: Diesel railcar.
Snap: Food carried in 'snap' tin—snap-lidded box.
Snow: Small silver coins.
Thin red line: A jam sandwich.
　　　　　　　　　Red mark on pressure dial indicating full head of steam.
Thrombosis: A bloody clot wandering through the system liable to foul it
　　up at any moment.
Toasting fork: An isolating handle on Diesel Multiple units.

Signalling Terms

Back 'un: Distance signal.
Big Dipper: High semaphore.
Biscuit: Signal line token.
Blackboard: Oblong ground signal.
Bullseye: Signal light.
Christmas tree: Multiple aspect signal.
Clear pop: Clear signal.
Dolly, Dodd, Dummy: Ground signals.
Double yolk: Two yellows.
Fairy land: Multiple aspect signals.
Feathers: Lunar lights.
Forever amber: Fixed distant signals.
Gun: Radar speed trap.
Harbour lights: Lunar lights.
Hitler salute: Upraised semaphore.
Iron Man: IBS Post.
On the block: In loop.
Orange peel: Plate-layers' orange jackets.
Peg, stick, board: Semaphore signals.
Persecuted Minority: Employed, over-65s.
Pounded: Inside clear.
Spider: Signal apparatus in four foot.
Stairway to the stars: Ladder to signal's arm.
Triple Crown: Three head lamps.

Places of Interest

Back Pan, the: Washwood Heath.
Big Stacks, the: Brickfield Chimneys, Bedford.
Block all Junction: Watford.
Bowling Green: Fast line.
Cupboard, the: Coppermill Junction, Eastern Region.
Drain, the: Waterloo.
Fernando's Hideaway: Plate-layers' cabin.
Goal Post, the: Cricklewood.
Hostile Territory: Another region.
Indian Country: Eastern Region.
Land of Plenty: Overtime.
Lawn, the: Fast line.
Maze, the: Clapham Junction.
Nerve Centre, the: Yard Foreman's cabin.
Orchard, the: Cricklewood sidings.
Plywood Sidings: Barking, Essex.
Ponderosa, the: Kentish Town to Barking.
Rat Hole, the: Euston Tunnel.
Shanty, the; also Library: Messroom.
Tea Gardens, the: Somers Town Sidings, St Pancras.

Diesel Terms

Bird Cage: Air compartment.
Death chamber: High-tension cubicle.
Mindbenders: Diesel instructors.
One-Arm Bandit: AWS equipment.
Paraffin burners: ⎫
Spam Cans: ⎬ Diesel trains.
Shunting Mike: 350 HP Diesel Eastern Region.
Side winder: Local Start DMU.
Windjammer: Blocked air pipe.

Nicknames

Abadan: Excessive oil user.
College of Knowledge: The depot union representative.
Dab hand: Painter.
Dead-end kid: Person not taking promotion.
Desk jockey: Clerk.
Florence Nightingale: Shunter with lamp.

Genial Menial: Shed labourer.
Glossies, the: Weekly notices.
Gozundas: Bridge equipment.
Gruesome twosome: Joint chairmen.
Gutta percha: Bird on shed roof.
Hackney ghurkas: Railway soldiers.
Hawkeye: Messroom attendant.
His Master's Voice: Deputy foreman.
Hush puppies: Silencers on DMU's.
Jumping Jack: Lively chargehand.
Limited company: Small meeting.
Mistletoe Men: ⎫
Out Riders: ⎭ Non-union men.
Pail hands: Office cleaner.
Set of grinders: Sheffield men.
Siamese twins: Branch and LDC secretaries.
Syndicate, the: Full meeting, management–unions.
Talkies, the: Local negotiating meeting.
Talking machine: Branch secretary.
Traps: Guard's equipment.
Wells Fargo: Original Pullman Cars.
Whispering Baritone: Noisy person.
Wigan blind: A grey puddeny mass. Dross, a mixture of dust found in coal
     wagons emanating from briquettes, cobbles, slack and nuts.
Woolley backs: Leeds men.
Yankee Clipper: American barber.

9

The Tyranny of the Clock

In the days of old, when knights were bold
Before watches were invented,
From dusk to dawn, with brain and brawn,
The serf toiled, unlamented.

The railway system changed this game,
The clock became the master,
The lifeless hands within their frame
Insisted—more, and faster!

—Ruptured Coupling (with apologies
to Rudyard Kipling)

For thousands of years mankind has been fascinated by time and its measurements. Saints, philosophers and writers of many kinds have speculated on the nature of time. The Greek philosopher Aristotle defined time simply as the measurement of duration. Parmenides taught that there was no such thing as becoming or movement, because the human mind could not conceive of a void. Later, St. Augustine taught that time and the human soul were inseparable. For the French writer Henri Bergson, time was the essential characteristic of life and mind. To the American Ralph Waldo Emerson, time was the surest poison. For others it has been the conqueror of conquerors, or a flash of lightning, existing and expiring at almost the same moment. Horace Mann wrote, 'Lost, two golden hours, each set with sixty golden minutes. Gone forever. No reward.' In our own time Einstein has argued that time and space are relative and that events are conceived in space-time terms. Confident of his subject, Bishop Usher argued a century ago that the first men appeared on 23 March 4004 BC. Charles Lamb, the English essayist, gave us another view, arguing, 'What a dead thing is a clock.'

Until 1752, Britain, as a Protestant country, refused to use the new style calendar introduced by Pope Gregory XIII in 1582. By 1751, there was a difference of eleven days between British calendars and their European counterparts. When Britain adopted the European version in 1752, New Year's Day was moved from 25 March to 1 January.

Concepts of time differ throughout the world. The anthropologist Malinowski was long baffled by the subtleties of temporal sequences employed by the Trobriand islanders. According to Margaret Mead, the only past for the Arapesh is the age of fable, where every tree and rock are characters from the timeless past. The Balinese, according to the same writer, differed again, for 'although they had ways of recording the passing of the years, and their monuments were occasionally dated, the calendar by which they lived was one of cycling days and weeks . . . new books were dated by the day and week, not by the year.'

The ability to think in specific time sequences is vital to our civilization. We have created a system of past, present and future as points on a line, and our tense system confirms the practicality of the method. We chop up time into chunks, not because it is so segmented but because our economic system could not function without such a linear, sub-divided concept of time. Standard time stands its components like a row of bottles, but we make an error if we believe that other human societies view time and space in a way identical to our culture.

Since we learned to judge the passing of time from the length and direction of shadows, the sun has been our primary source of timekeeping and time, for our general purpose, has meant the day and its sub-divisions. A day is marked by one rotation of the earth in relation to the sun. In our own time standard timepieces, stop-watches and other kinds of clocks have introduced many new concepts of what is meant by a day. Our modern, highly integrated social system is possible only because we share a common approach to time. Without this common approach appointments could not be made and commercial and labour relationships would be impossible.

The inconvenience of non-standard time was evident in the 1780s. At this period, except for special purposes, the time was based upon the meridian of the place concerned. Different communities had different times—local time in London and Plymouth, for example, varied by six-teen minutes. In 1782, Mr John Palmer, manager of the Bath Theatre, proposed that the mail coaches be timetabled on the basis of a standard-ized timepiece. The success of the system he instituted eventually earned him the job of Comptroller of Mails.[1] Mail-coach guards were civil ser-vants, red-coated, top-hatted, and carried firearms. On departure they were given a flat brass case containing a chronometer which was handed to the postmaster at the terminus. On the eastward journey, the time-pieces were regulated to gain about fifteen minutes every twenty-four hours, so that the watch might accord with actual time; a correspond-ing allowance was made for east to west journeys. The coach guards were responsible for repairs to their coaches and for the compilation of way-bills and time-sheets en route. Incidents on the journey were written up and submitted; this form of information report spilled over into the railway age, where such correspondence was nicknamed 'skins and blisters'.

'London Time' was the basis of timekeeping on the mail coaches, but it appears to have been an unofficial categorization. In 1829, when a new General Post Office was opened in St Martin-le-Grand, London, a turret clock made by B. L. Vulliamy was placed in the portico, and this timepiece, which cost £1,800, seems to have established London Time. When the building was demolished in 1919, the clock was still giving satisfaction.

H. D. Howse of the National Maritime Museum has outlined how time in Britain came to be standardized:

> The rotating earth is the fundamental time-keeper. Until 1825, few people travelled very far and journeys were slow. The period from 1830 to 1850, however, witnessed far-reaching developments which changed public attitudes to time and timekeeping. Mail was rail-borne from 1838; by 1839 Bradshaw's railway timetable was available to those who could afford it, and by 1843 the first public telegraph line was in position alongside the Great Western Railway, between Paddington and Slough. In the 1840s, three major undertakings found it most inconvenient that different communities should keep different times—these were the private telegraph companies, the Post Office, and the railways. It was the railway which inaugurated a uniform time system upon Britain—and later the world.

In 1837, the inventors Cooke and Wheatstone took out a joint patent for an electric telegraph, and in the same year the London and Birmingham Railway experimented successfully with the equipment between Euston and Camden. By 1852, the Great Western Railway had run electric cables as far apart as south Wales and Birkenhead. However, it was the Board of Trade inspector, Captain Melhuish, who suggested in his first report for 1840 that station clocks should all keep London Time, so originating railway time as a countrywide theory.

A precedent for this idea could be found in 1837, when Mr C. A. Bagster, Coaching Superintendent of the London and Birmingham Railway, decided that action was necessary to ensure that guards' watches on his trains should take their time from a central timepiece. He wrote to Richard Creed, who was a joint secretary of the company: 'It will be found necessary to have a regulator clock to adjust our guards' chronometers with greater accuracy than is possible with our present clocks in the office.'[2] It is remarkable that such a proposal should still be necessary fifty-five years after John Palmer's suggestion. In any case, following Bagster's recommendation, a pendulum clock was made by Thwaites and Reed of London and was placed in the London boardroom, and all clocks on the line were regulated from this master timepiece. The clock remained in the possession of the London and North-Western Railway and the London, Midland and Scottish Railway and now stands in the chairman's room, British Rail Headquarters, London. The pendulum is still working and Bagster's letter to Creed is still inside the clock case.

The Great Western Railway adopted London Time in 1840. Though this was also called 'Railway Time', it was really Greenwich Mean Time. In the same year the GWR proposed to provide outside clocks for each station. These would be visible from passing trains by the engine-men and would ensure punctuality. The Great Western Railway did not therefore need to provide its foot-plate staff with watches. Another feature of the preoccupation with time on the Great Western was the provision of a 'tell-tale' clock at Swindon Works in 1848. A tell-tale clock was a long case pendulum sprung clock. Its dial consisted not of numerals but of steel pins. There was one pointer only. A watchman on his rounds was obliged to press a pin to prove he had visited the area. Unpressed pins indicated dereliction of duty. The tell-tale clock is the originator of all time clocks, and a version of it can be seen at the Horological Department of the British Library.

By June 1841, the Great Western was using through timetables which advertised that London Time was kept at all stations and that London Time was:

4   minutes earlier than Reading
5½   minutes earlier than Steventon
7½   minutes earlier than Cirencester
8   minutes earlier than Chippenham
11   minutes earlier than Bath and Bristol
14   minutes earlier than Bridgwater

In 1847, the London and Birmingham became part of the London and North-Western Railway. Later, when that company opened the Trent Valley line for through traffic, it placed all stations under Greenwich Mean Time. In a circular signed by General Manager Mark Huish it was stated that Greenwich Mean Time was:

7   minutes before Birmingham clocks
12   minutes before Liverpool clocks
10   minutes before Manchester clocks
10   minutes before Preston clocks
10   minutes before Chester clocks

The Bristol and Gloucester Railway opened in 1843, and in 1850 came the South Wales Railway; both of these companies advertised London Time at all stations. However, that later arrival, the Taff Vale Railway, unconnected with any main-line railway, always kept local time.

After the Nine Elms disaster of 17 October 1840, station clocks were given two faces, one visible to engine-men and regulated by the guard of the first train each day to halt at the station. Eighty years later on the Lancashire and Yorkshire Railway recalcitrant station clocks were the responsibility of office boys, who simply opened them up and swilled the works with paraffin.[3]

L. T. C. Rolt records:

> . . . for some years railway station clocks continued to be somewhat erratic. A passenger train which ran into the rear of a goods train which had stalled in a tunnel near Bootle on the East Lancashire Railway in 1849 had been despatched from Bootle only three and a half minutes behind it. In explaining this perilous proceeding to the inspector afterwards a witness candidly admitted that the Bootle station clock 'went wildly'.[4]

The accolade for self-confidence in this area must go to the Great Western for a GWR order dated 30 October 1852 declared: 'Commencing 1 November 1852, hourly signals will be transmitted regularly at stated times and operators are warned to keep the lines clear for two minutes preceding the hour. You are at liberty to allow local clock and watch makers to have Greenwich Mean Time providing such liberty shall not interfere with the company's services.'

The London and North-Western Railway made a special contribution to the establishment of London Time. Every day from 1848 to 1939, the guard of the down Irish Mail carried a London Time watch. At Holyhead, a postal official saw that the watch was conveyed safely to Dun Laoghaire, from where it went to Dublin to ensure that the GPO clock showed London Time.[5] The London and North-Western Railway was always a power in the north-west of England, so much in fact that in the early 1840s it persuaded the Corporation of the City of Manchester to adjust the municipal clocks to 'Nor'west railway' time.

From 1848, 'Railway Time' was seen to be in the ascendant as more and more towns adopted it. Nevertheless, many towns continued to retain local time. The great divide was between 'High Church' (local time) and 'Nonconformist' (railway time). In the east, Norwich, Ipswich, Cambridge and Yarmouth attempted to hold out against railway time; in the west, Bristol, Bath, Exeter and Portsmouth tried the same. Oxford as the centre of England put two hands on the great clock on Tom Tower, Christ Church, one set to local and the other to Greenwich Time.

This system was even more exaggerated in America, where the greater length of the railroad system meant that individual railways required independent time systems. On large stations, three clocks would be needed; one for local time, and other faces for eastward and westward meridians. On the German railways in the 1880s, time posts were set along the route; guards and drivers had to adjust their watches as the markers were passed.

In 1863, a time gun, controlled by current from Greenwich, was installed in the old Norman keep at Newcastle. Guns at North and South Shields were fired by the same method. The one o'clock guns at these sites were regulated from Greenwich to an accuracy of the twentieth part of a second.

Although railways put the mail coaches out of business and enforced a new concept of time upon the public it was not until July 1872 that the following notice appeared in a Post Office circular:

> Greenwich time is to be observed at all Post Offices in England and Scotland. Hitherto it has been the rule of the service to observe local time for certain purposes at County Post Offices, while Greenwich Time, spoken of in the *Book of Rules* as 'London' or 'Railway' Time has been used for other purposes. In future Greenwich Time, which is notified daily to all postal Telegraph Offices, is to be observed solely at all Post Offices in England and Scotland.

In 1872 the Post Office provided through its Central Telegraph Office the correct time to sixteen of the largest cities in the kingdom. The instrument which performed this task was a chronopher. The principal watchmakers of London, including Messrs. Dent and Benson, who supplied railway watches, received time daily from this instrument.

As early as 1845 the Liverpool and Manchester Railway had petitioned Parliament to grant uniformity of time for all ordinary and commercial purposes throughout the land. But it was not until 1880 that the requests by the Post Office and the railways for a standard time finally became a reality. In that year was passed the Definition of Time Act (43 and 44 Vict., C.9.) of which Clause 1 states: 'Whenever any expression of time occurs in any Acts of Parliament, deed or other legal instrument, the time referred to shall, unless it be otherwise specifically stated, be held, in the case of Great Britain, to be Greenwich Mean Time.'

Keeping the line clear for the time signal was a fetish on the Great Western Railway, right up to nationalization in 1948. Mr David Trimbell, who was a signalman on the company for many years, has recalled:

> I joined the Great Western Railway telegraph office in Gloucester in 1928. This office was a bewilderment of chattering instruments and a telephone exchange which was in itself a remarkable machine. At 9.58 a.m. the chief clerk would call out 'time, please everybody, time'. An industrial and commercial armistice followed. At 10.00 a.m. the morse code sounder broke the silence with the railway time—10.00 a.m.

Every day for many years, a representative of Mann and Company,

Gloucester, timepiece makers for the Midland Railway, appeared at the telegraph office door and upon receipt of 10.00 a.m. this gentleman thanked the office staff, replaced his watch and left. In the 1930s the Gloucester General Post Office and Mann's shop each had a clock which advertised 'Railway Time.'[6]

Despite the importance of the driver's watch, it was the watch displayed by the guard which gave 'Railway Time'. The pomposity of any express driver and the auspiciousness of the moment could always be punctured when the guard produced 'the time'.

For engine-men, time had many dimensions. 'Mileage' was one of these. Here, a run of 150 miles was translated into 'nine hours'. The phrase 'King's Cross to Doncaster is nine and a half hours' would baffle any foreign visitors to London who anticipated reaching York according to the advertised schedule. Another version of time would be presented during a journey. At intermediate stops the driver would advise the fireman not of 'actual time', but only 'two late away' or 'two down', this being a spur to greater activity. On arrival, the only remark would be 'right time' or 'two late arrival'. The position of the watch hands was never described.

There is another, darker side to the economics of time on the railways wholly apart from the standardizing of timekeeping and the efficiency of service. Here the battles were fiercer and the stakes higher. This is the question of whether the worker or his employer is in control of the amount of time spent on the job.

In the 1830s, when the railways were making their first ostentatious appearances over the countryside and cities of Britain, it was inconceivable that workers could collectively question their hours of labour. The economy at this time was already complex but was independent of a literate and numerate workforce. Education of workers was determined by bare necessity, and was free only if those desirous of learning could not afford a minimum fee. It was thought best to retain Bible studies as the basis for learning, and what education there was was generally limited to Sunday, the only day children were free from the factory.

In the factories, the only education was the minimal training necessary for the worker to perform his job adequately. Most workers were on the site at 6.00 a.m. and, except for short periods, were occupied until 7.00 or 8.00 p.m. A day was determined by the whim of the foreman, the nature of the task or the needs of the market. A twelve-hour day was the norm.

The coming of the electric telegraph and the railways changed all that, however. Though speculation on the nature of time rarely troubled transport workers, time and space were the twin axes in the physical process of moving people and things at agreed intervals and at agreed prices and were therefore of vital importance to their jobs. As we have seen the railways quickly provided a plethora of clocks. The station clock often became a civic institution, the railway telegraph office the main contact with other areas. As previously inaccessible or even unheard of areas were brought nearer by the great advances in transport and communication, people learned new relationships between time and space. Time became related to aspects of moor, hill, heath and coast. The conquest of time by the railway advanced the education, entertainment and awareness of the people in an unprecedented way.

For transport workers, duty rosters tightly governed the weekly, daily and even hourly activity of their lives. Nothing was really permanent, even though it was advertised in black and white; the critical moments of departure and arrival, the last-moment alteration to schedules, demanded constant access to an accurate version of the time. For such a service to run efficiently, it was esential that its workers have access to reliable timekeeping through the possession of their own watch. This was something radically new. The idea of a worker possessing a watch and checking his output was hitherto at best a novelty, at worst an abrogation of managerial prerogative. A good pocket watch was always a status symbol, especially in the days when watches were part of jewellery collections, not aids to workday performance. This can be seen even in the present day in the ritual of presenting an engine-driver with a watch on completion of fifty years on the railway. Status was joined with necessity to the point where a driver without a watch was like a symphony conductor without a baton.

Minus a watch a driver depended upon the station clocks or fleeting glimpses of the signal-box timepiece. This impossible situation could only be rectified by the purchase of a watch by an engine-man. Drivers of steam trains were rarely without watches and often paid the equivalent of a full week's wages for a timepiece. Watchmaking firms had agents in the depots who sold good watches on an instalment/commission basis.

However much the purchase of a watch may have put him in debt, it certainly helped reinforce his authority on the foot-plate. An engine-driver drew a watch like a gunfighter drew a Colt, and rarely did a fireman challenge the driver's version of the time, for to do so was to call into question the traditional relationship between the two men. There was a subservience and it was indicated by the holder of the watch, who drew it from its secret place if time was being 'lost'.

The pocket watch had a similar glory and status on the American railways. J. F. Stover records: 'In an early day the gold watch in the vest pocket, the bright hash marks on the sleeve marking years of service, and the shiny brass buttons on the dark blue jacket all marked the well-paid conductor as an aristocrat among wage earners in the nation.'[7]

The pocket watch eventually went the way of steam: surrendering to the more streamlined, efficient versions of wristwatch and diesel respectively. While the wristwatch had been regarded as effeminate in the days of steam, it now has a use and status of its own.

In its heyday, the pocket watch issued to railway workers was a token of responsibility and confidence. It brought key grades onto the level of the top-hatted, watch-chained aristocrats of labour—the engineers. The new, hand-held technology could not, however, remain neutral. The watch demonstrated the relationship between labour time and labour wages—the unforgiving minute had arrived. With the sharp segmentation of time came the militarization of the railway staff.

The process of the workers turning time to their own advantage was a long and difficult one, however. Railway management and workers have rarely agreed on the question of time. For management, time is a cost, something to be minimized; for a railway worker, time is what is surrendered to achieve living standards, and it must be sold as dearly as possible. In the 1840s, the approach of the railways to time was simply that of a feudal barony—'all of a man's time, waking or sleeping, belongs to the employer'. The railway workers were in a new category of labour. They were not casual workers or seasonal employees. They did not scramble like dock workers for a day's toil in a ship's hold, nor did they, like building workers, work on a 'job and finish' basis. They were, in the main, quite unlike the ponderous, frock-coated and careful men of the New Model Unions, the engineering unions of the 1870s, who fondled their watches and advocated co-operation with employers. Railway workers, although they were a highly competent breed of men, found themselves in a clock- and watch-bound bondage, wherein every tortured movement was accounted for and logged, and where every second was a rubbing knot within a roped existence.

The railway worker was a career man—an industrial soldier, a man who commissioned himself to a lifetime of service in which time was of the essence and the timepiece the supreme commander. To the engineman and signalman, the guard and the shunter, but no less to the office clerk, the tyranny of the clock was as meaningful as an empty pay tin. Nothing was allowed to interfere with the strict scheduling of the trains; responsibility had to be shouldered long after the body and mind demanded rest. The wealth of the railway companies was based upon the exploitation of labour time—the exhortation 'time is money' entered the directory of industrial relations. This became a managerial edict while the pleas of the overworked staff were ignored.

In the 1840s, two opposed views on labour and time were raging in Europe. For the classical economists, Mr Nassau Senior was arguing that only after a worker had laboured for twelve hours did he produce a surplus value for his employer. The socialist opposition, led by Karl Marx, argued that as soon as a worker created value to the level of his own subsistence everything else became profit to the master. Senior's argument prevailed and the twelve-hour day was the norm in many industries for many years.

The railway companies, however, went beyond the twelve-hour day. They insisted that all of a man's time belonged to them; he was ordered to live within call of his depot—usually a radius of one mile—and had to be available for work at a moment's notice. Before the railways came, the peaceful slumber of workers in mine, mill, office and shop had been broken by the nightwatchman marking the hours and waking early starters. The railway companies followed this practice and instituted the railway knocker-up; with hand-lamp and timepiece he made his rounds and snatched men from the anonymity of the deepest hours. For some men, the lightest tap on the window would suffice, followed by a whispered check on the time. For others, it was 'Walls of Jericho' stuff, the door being pounded until a tired and angry affirmation was received that the man was up and, however grudgingly, ready to go. A new definition of time consciousness had arrived—'the train must go through'. To achieve this, punctuality moved into the realm of obligation. The inexorable hands of the timepiece had to synchronize with the work-speed of the men.

Even as late as 1960, the injunction of punctuality could induce terrible fear into the men. In that year I heard a story about a Kentish Town driver on the Midland. This man's wife was in the last few days of pregnancy. Rising one morning at 3.00 a.m. to prepare for work, the driver discovered his wife in urgent need of midwife and doctor, so he hurried out to make a call from an adjacent telephone kiosk. After half an hour a tired and dishevelled doctor arrived to find the driver pacing the hallway of the little house and constantly checking his watch. The doctor hurried upstairs and made his examination, returning after a few minutes to give the driver the sad news that either the mother or the baby could be saved, but not both, and that the driver must make a decision. The Midland driver, knowing the penalty for missing a shift, picked up tea can and bag, stared at his watch again, and, as he made for the door, said, 'You're the doctor, you decide. I'm due on duty in ten minutes'.

The earliest trains were run on the unsatisfactory 'time interval system'. This generally meant a five-minute headstart for a passenger train, and fifteen minutes for a goods train. This time interval system placed a grave responsibility on the engine-men and guards. Far too often the safety of the line depended on decisions taken under stress conditions by overworked and exhausted men. This was particularly dangerous when station clocks observed local time and engine-men were not in the possession of watches. God and guesswork became components in situations where indecision and procrastination could, and did, have fatal results.

It wasn't until the 1860s that the labour movement joined together to try to break the companies' stranglehold on their time. It was at this time that the concept of the tripartite day arose. The centenary volume of the Trades Union Congress acknowledges this by including a metal watch case emblazoned with the words: 'Eight hours for sleep, eight hours for work, and eight hours for our own instruction'.

A major victory on the issue of time was achieved by workers in 1919 when a bitter three-day strike by London Underground train drivers at last won them a meal break within the eight-hour day. Norman McKillop records:

> The London Tube men had to partially paralyse the transport of the metropolis by coming out on strike, before the electric companies would grant them the facilities given even to a beast of burden. The electric railway companies contended that the motormen should be compelled to work every minute of the eight hours, without a break for meals or for any other purpose—and were adamant on the point.[8]

It was another four decades before the forty-hour week was conceded on the railways. The word conceded is important, for railways in Britain have always grudgingly reduced the hours of labour. Once you have a man at work you can exploit his ability to labour—'on the payroll, but off the premises' is a motto of little use to management.

When the eight-hour day was conceded, railway management turned to other methods of exploiting a man's time on the premises. For the engine-men it was the 'big-engine policy', with the giants of steam making their debut. Bigger engines, longer, heavier, faster trains—but no increases in pay. It was a simple idea—the shorter the day the more intensive the work.

Another method of increasing productivity was the 'trip system', a form of bonus dependent upon right time away and right time arrival with freight trains between marshalling yards. This had engine-men and guards scrambling like demons in an early version of 'beat the clock', which they rarely did. In the trip system, the hand of every man was against his co-worker—each blamed the other for suspected dilatoriness and for consequent loss of bonus.

In the 1960s, the stop-watch, work measurement, time studies and bonus schemes based upon time were introduced in order to increase productivity and to gear the human and mechanical into a new relationship. The problem was always that a 'rater's' watch was an assessment, not a scientific appraisal. A man and a stop-watch are not interchangeable. The dream of stop-watch engineers has always been increased productivity; the argument today is the same as it has always been—who benefits from increased productivity?

GLOSSARY

There is another aspect of railway time—the relationships between time and work as described by working railwaymen. Through the comments on time, from the acidulous to the anachronistic, we can recover some sense of the human relationships which were born and rooted in the age of steam. There follows some slang terms on the subject of time not covered in the chapter on language.

After lemon time: This is the second part of a shift, 'after the break'. In early days, when shifts were a minimum of twelve hours, engine-men were often forbidden to leave their engine to take food in a warm cabin, even if the cabin was only a few feet from the engine.

Australian days: Night work. Men working at this time live in an inverted bowl and thus christen night work as an upside-down life—an industrial antipodes.

Bare twelve: A bare twelve was a twelve-hour shift, ie, four hours' overtime, usually worked in fog, falling snow, or on congested lines. In days of steam, drivers and guards could make twelve hours regularly in the winter months; they could organize the running of the train to suit themselves, not the train service.

Bare week: A bare week was a wage packet devoid of bonus payment, mileage money, overtime or night-duty enhancements.

Birth control hours: For trainmen, signing on for duty between 2.00 AM and 5.00 AM was a method of keeping down the population.

Copper weeks: A copper week was organized well in advance. Certain trains, especially freighters, regularly ran hours behind schedule. Many drivers developed the art of pre-planning to gain maximum overtime.

Dark money, Dark time: The extra money paid for duties between 10.00 PM and 6.00 AM. 'A little dark money' meant that only half the shift entered the hours when dark time was paid. Usually 25 per cent extra.

Daylight saving: Darkness, particularly an electric socket minus a bulb, either on a train or in the shed. 'Sods Law' applied here—the more important the need for light, the more frequently the bulb would be missing.

Exhausted time: A definition used by work-study engineers to differentiate between real and estimated time.

First eleven: Eleven continuous hours on duty—one hour short of a rounder (a twelve-hour duty shift).

Gobblers: A title for railway workers who would snatch or gobble up any overtime offered or possible.

Green pastures, Ham—or fatty ham: Ham was a general term for overtime. Fatty ham meant overtime easily performed, ie, in comfortable surroundings—green pastures.

Land of plenty: Overtime, mileage, bonus, shift premiums. Any week which contained most or all of these was the land of plenty.

Limbo: Back-shift or split-shift working which simply withdrew men from social contact. Such starting times were 7.00 PM and 3.00 AM.

Magic moments: When a foreman or his assistant was proven wrong or incorrect, magic moments ensued.

Minutemen: Work-study engineers: raters of the 'unforgiving minute'. Counterposed by magic moments.

Miser rate: Minimum bonus. A term 'stolen' from gas advertisements of the 1960s.

Mumford's time, in: Beyond living memory. Mumford was a railway foreman of antiquity who lives on in jargon.

Night hawks: These were engine-men and guards who would volunteer for night work in order to earn extra money.

Owls: Men on almost permanent night work, not from choice but due to the nature of the work. It was said that their badge was two grey owls against a dark blue background.

Petticoat government: A nagging wife, but also wifely complaints and sanctions against night work.

Pig-shearing time: A countryman's term for 'never' introduced to the railway many years ago.

Rip Van Winkle money: In bad weather a train crew might be on long hours with their train. Relieved en route, they would travel back to the depot 'on the cushions', usually fast asleep, often raising derisory remarks from passengers. This was overtime money earned while sleeping.

Rounder: A twelve-hour shift. A rounder was usually hard earned; a full twelve hours in charge of an engine in dense fog, snow drifts, storms, with little food or sustenance against the weather.

Twilight zone: A period when a railway worker was operating in a hybrid capacity—a cleaner not yet promoted into fireman or a fireman, passed for driving, who had not reached full driver's status in pay.

Wages of sin: Money earned by falsification of time sheets. Sometimes 'white lies' to cover an easy day. Instant dismissal if caught.

Appendix to Chapter 5

List of grades employed on an engine shed.

Administrative:
>Running Foreman
>Shift Foreman
>Yard Foreman
>Foreman's Assistant
>Roster Clerk
>Telephone attendant

Locomotive staff:
>Engine-drivers and firemen included
>Shed drivers and mates
>Shunting drivers
>Trip drivers and mates
>Main-line drivers and mates

Engine Cleaners:
>Foreman cleaner
>Engine cleaner
>Passed cleaner

Labourers:
>Foreman labourer
>Boiler washout men
>Brick archmen
>Tube blowers
>Firedroppers
>Messroom attendants
>Shed sweepers

Appendix to Chapter 9

The following information on time differences, clocks, watches and repair work is supplementary to Chapter 9, 'The Tyranny of the Clock'.

In 1935 the Rev R. B. Fellows provided details of the situation on the London and Birmingham Railway in 1838:

TIMETABLE

Calculated on the difference of longitude between London and Birmingham. Selected stations only.

Station	Slower than Euston mins. secs.		Faster than Birmingham mins. secs.	
Camden	0	0	7	15
Harrow	1	0	6	15
Watford	1	0	6	0
Tring	2	0	5	0
Wolverton	3	0	4	15
Blisworth	3	15	4	0
Rugby	4	45	2	30
Coventry	5	45	1	30
Hampton	6	30	1	0
Birmingham	7	15	0	0

Station clocks were regulated by the above table. Office clocks in London and Birmingham were set three minutes later than the correct time. These figures were advertised in the *Railway Times* of 22 September 1838.

Specification for a station clock at Bowden, Cheshire, on the Manchester South Junction and Altrincham Railway:

Single piece wood frame.
Engine finished wheels of hammer-hardened brass.
Pinions of hard and tempered solid steel.
Main wheel diameter of 10 in.
Iron pulleys with turned grooves.

Escapement	Denison's Gravity.
Dials	Four, diameter of each 5 ft. Best plate glass. Painted, strippled, figured 3/8 in. thick.
Lighting	Gas.
Estimate	£60 plus Bell, Mason's and Carpenter's work, fixing, glaz-

ing and gas fitting. *Cost not to include later cleaning
of clock.*

Specification by   Arnold & Lewis Ltd, 7, St Ann's Square, Manchester, 3
March 1882.

Examples of railway watches. From *Locomotive Journal*, November 1937.

1. Maker   Benson, London.
   Type   Solid gold—half-hunter 'Triumph'.
   Details   Side winding. Roman numerals—not upright. Num-
                      ber VI missing.
   Price   £9 0s. 0d.
   Price to engine-men   £8 8s. 0d.

This watch equalled two weeks' wages for a top express driver.

2. Maker   Winegarten, London.
   Type   'Watch of the Century' for railways.
   Details   Solid nickel screw back and front case. No number
                      VI. Roman numerals, not upright. Supplied to
                      Continental Government Railways.
   Price to public   £2 0s. 0d.
   Price to engine-men £1 12s. 0d.

Approximately one third of a driver's wage.

3. Maker   W. E. Watts, 9, Market Street, Derby.
   Type   'Meridian'.
   Details   Hall-marked silver. Straight line lever escapement.
                      Chronometer balance—Breguet hairspring. More
                      expensive model fitted with micrometer regulator
                      and 17 jewels.
   Cash Prices
   'Greenwich'   Ten years warranty. £3 3s. 0d.
   'Standard'   Keyless only. Twenty-five years warranty. £4 4s. 0d.
   'Heavy Standard'   With special heavy case. £5 5s. 0d.
   'Super Quality'   Fifty year warranty. Compensated, Breguet spring.
                      Micrometer regulator. £6 6s. 0d.

In 1909, Graves of Sheffield offered the 'Express' English lever for £2 10s.,
twice the weekly wage of most unskilled workers. In 1922, the Leeds firm of
Yewdall offered a Keyless silver watch at £3 15s. and requested details of social
rank (!) before sending the watch for a seven-day trial. Stones of Leeds
offered English lever watches at £5 12s. 6d. and railway staff could test any
watch free. When Stones were advertising, the wage of a top-flight engine-man
was £4 10s. weekly.

In 1977, Mr Harry Evans allowed me a look at a Great Western Railway
watch, made about 1921. This Swiss Limit timepiece, still in perfect working
order, was stamped and numbered GWR 0–2745. It was made with fifteen

jewels and still responds beautifully to the winder. The gunmetal case is numbered 246218 and it is milled at the rim.

England had for many years a fine reputation for high-class watches, and it was not until the later years of the Industrial Revolution that the country was swamped with watches from France, Germany, the USA and Switzerland. The latter's products were denigrated by the British Horological Association as 'slop trade'. The Americans and the Swiss, however, went into mass production of watches and scored heavily in the British railway industry with 'Limit' and 'Waltham' models.

RAILWAY CLOCK AND WATCHMAKERS

Company	Address	Company supplied
Potts	Leeds	Great Northern
Arnold, Lewis	Manchester	London and North-Western
Mann, W. C.	Gloucester	Midland
Sharrats	Worcester	Great Western
Palmer	Chatham	South-East and Chatham
Benson	London	All companies
Watt	Derby	All companies
Lancashire Watch Co.	Prescot	All companies

In December 1900 an agreement was signed between the Great Northern Railway and William Potts and Son of Guildford Street, Leeds. The contract was for the repair of railway-owned watches and clocks, for the supply of new parts and for the cleaning of timepieces if necessary. This was a valuable contract for Potts and Son for it covered a territory which included the whole of the Yorkshire district, and Great Northern premises in Liverpool, Manchester, Lincoln and Worksop. Here is a scale of charges for 1900:

	Maintenance per annum		
	£	s	d
Ordinary single-dial clocks		2	6
Ordinary double-dial clocks		5	0
Watches		3	0

Special Rates Clocks
Site:

	£	s	d
Doncaster Plant striking clock	5	0	0
Running Shed. Four Dials	10	0	0
Platform, Station-Master's Office	2	0	0
Refreshment Rooms:			
Leeds Central	3	0	0
Retford	1	0	0
Lincoln	1	0	0
Wakefield		10	0

Under this agreement, Potts and Son provided efficient workmen who worked with great despatch. The essence of the contract was that every watch and clock was maintained as a thoroughly efficient timekeeper. Should the Great Northern become dissatisfied with the performance of Potts and Son, the company reserved the right to terminate the agreement and to pay out only what sums were outstanding.

The London, Midland and Scottish Railway held no standard watch patterns, but bought Swiss Jewelled Movements. The watches on this railway were not inspected, the holder being held responsible for the reporting of inaccuracies. LMS watches were repaired at Osborne Street, Manchester, in a repair shop opened by the Lancashire and Yorkshire Railway in 1894. Balance staff breakages seemed to be the most common problems.

The process today for general repair is (a) completely dismantle; (b) clean with chemical solution; (c) fit and assemble new parts; (d) test run for seven days. The present watch is the 'Montine', an Incabloc Swiss product, wholesaled at about £10 each. In 1949, the cost of a similar unspecified watch was £3 3s. plus purchase tax. The following is a list of watches and suppliers to the private railway companies:

Watch	*Distributor*
Limit	Agar
Recta	Walkers—Derby
Jaeger le Coutre	Fatterini—Leeds
Lancs. Watch Co.	Hirst Bros.
Seth Thomas	Pringle and Son
Elgin*	Marchand and Jobin

*Key and stem wind
All others stem wind only.

Notes

CHAPTER 1   The Railway Company: A Victorian Leviathan

1. M. Wellesley, *Wellington in Civil Life* (Constable, 1939), p. 345. In 1817, a group of starving Lancashire weavers, displaced by steam-driven machinery, assembled at St Peter's Fields, Manchester. On their shoulders were rolled-up blankets, a symbol of their determination to walk to London and to present to the Regent a petition asking for relief from their poverty and a measure of reform. The leaders, Drummond and Bagulay, were soon arrested, and the assembly was dispersed with great violence by the soldiery. Many of the would-be marchers were imprisoned without trial; others were jailed as vagrants. Many were seriously injured. So ended the 'March of the Blanketeers'.

2. A. Paul, *History of Reform* (Routledge, 1884), pp. 94 ff. In 1818, the desire for reform was so strong that the Home Secretary, Lord Sidmouth, instructed the Lord-Lieutenants of the counties to watch reform meetings and to have yeomanry standing by to preserve the peace. In the carrying out of these instructions the authorities of Manchester achieved a notorious distinction. In August 1819, some 50,000 citizens of Manchester gathered to hear the radical orator Henry Hunt speak on the subject of Parliamentary reform. The Manchester Yeomanry, at the call of 'at the flags', drew swords and attacked the crowd, in which they were soon swallowed up. The stand-by Hussars, in a rescue attempt, attacked the peaceful demonstrators with the flat edges of their swords. Eleven people died and over 600 were injured. This demonstration, and the attack of it by the soldiers, was canonized the 'Peterloo Massacre' because of its nearness in time to Waterloo.

3. H. Pollins, *Britain's Railways: An Industrial History* (David and Charles, Newton Abbot, 1971), p. 74.

4. K. Chesney, *Victorian Underworld* (Penguin, Harmondsworth, 1975), p. 137.

5. R. H. G. Thomas, *London's First Railway—The London & Greenwich* (B. T. Batsford, 1972), pp. 16–17.

6. R. M. Robbins, *The Railway Age* (Routledge and Kegan Paul, 1962), p. 81.

7. D. Morgan, *Harvesters: Village Life and Labour* (Routledge and Kegan Paul, 1976), p. 52.

8. M. Harlow, 'The Railway Town, 1840–1919' (undated manuscript).

9. P. W. Kingsford, *Engineers, Inventors and Workers* (Edward Arnold, 1964), p. 133.

10. *Ernest Struggles* (published anonymously by J. J. Beechcroft, Reading, 1879), vol. I, pp. 2–3. The book has been reissued as *Memoirs of a*

Station-Master, H. A. Simmons (edited by Jack Simmons) (Adams and Dart, Bath, 1974).

11. ibid., p. 85.
12. Trades Union Congress, *Centenary Booklet*, 1968.
13. 'The Porter', 'Our Railway Men', *South-Western Gazette*, 1 October 1881, p. 6.
14. E. Glenny Cory, *East London Industries* (Longmans Green, 1876), p. 189.
15. R. Graham, in correspondence with the author.
16. J. Swain, in correspondence with the author.
17. A. Williams, *Life in a Railway Factory* (David and Charles, Newton Abbot, reprinted 1969), pp. 278–9.
18. H. Core, in correspondence with the author.
19. R. Kenney, *Men and Rails* (Fisher Unwin, 1913), p. 4.
20. B. Evans, *When Railways Came to Romford* (Havering Public Library publication, undated).
21. 3rd and 4th Vict.
22. W. W. Tomlinson, *The North-Eastern Railway*, quoted in C. J. Allen, *The North-Eastern Railway* (Ian Allan, 1974), p. 230.
23. The account of Mark Huish's career is based on T. R. Gourvish, *Mark Huish and the London and North-Western Railway* (Leicester University Press, 1972).
24. R. Kenney, op. cit.
25. W. Stephens, in conversation with the author.
26. W. Thorne, in correspondence with the author.
27. G. Smith, in correspondence with the author.
28. G. A. Brown, J. D. C. A. Prideaux and H. G. Radcliffe, *The Lynton and Barnstaple Railway* (David and Charles, Newton Abbot, 1971).
29. H. A. Simmons, op. cit., pp. 18–21.
30. M. Reynolds, *Engine-Driving Life* (Crosby, Lockwood and Son, 1889), p. 2.
31. F. S. Williams, *The Midland Railway* (Strahan and Co., 1876), p. 629.

CHAPTER 2   The Rise and Fall of Company Loyalty

For a pertinent insight into the growth of loyalty to organizations and ideologies we are all indebted to Eric Fromm's *Fear of Freedom* (George Allen and Unwin, 1966).

1. O. Newman, *Defensible Space* (Architectural Press, 1973).
2. J. E. Campbell, *The Iron Track Through the Highlands*, quoted in O. S. Nock, *The Highland Railway* (Ian Allan, 1965), p. 78.
3. ibid., p. 84.
4. A. Butler, in correspondence with the author.
5. Sir F. B. Head, *Stokers and Pokers: The London and North-Western Railway* (Frank Cass and Co., 1968), p. 82.
6. W. F. Mills, *The Railway Service* (W. J. Adams, 1867).
7. *South-Western Gazette*, 1 September 1881, p. 5.

8. MAS, *Centenary Report*, 1965.
9. *On the Line* (Tullie House, Carlisle), vol. XXVI, March 1908.
10. *Railway Signal*, 1883.
11. N. Longmate, the *Observer Colour Magazine*, June 1973, pp. 15–18.
12. T. Brassey, *Work and Wages* (Bell and Daldy, 1872).
13. R. H. G. Thomas, *London's First Railway—The London & Greenwich* (B. T. Batsford, 1972), p. 52.
14. C. H. Ellis, *British Railway History* (George Allen and Unwin, 1959), p. 19.
15. W. J. Gordon, *Every-day Life on the Railroad* (The Religious Tract Society, 1898), pp. 188–9.
16. Mrs Beryl Woods of St Pancras quoted this book to me in correspondence.
17. J. Thomas, *The West Highland Railway* (David and Charles, Dawlish, 1965), pp. 101–2.
18. C. J. Allen, *The Great Eastern* (Ian Allan, 1955), p. 17.
19. P. S. Bagwell, *The Railwaymen* (George Allen and Unwin, 1963), p. 21.
20. G. Dow, *Great Central* (Ian Allan, 1969), vol. II, p. 11.
21. Sir F. B. Head, op. cit., p. 82.
22. ibid., p. 110.
23. J. Thomas, *The North British Railway* (David and Charles, Newton Abbot, 1969), vol. I, pp. 104–5.
24. W. McLagan, in correspondence with the author.
25. This material is the result of various interviews conducted by the author in 1971.
26. ibid.
27. 'North-Western Servants', *Railway Review*, 3 December 1880, p. 8.
28. ibid.
29. Parliamentary Papers 1891, vol. XVI, p. 222, evidence of G. Findlay.
30. J. R. Raynes, *Engines and Men* (Goodall and Siddick, Leeds, 1921), p. 153.
31. H. Evans, in conversation with the author.
32. N. McKillop, *The Lighted Flame* (Thomas Nelson and Sons, 1950), p. 131.
33. S. Mosley, in correspondence with the author.
34. F. Almond, in correspondence with the author.

CHAPTER 3 Signalmen and Guards

1. O. S. Nock, *The Great Western Railway in the Nineteenth Century* (Ian Allan, 1962), pp. 109–10.
2. P. W. Kingsford, *Builders and Building Workers* (Edward Arnold, 1973), p. 77.
3. P. W. Kingsford, *Victorian Railwaymen* (Frank Cass and Co., 1970), p. 24.
4. A. Williams, *In a Wiltshire Village* (Duckworth, 1938), p. 217.
5. *Railway Review*, January 1889, p. 1, for a discussion of signalmen on the Great Northern Railway.
6. Letter to the Editor from 'A Signalman', *Railway Service Gazette*, 3 February 1872, p. 7.

7. Letter to the Editor from 'Another Black Country Signalman', *Railway Service Gazette*, 4 January 1873, p. 11.

8. *Railway Service Gazette*, 4 January 1873, p. 4.

9. ibid., 23 October 1874, p. 3.

10. 'Railway Accidents and Railway Signalmen', *Railway Service Gazette*, 11 April 1874, p. 14.

11. Parliamentary Papers 1891, vol. XVI, p. 82.

12. *Ernest Struggles* (J. J. Beechcroft, Reading, 1879), vol. I, pp. 30–2 (see Chapter 1, note 10).

13. *Railway Herald*, 8 February 1890, p. 8.

14. Letter to the Editor from 'One who would like to have Justice', *Railway Herald*, 1 March 1890, p. 12.

15. 'Hours on the GWR', *Railway Herald*, 15 February 1890, p. 13. Like most letters of complaint by railwaymen at this time, this one carried a pseudonym owing to the writer's fear of dismissal.

16. 'Manifesto to the men of the North-Eastern Railway', *Railway Herald*, 15 February 1890, p. 2.

17. *Railway Herald*, 26 July 1880.

18. Letter signed 'Nero', *Railway Herald*, March 1890, p. 14.

19. *Pembroke Guardian*, 25 August 1911.

20. *Leeds Mercury*, 25 August 1911.

21. ibid.

22. ibid.

23. *Wolverhampton Express and Star*, 19 August 1911, p. 6.

24. A. Waterman, in correspondence with the author.

25. A. Young, in correspondence with the author.

26. A. Lyon, in correspondence with the author.

27. ibid.

28. A. Butler, 'Seven Bells', unpublished manuscript.

29. ibid.

30. The poems by Walter Sinkinson are from *See How They Run (Railway Rhymes)* (Leslie Brook, Royd Printing Works, Mirfield, 1961) and from original manuscripts supplied to the author.

31. J. Greenwood, 'Guards and Drivers Off Duty', *Daily Telegraph*, 4 December 1871, p. 2.

32. S. Mosley, in correspondence with the author.

33. F. Almond, in correspondence with the author.

34. A. Young, in correspondence with the author.

35. W. Bishop, in correspondence with the author.

CHAPTER 4   Ashpits and Offices: The Engine Shed

1. Letter from Joseph Alexander of the North Midland Railway, Derby, 6 February 1844, published in *Railway Times*, 10 February 1844, p. 13.

2. N. McKillop, *The Lighted Flame* (Thomas Nelson and Sons, 1950), p. 82.

3. R. Smith, in correspondence with the author.

4. J. Hulme, in correspondence with the author.

5. ibid.
6. W. McLagan, in correspondence with the author.
7. ibid.
8. W. Bishop, in correspondence with the author.
9. Mrs P. Foreman, in correspondence with the author.
10. Mrs. V. Tansley, in correspondence with the author.
11. L. Housden, in correspondence with the author.
12. M. F. Higson, *London Midland Firemen* (Ian Allan, 1972), p. 69.
13. *Ernest Struggles* (J. J. Beechcroft, Reading, 1879), vol. I, pp. 4–5 (see Chapter 1, note 10).
14. J. Thomas, *The North British Railway* (David and Charles, Newton Abbot, 1965), vol. I, pp. 111–12.
15. 'Nil Desperandum', 'Clerk's Wages', *Railway Service Gazette*, 9 March 1872, p. 8.
16. J. Davis, in correspondence with the author.
17. F. Almond, in correspondence with the author.
18. H. Evans, in correspondence with the author.

CHAPTER 5   Engine Cleaners and Firemen

1. *Ernest Struggles* (J. J. Beechcroft, Reading, 1879), vol. I, pp. 61–2 (see Chapter 1, note 10).
2. *Railway Service Gazette*, 22 February 1873, p. 2.
3. ibid.
4. J. Swain, in correspondence with the author.
5. J. Walker, in correspondence with the author.
6. A. Bradshaw, in correspondence with the author.
7. W. McLagan, in correspondence with the author.
8. J. R. Raynes, *Engines and Men* (Goodall and Siddick, Leeds, 1921), pp. 47–8.
9. W. Turner, in correspondence with the author.
10. A. Sperdutti, in correspondence with the author.
11. C. Brooks, 'How It Was', unpublished essay.
12. L. Housden, in correspondence with the author.
13. A. Sperdutti, in correspondence with the author.
14. N. McKillop, *The Lighted Flame* (Thomas Nelson and Sons, 1950), p. 204.
15. W. McLagan, in correspondence with the author.
16. ibid.
17. R. Smith, in correspondence with the author.
18. H. R. Chubb, 'The Rule Book—Ancient Version', *GWR Magazine*, vol. 51, no. 12, December 1939 (1939 British Rail Archives), p. 491.
19. R. Smith, in correspondence with the author.
20. ibid.
21. N. Cox, in correspondence with the author.
22. J. Hulme, in correspondence with the author.
23. F. Frost, in correspondence with the author.

24. A. Bradshaw, in correspondence with the author.

25. B. Lunniss, in correspondence with the author.

26. Four men of very different views rose from the position of engine cleaner to play significant roles in trade-union and political life. Two became prime ministers, one attained eminence as the most controversial figure of the General Strike of 1926, and another contested the presidency of the United States on no less than four occasions as the candidate of the Syndicalist Movement of America. J. H. Thomas began his career as an engine cleaner on the Great Western Railway and became President of the ASRS in 1905–6. In 1907 he was involved in the Osborne Judgment, a famous legal case which prevented the Labour Party from levying trade unionists on behalf of its political fund. In 1910 he entered Parliament, later becoming Colonial Secretary. In 1917 he was elected General Secretary of the NUR. He played a role in getting the General Strike called off, losing him much support. He resigned from Parliament in 1936 after a budget leak. Sir Roy Welensky started as an engine cleaner on Rhodesian Railways and in 1941 founded the Labour Party, an organization formed to protect the white worker from African competition. He became Federal Prime Minister in 1956, but in the mid-sixties his world began to shrivel and crack before the winds of political change in Africa, and even though his attitudes softened, the events of the period brought about his retirement from active politics. Ben Chifley started as an engine cleaner on Australian Railways and eventually worked his way up to driver. Trade unionist and labour leader, he was Prime Minister of Australia from 1944–5. Another trade unionist turned politician is the American Eugene V. Debs. He founded the IWW, the famous Wobblies, a militant organization which was subjected throughout its life to a reign of terror by right-wing elements in American society. Debs contested the Presidency of the United States in 1900, 1904, 1908, and 1920, his highest vote being 1,000,000. In 1918 he was arrested under the Espionage Act and sentenced to two terms of ten years each, but was released in 1921. His life and work have assured him of a special place in the labour movements of the world.

27. W. Hannington, *Ten Lean Years* (Left Book Club, 1940), pp. 231–5. The NWUM hit on the idea of a mock funeral procession to take place at midnight, 31 December 1938. The coffin itself, with glass-sided hearse lanterns to heighten the effect, and painted with the words 'He did not get winter relief', was paraded through the West End of London. In Piccadilly, the marchers fought with police to retain possession of the coffin. It was later delivered to 10 Downing Street and to Lord Rushcliffe at the headquarters of the Unemployed Assistance Board.

28. 'North London Servants', *Railway Review*, 16 July 1880, p. 3.

29. W. Turner, in correspondence with the author.

30. A. J. Street, *I Drove the 'Cheltenham Flyer'* (Nicholson and Watson, 1951), pp. 23–4.

31. R. Smith, in correspondence with the author.

32. A. J. Street, op. cit.

33. Great Western Railway, *Conciliation Board Minutes*, 1917.
34. R. M. Ballantyne, *The Iron Horse, or Life on the Line* (James Nisbet and Co., 1871), p. 375.
35. A. J. Street, op. cit.
36. J. Morgan, in correspondence with the author.
37. A. Sperdutti, in correspondence with the author.
38. ibid.
39. ibid.
40. L. Housden, in correspondence with the author.
41. N. McKillop, op. cit., pp. 280–1.
42. J. Hulme, in correspondence with the author.
43. ibid.
44. ibid.
45. ibid.
46. ibid.
47. ibid.
48. R. Smith, in correspondence with the author.
49. ibid.
50. R. Graham, in correspondence with the author.
51. ibid.

CHAPTER 6 Engine Drivers

1. R. M. Robbins, *The Railway Age* (Routledge and Kegan Paul, 1962), p. 81.
2. N. McKillop, *The Lighted Flame* (Thomas Nelson and Sons, Ltd, 1950), p. 18.
3. P. Kingsford, *Victorian Railwaymen* (Frank Cass and Co., Ltd, 1970). p. 14.
4. R. M. Robbins, *Journal of Transport History*, vol. IV, 1959–60, p. 180.
5. London and South-Western Railway, *Rule Book*, 1847, Rule 72.
6. J. Raynes, *Engines and Men* (Goodall and Siddick, Leeds, 1921), p. 100.
7. J. Thomas, *The North British Railway* (David and Charles, Newton Abbot, 1969) vol. I, pp. 57–71, for a discussion.
8. N. McKillop, op. cit., p. 377.
9. *Ernest Struggles* (J. J. Beechcroft, Reading, 1879), vol. I, pp. 88–9 (see Chapter 1, note 10).
10. R. M. Ballantyne, *The Iron Horse, or Life on the Line* (James Nisbet and Co., 1871), pp. 5, 23, 215.
11. C. J. Bowen Cooke, 'Engine-Drivers and their Duties', *Railway Magazine*, August 1897, pp. 113–15.
12. *The Times*, 31 July 1862.
13. *Railway Review*, 8 February 1889.
14. J. Thomas, *The West Highland Railway* (David and Charles, Dawlish, 1965), p. 134.
15. *Ernest Struggles*, op. cit., pp. 100–1.
16. W. Cameron, in correspondence with the author.
17. P. Kingsford, op. cit., pp. 115–20.

18. 'Engine-men's Hardships', *Railway Service Gazette*, 1 March 1873, p. 7.
19. 'A Constant Observer', *Railway Service Gazette*, 12 April 1873, p. 14.
20. *Railway Service Gazette*, 10 January 1874, p. 7.
21. Letter from John Graham, *Railway Service Gazette*, 14 February 1874, p. 13.
22. 'The Scotch Strike', *Railway Review*, 30 January 1891, p. 54.
23. M. Reynolds, *Engine-Driving Life* (Crosby Lockwood and Co., 1881), p. 25.
24. *Railway Service Gazette*, 13 June 1880.
25. *Railway Review*, 30 September 1881, p. 1.
26. ibid., 28 October 1881.
27. Taff Vale Policeman, 'Work Without Wages', *Railway Service Gazette*, 18 April 1874, p. 4.
28. 'How to pay good dividends and high wages', *Railway Herald*, 1 February 1890.
29. Parliamentary Papers 1891, 'Railway Hours', vol. XVI, Qq 7791–7877, p. 369.
30. ibid., Qq 8672–8691, p. 420.
31. *Railway Review*, 2 February 1891, p. 66.
32. Parliamentary Papers 1891, vol. XVI, Qq 8428–8547, pp. 406–10.
33. J. Thomas, *The West Highland Railway*, op. cit., p. 82.
34. Letter from 'West Dock', 'North-Eastern Pilotmen and Shunters', *Railway Review*, 18 November 1881, p. 6.
35. N. McKillop, op. cit., pp. 28–9.
36. C. H. Ellis, *The Trains We Loved* (George Allen and Unwin, 1947), p. 22.
37. J. Thomas, *The Callander & Oban Railway* (David and Charles, Newton Abbot, 1966).
38. J. Thomas, *The North British Railway*, op. cit., p. 16.
39. C. H. Ellis, *British Railway History* (George Allen and Unwin, 1959), vol. II, p. 204.
40. O. S. Nock, *The Highland Railway* (Ian Allan, 1955). p. 88.
41. G. Smith, in correspondence with the author.
42. W. Turner, in correspondence with the author.
43. G. A. Brown, J. D. C. A. Prideaux and H. G. Radcliffe, *The Lynton and Barnstaple Railway* (David and Charles, Dawlish, 1964), p.66.
44. A. Sperdutti, in correspondence with the author.
45. ibid.
46. *Southern Railway Magazine*, May 1928, p. 43.
47. R. Graham, in correspondence with the author.
48. ibid.
49. L. T. C. Rolt, *Red for Danger* (David and Charles, Newton Abbot, 1976), pp. 198–200.
50. J. Walker, in correspondence with the author.
51. M. F. Higson, *London Midland Firemen* (Ian Allan, 1972), p. 30.
52. ibid., p. 31.
53. C. Brookes, 'How It Was', unpublished manuscript.
54. W. McLagan, in correspondence with the author.

55. The figures in this table were supplied by ASLEF.

56. ASLEF Circular, 29 January 1924.

57. ASLEF Strike Bulletin, 1924, p. 21.

58. 'The Dispute', *Locomotive Journal*, July–August 1955, pp. 222–7.

59. ASLEF Circular 54, 1955.

60. ASLEF Circular 53, 1955.

61. ibid.

62. London School of Economics, 'Abstract of Statistics', Railways, 1956.

63. The information on the Southern Region comes from Dave Bush, a driver and ASLEF representative at Slade Green depot, London.

64. N. M. Lera, in correspondence with the author.

65. G. Bishop, in correspondence with the author.

CHAPTER 7   The Double Homers

1. P. W. Kingsford, *Victorian Railwaymen* (Frank Cass and Co., 1970), pp. 108–9.

2. S. Mosley, in correspondence with the author.

3. O. S. Nock, *The Great Western Railway in the Nineteenth Century* (Ian Allan, 1962), p. 110.

4. W. Turner, in correspondence with the author.

5. A. Sperdutti, in correspondence with the author.

6. S. Packwood, in correspondence with the author.

7. W. McLagan, in correspondence with the author.

8. W. Chalmers, in correspondence with the author.

9. W. Parker, in correspondence with the author.

10. Mrs Hines, in conversation with the author.

11. S. Mosley, in correspondence with the author.

12. Parliamentary Papers 1891, vol. XVI, p. 224, evidence of G. Findlay.

13. Mr Davis, in correspondence with the author.

14. *Railway Service Gazette*, 23 March 1872, p. 9, and *Blechley Railman*, April 1970.

15. Mr Davis, in correspondence with the author.

16. A. E. Grigg, *Railway Service*, (NUR, Bletchley, 1971).

17. J. Cox, in correspondence with the author.

18. A. E. Grigg, op. cit.

19. J. Walker, in correspondence with the author.

20. Letter from 'Hawk', 'Treatment at the Birmingham Barracks (LNWR), Curzon Street', *Railway Review*, 21 October 1892, p. 7.

21. F. S. Williams, *The Midland Railway* (Strahan and Co., 1876).

22. A. E. Grigg, op. cit.

23. J. Walker, in correspondence with the author.

24. W. Chalmers, in correspondence with the author.

25. Parliamentary Papers 1891, vol. XVI, Qq 7606.

26. Guard Ellis, evidence to 1891 Parliamentary Select Committee.

27. G. Barnes, *A Railwayman Looks at Railways* (ILP Publications, 1955), p. 13.

28. R. Lunniss, in correspondence with the author.
29. F. Frost, in correspondence with the author.
30. *LNER Magazine*, June 1928, p. 274.
31. O. S. Nock, *The Highland Railway* (Ian Allan, 1965), p. 90.
32. W. Watt, in correspondence with the author.
33. Parliamentary Papers 1891, vol. XVI, Qq 8332–8354, p. 403.
34. ASLEF *Conditions of Service Book*, 1922, p. 13. This volume giving agreements relating to 'lodging out' kindly loaned to the author by engineman Jim Walker of Eccles.

CHAPTER 8   Language on the Railway

Select bibliography

Bolinger, D., *Aspects of Language* (Harcourt Brace, New York, 1968).
Honeycombe, G., *Red Watch* (Hutchinson, 1976).
Mead, M., *Culture and Commitment* (Bodley Head, 1970).
O'Neil, W. M., *Beginnings of Modern Psychology* (Penguin, Harmondsworth, 1975).
Open University, *Language in Education*, Source Book (Milton Keynes, 1972).
Orwell, G., *Politics and the English Language* (Penguin, Harmondsworth, 1967).
Sapir, E., *Language* (Hart-Davis, 1970).
Sinclair, A., *The Savage* (Weidenfeld and Nicolson, 1973).
Trudgill, P., *Sociolinguistics* (Penguin, Harmondsworth, 1970).
Whorf, B., *Language, Thought and Reality* (M.I.T., 1965).

CHAPTER 9   The Tyranny of the Clock

For a discussion on various approaches to time, see F. N. Cousins, *Sundials* (John Baker, 1979); for a general background to this chapter, see D. S. Landes, *A History of Watches* (Harvard University Press, 1979), and for an important discussion on the history of timekeeping, see D. S. Landes, 'Watchmaking: A Case-study in Enterprise and Change', *Business History Review* (U.S.A.), vol. LIII, spring 1979.

1. D. Mountfield, *The Coaching Age* (Robert Hale, 1976), p. 61.
2. British Transport Records, General A, pp. 568–609.
3. A. Taylor, letter to Leonard Lean, April 1977.
4. L. T. C. Rolt, *Red for Danger* (Bodley Head, 1955), p. 37.
5. J. Edgington, in correspondence with the National Railway Museum, 1 December 1976.
6. D. Trimbell, in correspondence with the author.
7. J. F. Stover, *Life and Decline of the American Railroad* (Oxford University Press, New York, 1970), p. 219.
8. N. McKillop, *The Lighted Flame* (Thomas Nelson and Son, 1950), p. 121.

Index

Abbots Ripton, 38
Abingdon, 35
accidents, 38–9, 175, 216–17; caused by overwork, 38–9, 69, 162, 165, 167; engine-men, 156, 172, 180–1, 216–17; engine sheds, 90; first passenger fatality, 23; fogmen, 66; guards, 82; lodging men, 216–17; poverty caused by, 42–3; staff, 38, 42–3, 66, 84, 165, 172; trip system, 84
Acton, 53, 54, 196–7, 216
Advanced Passenger Trains, 156, 229
Ais Gill, 76, 175
Alexander, Joseph, 89–90
Allen, William, 226
allotments, 219
Almond, Francis, 105
Amalgamated Society of Railway Servants (ASRS): 1887 strike, 181; loyalty to grade and union, 57; opposition to, 35; working hours, 162, 165, 166
Amphlett, Baron, 69
Annesley, 209
Ardrossan, 194
Aristotle, 242
Armstrong, John, 137–8
ashpits, 90–3
Ashworth, John, 48
ASLEF: foundation, 158–9; and lodging away, 224, 225, 226, 227; membership, 187; strikes, 130, 133; 1887 strike, 181; 1924 strike, 130, 182
Asquith, H. H., 58
Attlee, Clement, 227
Augustine, Saint, 242
Austin, A., 210
Aviemore, 212

Bagster, C. A., 244
Ball, Inspector, 122
Ball, Joe, 172
Ballantyne, R. M., 139–40, 157
Bambra, J., 210

Banbury, 44, 228
Barry, Jim, 114
Bath, 246
Bathgate, 211
Batho, Sir Charles, 210
Baty, Mr, 227
Beattock, 76
Bell, driver, 160–1
Bell, Peter, 126
Bergson, Henri, 242
Bermondsey, 24
Bethnal Green, 24
big-engine policies, 141–2, 252
Binstead, Captain, 31
Birkenhead, 143, 194
Birmingham, 177, 201, 205, 228
Birt, Mr, 206
Bishop, G., 189
Bishop, W., 86, 95, 100
Blackburn, 129
Blackett, Christopher, 21
Blackpool, 130, 194
Blair Atholl, 211
Blake, fireman, 195
Blazey, engine-man, 224, 226
Bletchley, 170, 191, 199, 200, 220
Board of Trade, 72, 106, 154, 162
boiler tube cleaners, 95, 96
boiler-washers, 95
Bolton, 129
Bootle, 246
Bordesley, 83
Bow, 27
Bradford, 74
Bradlaugh, Charles, 167
Bradshaw, Adam, 111, 130
brakemen, 82, 166
brake vans, 82, 83
Brandreth, Major, 32
Brassey, Thomas, 46
brick-arch men, 94, 95
Bricklayer's Arms, 195
Bridle, W. J., 210
Bristol, 113, 165, 214, 228, 246

Bristol and Gloucester Railway, 245
British Rail, lack of corporate identity, 64
Bromley, J., 58
Brooks, Charles, 113
Brown, driver, 181
Bruce, secondman, 181
Brunel, Isambard Kingdom, 50, 53, 152
Bulleid Pacifics, 143
Bullock, William, 25
Burlinson, Mr, 72
Burnett, Reg, 228–9
Burnley, 134
Bury, 129
Bush, Dave, 118
Butler, Alan, 42, 76–7, 78, 79

Cairn, J. F., 210
Caledonian Railway, 31, 179; accidents, 156; hours of work, 166; housing, 53; signalmen, 70
Callander and Oban Railway, 169
Cambrian Railway, signalmen, 70
Cambridge, 130, 246
Camden, 114, 142, 178–9, 198, 201, 214
Cannon Street, 187, 188
Cardean, 141
Cardiff, 194, 214, 228
Carlisle, 28, 172; company loyalty, 179; engine cleaners, 117–18; engine decoration at, 169; knocking up, 125; lodging away, 190, 191, 194, 198, 201, 214, 216; staff housing, 53, 55; *see also* Durran Hill; Kingmoor
Carmarthen, 36, 195–6
Caudle, driver, 175
Chalk Farm, 198, 199
Chalmers, Wally, 195, 206
Chance, Blind Charlie, 179
Charing Cross, 187, 188, 221
Chat Moss, 22
Cheltenham, 44
Chester and Shrewsbury Railway, signalmen, 71
Chomsky, Noam, 231
church attendance, 46–50
Churchward, J. F., 141
Clapham Junction, 76
Clarke, William, 130
cleaners, *see* engine cleaners
clerks, 101–8

Clifford, Alfred, 132
Clifton Down, 42
clocks and time-keeping, 242–54, 256–9
clothes, *see* uniforms
coaches, as lodgings, 220–1
coaling engines, 97
Cobbett, Mr, 159
Cockermouth, Keswick and Penrith Railway, 72
Coddington, Captain, 31
concessionary travel, 55, 138, 219
Conciliation Boards, 58
Cooke, W. F., 244
Core, Harry, 29, 126
Corkerhill, Glasgow, 122, 194
Cottrell, Fred, 237
countrymen, as railway workers, 26–9
Cox, Jim, 200
Cox, Noel, 125, 205
Craven Hotel, London, 221
Creed, Richard, 244
Crewe, 56; church attendance, 48; housing, 51; lodging away, 192, 198, 199, 200, 201, 214, 216; mess rooms, 100
Cricklewood, 97, 113, 179, 202, 216
Crown Street, Liverpool, 144
Crystal Palace, 74

Dairycoates, Hull, 125, 126
Darlington, 226
Davis, driver, 198, 199
Davis, J., 104
Davis, Mrs, 192
Day, J., 210
Decayed Southwestern Clerks Fund, 43
Definition of Time Act (1880), 247
Denison, Edmund, 33
Dent and Benson, 247
Derby, 48, 74, 83, 89
Dewsbury, 105
Didcot, 138
dining-car attendants, 191, 213
discipline, 34–9; drivers, 137–8, 154–6; engine cleaners, 114, 122; engine sheds, 30; fines, 65–6; firemen, 137–8; guards, 82, 83, 85–6; railway police, 34; in staff housing, 55
District Line, 107, 108
Doncaster, 208, 214
D'Onion, Ramon, 126–8
Doody, Eric, 221
Dorchester, 163

double crewing, 209–10
double homers, 190–229
Dover, 195
Doyle, Henry, 130, 134
drivers, *see* engine-drivers
'Duke' class, 147
Dumfries, 191
Dundee, 211
Durham, 69
Durran Hill, Carlisle, 28, 117, 148, 173

Easingwold and Avonmouth Light Railway, 60
Eastern Counties Railway: discipline, 30; double homers, 206–7; effect on Bethnal Green, 24; Euston Confederacy, 33; housing, 51; police, 34
Eastern Region, lodging, 226–7
Eastfield, 211, 212
Eastleigh, 100, 166, 189, 206
Eborall, Captain, 13
Edge Hill, Liverpool, 93, 94, 125, 143–5, 172, 194, 217
Edinburgh, 75, 102–3, 130, 155
Edinburgh and Glasgow Railway, 52, 86, 155
education, 51
Edwards, J. Passmore, 165
Elliot, Dr, Bishop of Gloucester, 27
Ellis, guard, 206–7
Ellis, Hamilton, 169
Eltingham, J. G., 210
Emerson, Ralph Waldo, 242
Enclosure Acts, 25
engine cleaners, 109–35; board boys, 113; discipline, 114, 122; eyesight, 116–17; as firemen, 112; hours, 110, 120–1; initiation ceremonies, 118; knocking up, 120, 125; leg-pulling, 114; materials, 115–16; methods, 112, 113, 114; and the 1923 reorganization, 130; promotion, 109, 110, 114–15, 116; trade unions, 109, 112, 128–35; wages, 110, 112, 116, 183
engine disposal, 90–2
engine-drivers, 151–89; accidents, 172, 180–1; attachment to their engines, 168–70; and big-engine policy, 252; and boys as firemen, 112; effect of modernization, 186, 187; engine allocation, 168–70; eyesight, 117, 151, 215; freight train overtime, 215;

health, 215; hours, 159, 161–8, 215; job loyalty, 171–4, 186; mess facilities, 100–1; militancy, 187–8; nicknames, 179–80; overnighting, 99, 190–229; overwork, 161–8; passed firemen, 137; pocket watches, 248, 249; promotion, 156; purchase own stores, 156–7; railway by-laws and, 156; recruitment, 152; redundancies, 186; relations with firemen, 135, 136–7, 161; relations with guards, 84; relations with signalmen, 78; retirement, 177; sanctity of the cab, 159–60; shed loyalty, 177–80; wages, 27, 61, 154, 155, 156, 158, 161–8, 182–8, 219; weather hazards, 158, 171–2, 173
engine sheds, 88–108; ashpits, 90–3; cabins and huts in, 93–4; cleanliness, 173; engine cleaners, 109–35; fitting shops, 98; foreman's office, 101; grades, 255; messing facilities, 99–101; overnight men, 99; personal hygiene, 91, 94, 100, 115; railway office, 101; repairs, 94–6; sandbox fillers, 94; women working in, 96–8
environment, impact of railways on, 23–4
Euston, Polygon Buildings, 54–5
Euston Confederacy, 33
Euston Day School, 44
Evans, Herbert, 60, 107–8
Evans, Mr, 68
excursion trains, 219
Exeter, 246
Ewart, W., 49

families, railway tradition in, 50
Farnley, 207–8
Fellows, R. B., 256
Figgins, Jim, 225
Findlay, George, 197–8
fines, 65–6
fireboxes: cleaning, 90–2, 111–12; repairs, 89–90, 94, 95–6, 111, 139
fire lighters, 95
firemen, 135–50; accidents, 172, 180–1; aircrews as, 220; and the big-engine policy, 141–2; classification, 135–6; engine cleaners on, 112; engine preparation, 138–9; hours, 138, 144; oiling the inside motion, 120; overnighting, 99, 190–229; passed firemen, 137;

promotion, 135–6; relations with drivers, 135, 136–7, 161; relations with guards, 84; Second World War, 143; shortage of equipment, 119; wages, 135–6, 138, 141–2, 154, 158, 182–8; weather hazards, 140
First World War, 60
Fishguard, 195
5XP's, 141
Fleetwood, 111
Fletcher, driver, 181
Flying Scotsman, 209, 210, 222
fogmen, 66
Forbes, Mr, 71
Foreman, Pat, 96–8
foremen, 101; wages, 184, 185
Fort William, 212
Fratton, Portsmouth, 95
Fretsum, Mr, 102
Frodingham, 228
'Frowd' radar speed recorder, 188
Furness Railway Company, 61

Galton, Lieutenant, 32
Gascoigne, J., 210
gate-keepers, 68
Gates, Francis, 130, 134
Gateshead, 214, 225
General Post Office (GPO), time unification, 244, 246, 247
Gideon Society, 198
Glasgow, 130; housing, 52; knocking up, 125; lodging away, 211, 213, 219; *see also* Polmadie
Glasgow, B., 210
Glasgow, Paisley and Greenock Railway, 32
Gloucester, 118, 247–8
Goddard, W., 210
Gooch, Sir Daniel, 159, 165
Goose Hill, 73
Gordon, W. J., 48
Gorton, 112
Gourvish, T. R., 32, 33
grades, 31, 255
Graham, Ritson, 28, 148–9, 173–4
Grand Junction Railway, 32
Grant, G., 192
Gray, Andrew, 169
Gray, F., 210
Great Bear, 141

Great Central Railway, engine cleaners, 112
Great Eastern Railway, 130; accidents, 38; double homing, 206–7
Great Northern Railway, 28, 130; accidents, 38, 166; brake vans, 82; clerical grades, 105; discipline, 35; and the Euston Confederacy, 33; housing, 51
Great Western Housing Association (London), 53
Great Western Railway (GWR), 28–9, 50; discipline, 35, 36, 66; double homing, 191, 192, 195–6, 197; drivers, 157, 160, 170–1; economies on materials, 104; effect on Swindon, 25; engine cleaners, 110, 112, 122; firemen, 135, 138; First World War, 60; General Strike, 62; housing, 55; introduce the electric telegraph, 244; introduce 'King' class, 141; loyalty, 42, 79; as a model employer, 159; 1911 receipts, 57; provident societies, 44; railway offices, 102; restrictions on staff, 138; *Rule Book*, 30; safety, 56–7; signal frames, 77; signalmen, 73; staff housing, 51, 53; testimonials required by workers, 25–6; timekeeping, 245, 246, 247–8
Green, driver, 195
Greenwood, James, 83
Gregory XIII, Pope, 242
Gresley, Nigel, 209
Gresley Pacifics, 141, 209
Grigg, A. E., 199–200, 203
guards, 82–7; double homers, 190–229; goods trains, 82–5, 87; passenger trains, 82, 85–7; pocket watches, 248
Gunther, Ray, 188

Halford, J. W., 210
Hamilton, 211
Hampden Club, London, 220–1
Harding, Colonel, 74
Harness, Captain, 31
Harris, John, 110–11
Harrison, George, 125
Harrow and Wealdstone disaster (1952), 216
Harvester, 209
Harvey Combe, 152
Hay, Bailie, 210
Hayes Garden Village, 53–4, 55

Head, Sir F., 51
Healey Mills, Liverpool, 145
Heard, Sam, 136
Heaton, 225
Heaton Norris, 200
Hedley, William, 21
Hellifield, 88, 205
Henderson, T., 210
Hereford, 192
Hewitt, John, 153
Higgins, Cormack, 172
Highland Railway: double homers, 211; driver, 169; engine cleaners, 110; loyalty, 41–2
Higson, S., 100
Higson, M. F., 177
Hill, George, 69
Hinehoe, 26
Hines, Mrs, 196–7
Holbeck, 89, 204
Holborn Low Level, 76
Holt, William, 107
honesty, 36–7
Hope, Lady, 45–6
Hornsey, 130
Horwich, 51–2
hostels, 197–229
hours: clerks, 103, 108; drivers, 159, 161–8, 215; engine cleaners, 110, 120–1; firemen, 138, 144; guards, 83; shunters, 56; signalmen, 66–9, 70, 71–2, 73, 74
Housden, Len, 99–100, 142
housing, 50–5
Howse, H. D., 244
Hudson, George, 153
Huish, Mark, 32–4, 245
Hull, 125–6
Hull and Barnsley Railway, 170
Hulme, fireman, 180
Hulme, Jimmy, 94, 143–5, 201
Hurcombe, 83
Hurlford, 130, 211
Huskisson, William, 23

Ilford, 228
Ipswich, 246
Isle of Wight Railway, 34

Joint Railways, 108
Jones, D., 169, 211
Jones, fireman of Crewe, 216

Jones, fireman of Wellingborough, 180, 216
Jones, John, 56

Kenney, Roland, 29
Kentish Town, 96, 98, 100, 113, 115, 179, 211, 227
Kilsby Tunnel, 50
'King' class, 141
Kingmoor, Carlisle, 88, 114–15, 117–18, 119
King's Cross, 130, 132, 133, 207, 214, 226, 227, 228, 229
Kingsbury, 28
Kingsford, P. W., 191
Kirtley, Henry, 44
Kirtley, Mr, 90
knocking up, 120, 125, 251

Labour Party, 107
Lackie, Charles, 130
Lady of the Lake, 141
Laing, S., 154
Laira, 205–6
Lamb, Charles, 242
Lancashire & Yorkshire Railway, 31, 130; engine cleaners, 111, 112, 116, 129; Euston Confederacy, 33; signalmen, 73; staff education, 51; time keeping, 246
Lancashire Witch, 21
Lancaster, 177
Landman, George Thomas, 31
language, railway, 230–41
Larkfield, Glasgow, 213
Laws, Captain, 31
Lawson, Wilfred, 46
'Leader' class, 143
Lean family, 50
Lean, Charles, 50
Lean, John, 50
Lean, Leonard, 50
Leeds, 89, 204–5, 207–8, 219
Leicester, 203
Leicester and Swannington Railway, 152
Lenten, Jack, 25
Lera, N. M., 188
list clerks, 103
Little Brickhill, 220
Liverpool, 93, 94, 143–5, 201
Liverpool and Manchester Railway, contracts for drivers, 153; Crown Street,

144; opening, 21–3, 152; orders of the day, 31; timekeeping, 247
Lockey, Victor, 161
Locomotion No. 1, 141
lodging overnight, 190–229
London and Brighton Railway, double homing, 191
London and Greenwich Railway, 31; church attendance, 46; viaduct construction, 24; wages, 27
London and North-Eastern Railway (LNER), 160, 175; drivers, 170; non-stop London–Edinburgh, 209–10; signalmen, 75
London and North-Western Railway (LNWR), 130, 180; church attendance, 48; double homing, 191; drivers, 156, 158, 173; engine cleaners, 111, 114; firemen, 140, 158; First World War, 60; guards, 84, 86, 87; hostels, 197–8; housing, 51; Huish's management, 32, 33; 1911 receipts, 57; Polygon Buildings, 54–5; *Rule Book*, 34; signalmen, 69; staff loyalty, 56; time keeping, 245, 246; trip system, 84–5
London and South-Western Railway (LSWR): accidents, 166; discipline, 34, 86; drivers, 154–5, 163–4, 171–2; guards, 86; police, 34; recruitment of countrymen, 27; staff welfare, 43
London, Brighton and South Coast Railway, drivers, 169
London, Chatham and Dover Railway: hours of work, 166; signalmen, 67–8
London Engine Cleaners' Vigilance Committee, 130
London Midland and Scottish Railway (LMS), 61, 175; diesel shunting, 132; drivers, 177; engine cleaners, 118–19; hostels, 201, 211; introduces 'Princess' class, 141; lodging facilities, 220; messing facilities, 99–100
London Midland Railway, signal frames, 77
London Midland Region, messing facilities, 100
London Time, 243–5, 246
London Underground, 252
Long Eaton, 203–4
Longstaff, 156–7
Lonsdale, Bishop, 48
loyalty, company, 40–64, 171–2, 192

Lunniss, Bob, 129, 130, 134, 207
Lynton and Barnstaple Light Railway, 36, 170
Lyon, J., 75–6

McCulloch, 156
McIntosh, J. F., 141
McKenzie, R., 210
McKillop, Norman, 61, 168, 252
McLagan, William, 94, 95, 112, 118–19, 122, 125, 194
Madge, driver, 181
Maillard, Mrs, 204
Malinowski, B., 242
Mallaig, 212
Manchester, 22–3, 125, 201
Manchester, Sheffield and Lincolnshire Railway, 160; drivers, 165; housing, 51
Mann, Horace, 242
Mann and Company, 247–8
Manuel, Archie, 134
March, 208–9, 216
Martin, driver, 180
Maryport and Carlisle Railway, 179
Masborough, 194
Mason, Frank, 115–16, 140, 175
Mathias, B., 138
Maynard, Percy, 73
Mead, Margaret, 242–3
Melhuish, Captain, 244
Meon Valley, 171–2
messrooms, 99–101
Metropolitan Railway, 60; clerks, 107–8; punctuality, 160
Middlesbrough, 227
Midland Railway, 32, 61, 130; discipline, 37; drivers, 174, 177; 1887 strike, 181; engine cleaners, 113; Euston Confederacy, 33; firemen, 140; housing, 51; introduces 5XP's, 141; 1911 receipts, 57; railway lodgings, 202–5; recruitment, 28; retirement, 177; standards, 173.
Miles, H., 210
military influence on railways, 30–2
Millbay, Plymouth, 113, 171
Miller, 49
Mill Hill, 93
Millhouses, 88
Mold Junction, 200, 201
Monument, 108

Moon, Sir Richard, 68, 165
morale, 63
Morgan, David, 25
Morgan, Jack, 141
Morris, Lord Justice, 185
Mosley, Sir Oswald, 134
Mosley, Sid, 61, 84, 194, 197
Motherwell, 53, 213
Mumford, Lewis, 88
Murphy, W., 183

National Union of Railwaymen (NUR):
growth, 59; and lodging, 224–5, 226–
7; 1955 footplate strike, 185; signal-
men join, 74
National Wages Board, 182
nationalization, 63–4, 108, 171
Neasden, 130
Neath, 138
Nelson, William, 130
Newburn, 75
Newcastle, 228, 247
Newcastle and Carlisle Railway, lodging
allowances, 191
New Cross, 187
New Lanark, 55
Newman, Oscar, 40
Newnes, F. R., 143
Newport Pagnell, 191–2
Newton, 74
Newton Abbot, 44, 228
Newtown, 70
nicknames, 225, 240–1
Night Hawk, 209
Nine Elms, 133, 245
Nock, O. S., 42, 65, 169, 192
non-stop trains, 209–10
Normanton, 73–4
North British Railway, 180; builds Ric-
carton, 52; conditions of service, 166;
double homers, 211; drivers, 155–6;
engine embellishments, 169; firemen,
139; guards, 86; railway offices, 102
North-Eastern Railway, 31, 130; attitude
to unions, 106; discipline, 35; guards,
84, 85
North London Incline, 76
North London Railway, church atten-
dance, 48
North Midland Railway, drivers, 153–4
North Shields, 247
North Union Railway, guards, 82

North-Western Railway, 31, 61; disci-
pline, 35
Norwich, 38, 246
Nuneaton, 193–4, 220

Oban, 212
O'Brien, William, 31
Oldham, 29
Old Oak Common, 136, 205, 214, 221,
222–3, 228
Oswestry, 56
overnighting, 99, 190–229
Owen, Robert, 55
Oxford, 246

'Pacific' class, 142
Paddington, 196
Palmer, John, 243, 244
Parker, Bill, 54, 196
Park Lane, Liverpool, 143
Parliamentary Select Committee on
Hours of Labour on the Railways
(1891), 56, 166, 206
passengers, first fatal accident, 23
Patricroft, Manchester, 125, 192
Paxton, Joseph, 65
Pearce, H., 138
Pennington, H., 210
Penzance, 196
Perth, 198, 212–13
Peterborough, 51, 216
Pibworth, A., 210
Pill, 77, 78, 79
plate-layers, 35–6
Plymouth, 113, 115, 192, 195, 196, 243
pocket watches, 248, 249–50, 257
pointmen, 65–6, 82, 86; fines, 65–6;
wages, 66
police, 34
Polmadie, Glasgow, 94, 95, 112, 119, 122,
180, 211, 214
Polygon Buildings, 54–5
Poor Law (1934), 25
porters, wages, 184
Portland Street Station, 107
Portsmouth, 95, 246
Preston, 201
Primrose Hill Tunnel, 172
'Princess' class, 141
Proctor, 73–4
provident societies, 43–4
Puffing Billy, 21

punctuality, 251

Q.I.'s, 143

Railway Clerks' Association (RCA), 105-6, 107, 108
Railway Commission, 32
Railway Disciplinary Procedure (1912), 37
Railway Executive, 225, 226, 228
Railway Mission, 49
Railway Nine Hours Movement, 165
railway police, 34
Railway Staff National Tribunal (1955), 184
Railway Temperance Movement, 45, 46
'Railway Time', 245-8
Ralph, Johnny, 125
Ramsbottom, 141
Ramsgate, 195
Rathbone, driver, 168
Raynes Park, 68
recruitment, 26-7, 63
Redpath, J., 210
Redrup, Ted, 146
redundancies, 62, 186
Rees, Dai, 196
Retford, 33
Reynolds, Michael, 28, 164
Riccarton, 52
Ridley, J., 210
Rigby, 51
Robbins, Michael, 25
Rolt, L. T. C., 151, 246
Romford, 30, 151
Roper, T., 210
Rowsley, 88
Royal Air Force (RAF), 220
Royal Commission on Railways (1867), 34
Royal Lancer, 209
Royal Scot, 222
royal trains, 97, 114, 151, 169
Rugby, 200
Rule Book, 30-1, 34, 37-9, 136, 195, 202, 232
Rutherglen, 156

Sadler, Mrs, 192
safety, see accidents
St Helens, 192

St Pancras Station, 48-9; Polygon Buildings, 54-5
Salop, 192, 200
Saltley, Birmingham, 177, 205
Sandburg, Carl, 231
Sandy, James, 160
Sapir, Edward, 231
Scratchwood, 93
Scunthorpe, 125, 205
Second World War, 63, 96, 143, 220, 224
Senior, Nassau, 251
Shandon Station, 168
Sharp, Shadrach, 179
Shaw, Richard, 134
Shawcross, Sir Hartley, 226
Sheddon, R., 210
Sheffield, 114, 165, 204
Shepstone, Mr, 123
Shotover, 209
signal boxes, 67, 70-1
signalmen, 65-82; and accidents, 69-70; bell codes, 79; box boys, 74-5; hours, 66-9, 70, 71-2, 73, 74; moving signals, 77; and the 1911 strike, 73-4; pay and conditions, 66-9, 70, 71-2, 73, 74; relations with drivers, 78; tedium, 75; travel difficulties, 79; visitors to the box, 75, 76, 78; wages, 66-9, 72, 73, 184, 185
Simmons, H. A., 26, 36, 70, 102, 110, 157, 160
Sinkinson, Walter, 79-81
slang, railway, 230-41
sleeping-car attendants, 191, 212, 213
Slinger, J., 210
Smith, George, 195-6
Smith, Ron, 93, 122-3, 137, 145-7
Smith, T., 210
snow-clearing, 171-2
Solomon Islands, 183
Somers Town, 222
South-Eastern Railway: accidents, 39; signalmen, 68, 71-2, 73; drivers, 170
South Shields, 247
South Wales Railway, time keeping, 245
South Western Railway: guards, 86; welfare funds, 43
Southall, 93, 113, 137, 146-7
Southampton, 163-4
Southern Railway: double homers, 195; firemen, 143; messing facilities, 100; railway lodgings, 206

Southern Region: Craven Hotel, 221; militancy, 187–8
Southwold Railway, 60
Spanish Civil War, 134
speedometers, 188
Sperdutti, Anthony, 113, 115, 141–2, 170–1
Spey Lodge, Aviemore, 212
Stafford, 201
Staffordshire Railway, drivers, 164
Stalbridge, Lord, 45
Stanier, 141
Starlight Specials, 219–20
station masters, wages, 107
steam, decline of, 188–9
Steam Engine-Makers' Society, 21
Stephens, Walter, 35
Stephenson, George, 21–2, 25, 141, 152
Steventon, 25
Stockton and Darlington Railway, 21
Stoke-on-Trent, 111, 177
stores, 104–5, 115, 176; drivers' purchase of, 156–7; economy of materials, 104–5, 216
Stover, J. F., 249–50
Stranraer, 130, 194, 212
Stratford, 30, 51, 130, 167–8, 185, 194, 206–7, 223
Street, A. J., 136, 137–8
strikes: drivers, 153, 154, 155–6, 164, 181–6; engine cleaners, 129, 132–3; 1836, 153; 1842, 154; 1850, 155–6; 1887, 181–2; 1890, 164; 1911, 57–60, 73–4, 158–9; 1919, 61, 252; 1924, 130, 182; 1926, 62, 130; 1949, 226–7; 1954, 228; 1955, 184–5, 186
Strome Ferry, 49–50
Sunter, Thomas, 155
Sutton Oak, 192
Swaby, driver, 216
Swain, Jim, 28, 111, 130, 134
Swindon, 26, 28–9, 53, 55, 89

Taff Vale Railway: church attendance, 48; engine-drivers, 162, 164; guards, 83; hours of work, 71, 162, 164, 165–6; signalmen, 71
Tait, Dr, 48
Tansley, Mrs, 98
Taylor, George, 130
Taylor, J., 210
Tebay, 188

telegraph, 244, 248
temperance, 44–6
Tennant, Henry, 166
Thomas, J., 139, 155, 168, 169
Thomas, James, 70
Thomas, J. H., 58
Thomas, John, 49
Thomas, Ma, 195
Thomas, R. H. G., 24
Thompson, driver, 168
Thompson, Mr, 167
Thorne, Will, 35
Thornhill, Wilf, 204
Thornton, driver, 168
Thornton, Mr, 156
Thwaites and Reed, 244
ticket collectors, 191
time, 242–54, 256–9
time clocks, 245
Todd, J., 210
Total Abstinence Movement, 48–9
Trade Disputes Act (1927), 106
trade unions, 128–35; clerks, 105–6; drivers, 158–9, 181–8; engine cleaners, 109, 112–13, 128; firemen, 158–9, 181–8; and literacy, 230–1; and lodgings, 223–8; 1911 strike, 58–60; 1919 strike, 61; and temperance, 46
Trades Union Congress (TUC), 106
traffic receipts, 57
training, 31
Transport Act (1947), 63
Transport Commission, 183, 184, 185, 186
travel concessions, 55, 138, 219
Trent, 72
Trevithick, 147
Trevithick, Richard, 50
Trimbell, David, 247–8
trip system, 84–5, 252
Truro, 196
Tuck, Raphael, 108
tunnels, 144–5
Turner, Wilf, 135–6, 138, 192
Tweedmouth, 226
Twin Sisters, 21

Ullyot, William, 158
uniforms and clothing, 34; drivers, 137, 171; engine cleaners, 119, 121, 137; firemen, 137; guards, 86–7; pointsmen, 86; railway police, 34; raker-

outs, 91; signalmen, 67
unions, *see* trade unions
Upperby, 88
Usher, Bishop, 242

viaducts, 24
Victoria, Queen, 32–3
Victoria Basin, 168
Vigilance Movement, 38, 129, 130–5
Vulliamy, B. L., 244

wages, 25, 31–2, 58, 61, 226; clerks, 103,
106, 107; drivers, 27, 61, 154, 155,
156, 158, 161–8, 182–8, 219; engine
cleaners, 61, 110, 112, 116, 183; firemen, 135–6; 138, 141–2, 154, 158,
182–8; fogmen, 66; foremen, 184,
185; gatekeepers, 68; guards, 86, 87;
lodging allowances, 191, 219, 223,
225; plate layers, 35; pointsmen, 66;
porters, 184; signalmen, 66–9, 72, 73,
184, 185; station masters, 107
Walker, Jim, 111, 125, 177, 201, 202,
205
Walker, Mr, 102–3
Walter, George, 31
Waterman, Alex, 74
Watkin, Sir Edward, 160
Watson, fireman, 180
Watt, William, 194, 218–19
Weatherburn, Henry, 152
Weatherburn brothers, 152
Webb, A. H., 48
Webb, Beatrice, 21
Webb, Frances, 48
Webb, Sidney, 21

Wedgewood, Sir R. L., 210
welfare funds, 43
Wellesley, Arthur, Duke of Wellington,
22–3, 233
Wellingborough, 202
Westbourne Park, 110
Western Region: lodging facilities, 222,
228; loyalty, 42; railway lodgings, 205
West Highland Line, 160; religious
views, 49–50
Westhouses, 194
Westland Row Station, Dublin, 166
Weymouth, 192
Wheatstone, Sir Charles, 244
Whitelaw, Mr, 210
Whitland, 73
Wigan, 61, 130, 192, 194
Willesden, 172, 178–9, 199–200, 216,
220
Williams, Albert, 67, 89
Williams, F. S., 37, 202
Williams, J. J., 210
Williamson, Joseph, 144
wives, 216–18
Wolverton, 42, 51
women, work in engine sheds, 96–8
Worcester, 126
'working to rule', 30–1, 38, 134, 187, 188
Workmen's Compensation Bill, 106
Wylam Colliery, 21

Yarmouth, 246
York, 130, 225, 226
Young, Alex, 75, 85

Zita, 194